IMAGES of America

# CATSKILL VILLAGE

*On the cover*: Generations of explorers and settlers thought of the Hudson River as America's Rhine. It was the resilient spine of the new nation in terms of culture, commerce, and convenient transportation. The river has also been a source of recreation from time immemorial. The particular occasion seen on the cover shows a lively group of local citizens crowding onto an experimental lifeboat that had just been made in nearby Athens. The photograph was taken during the First World War by one of Catskill's preeminent photographers, Paul Morrison. One of the most famous among the river spots for frolicking was known as Cole's Grove, located at the north end of the village. After the death of the painter Thomas Cole in 1848, his older son, Theodore, built a recreation park on family property along the river. Cole's Grove could be rented by the day for a small fee, the family sold refreshments, and there were picnic tables, a wooden pavilion, bathhouses, a playground, and a dock for boats that brought people from as far away as Poughkeepsie and Troy. Cole's Grove was sold and closed in 1901. Today the Rip Van Winkle Bridge joins the shoreline approximately where Cole's Grove once operated. (Photograph by Paul Morrison, courtesy of Peggy Ahwesh.)

IMAGES
*of America*

# CATSKILL VILLAGE

Richard Philp

ARCADIA
PUBLISHING

ISBN 978-0-7385-5794-6

Published by Arcadia Publishing
Charleston, South Carolina

Printed in the United States of America

Library of Congress Control Number: 2008923565

For all general information contact Arcadia Publishing at:
Telephone 843-853-2070
Fax 843-853-0044
E-mail sales@arcadiapublishing.com
For customer service and orders:
Toll-Free 1-888-313-2665

Visit us on the Internet at www.arcadiapublishing.com

*For Gladys, Ruth, Margaret, and Edith; they will each know why.*

# CONTENTS

# ACKNOWLEDGMENTS

Many people have been very patient with me during the making of this book; many have offered advice, help, and encouragement; and some have contributed crucially in ways known only to us. In the first two of these categories, I have to include Richard Frisbie of the Hope Farm Bookshop, who first suggested I go after this project; Raymond Beecher, recently deceased, a friend over the past 35 years, who told me I would be better off collecting the photographs for this book from scratch myself (over 800 of Catskill Village were subsequently scanned); Wanda Trevor, who made available to me her research in and photographic memory of the village over the past 70 years; Edith Cole Silberstein, a dear family friend who has let me root through (and copy) over many years extensive material on her great-grandfather Thomas Cole; and Dawn Augsberger, without whose support—well, I do not know what would have happened without her support, it is that important. The people who gave me access to their collections, assisted my research, and offered encouragement include especially Peggy Ahwesh, Frances Binder, James Cancienne, Robert Carl, Rebekah Collinsworth, Mark Cooper, Norma Cross, Joan Jacobs, Mark Krstovich, Dr. Robert Mantica, Robert Meo, Shirley Overbagh, Damon Pouyat, Rich Rappelyea, Michael Smith, Bob Stackman, Charles Swain, Nancy Ursprung, Kevin Van Vechten, Pat and Stephanie Walsh, and Barbara and Walter Weber. In the third category—much smaller—I have to include, as always, Dr. David Herman, who has put up with me now for 40 years, and Martin Freidman, who has put up with me now for 16 years. There are others, but I have run out of space.

# INTRODUCTION

The 130-mile stretch of the Hudson River from New Amsterdam (today's New York City) up to Fort Orange (today's Albany) winds through a fertile land of exceeding beauty and ready water transportation once called New Netherland. By the late 1600s, it formed the spine of the new nation that became the United States, and for centuries it was the commercial, cultural, and agricultural center of the New World. Settled by the Dutch in the early decades of the 17th century, this area so full of promise became a magnet for generations of pioneering settlers from many nations. The Dutch influence remains embedded in the culture and landscapes to this day as visible and verbal testimony to celebrated Dutch stubbornness, tolerance, government, thrift, and domesticity. We are very much part today of what we have been in the past.

Two-thirds of the way up the Hudson River on the west bank is the historic village of Catskill. Its population today is around 5,000 people—just as it was a century and a half ago. Located along both sides of the Catskill Creek, the village is only 11 miles (a half-day's ride by horse in the old days) from the Catskill Mountains. The Catskill Creek is joined not far from the center of the village by the Kaaterskill Creek, a far more animated sister stream that tumbles and falls and rushes over lofty precipices and through some of the most spectacular wild mountain scenery anywhere in the world. The name *Catskill*, subject of much speculation and curiosity over the centuries, derives from a Dutch tradition of honoring a distinguished person by naming a geographical site after him or her, in this case the early-17th-century statesman and poet Johannes Katz. *Kill* is the Dutch word for "creek" and thus Katzkill, or Catskill, which has nothing to do with the wildcats that once roamed the primeval forests or with hunting and killing them.

The region has been inhabited by man for at least 13,000 years, according to archaeological digs a few miles up from the village at the West Athens Hill site. The district includes many breathtaking mountain landscapes that draw travelers and artists in search of nature's beauty; rivers, creeks, and streams that are used for commerce, transportation, and recreation; rolling, fertile farmland, a veritable breadbasket that once provided milk, grain, vegetables, and meat for the nascent nation; historic settlements (Dutch was spoken in Catskill Village until the middle of the 19th century) and haunting romantic ruins and legends that tell of past accomplishments; peaceful country idylls for city dwellers escaping the pollution and frantic pace of New York City or Albany; architecturally significant buildings that represent centuries of diverse fashion and ever-changing ideas of taste; and centers of profitable industry, advanced learning, tourism, and longed-for culture.

Incorporated in 1806, the officially designated village as it is known today (the town was incorporated in 1788) languished in rather humble circumstances until late in the 18th century when farmers, entrepreneurs, lumbermen, and land developers of English, Irish, and German descent migrated from New England and fueled a land boom. There were 10 houses in the village in 1796; there were over 200 only 10 years later. Catskill's new prosperity was due to several factors. An early-20th-century historian wrote,

> The building of the Susquehanna Turnpike [in the early years of the 19th century], which started in Catskill and extended to Wattle's Ferry [today's Unadilla in Otsego County] on the Susquehanna River was one of the greatest events next to the building of the New York Central Railroad and the Erie Canal, and for a great many years Catskill was the outlet of trade from the interior of the state . . . and all this helped to make Catskill the most important place on the Hudson.

In other words, the source of Catskill's wealth can be described in terms familiar to anybody interested in real estate: location, location, and location.

Even location could not help prosperous little Catskill Village when, in the 20th century, the ice industry died due to electric refrigeration; the fishing succumbed to pollution; the commercial river traffic was supplanted by trucks and cars; the Catskill Mountain resorts were replaced by resorts in the Alps or the Caribbean easily accessible by air; polluting brick and shale yards moved away or went bust; cement plants were put out of business due to new regulations to control pollution; and the village greengrocer, hardware store owner, shoemaker, and baker were knocked out of commission by the sprawling malls and shopping centers that were located just a bit outside the village nearer the super highways.

Located in the heart of a vicinity of vast resources originally marketed back home in Europe as the biblical land of milk and honey, Catskill, after almost three centuries of prosperity, suffered a long period of decline as a result of the 20th century's technical and transportation advances. However, the word *renaissance* has been used by many in recent years, as is happening with so many towns and villages along the river, and Catskill Village has entered the 21st century with renewed spirit and hope.

New sources of income have been found, and old resources are being retooled to adapt to changing times. By the mid-1980s, an age of heightened awareness caused people—many of them younger people—to look for alternate uses for the old buildings (some of them very old) rather than just tearing them down. Since the early 1970s, the problems in the river caused by raw sewage and chemical waste have been addressed, and the wildlife—including the ancient sturgeon and nesting American eagles—has started to return. People with financial resources to spend on village homes have discovered time and time again the wonder and the beauty masked behind crumbling exteriors and are now preserving for future generations two of Catskill's most valuable assets—its architecture as well as its history.

A new Catskill Village is emerging to the delight of many old-timers and newcomers, and new values and ideas have begun to penetrate the old. This is an enlightened generation. The work and vision of these pioneers has become the backbone of the new Catskill—rooted firmly and with great pride in the old.

# One

# The Point

The Dutch settlers called the small rocky islands Bomptjes Hoeck, located just offshore where the Catskill Creek empties into the Hudson River. By 1820, the two islands were combined and joined to the mainland by the man-made Long Dock. Wetlands along the river to the north were filled in during the 19th century and are today the site of the park called Dutchmen's Landing, a boat launch, and a recreational facility. Catskill's river port is at the end of the Susquehanna Turnpike, one of the early principal sources of Catskill's commercial success. Catskill resident Benjamin W. Dwight writes in 1869 about the creation of the Point: "From the junction of the Hudson and the Catskill Creek, a wharf has been extended, about one fourth of a mile, to a small island in the Hudson formed by opposing currents of the two streams. . . . The whole of this ground is now called the Point. On it several dwelling houses, stores, and other buildings have been erected."

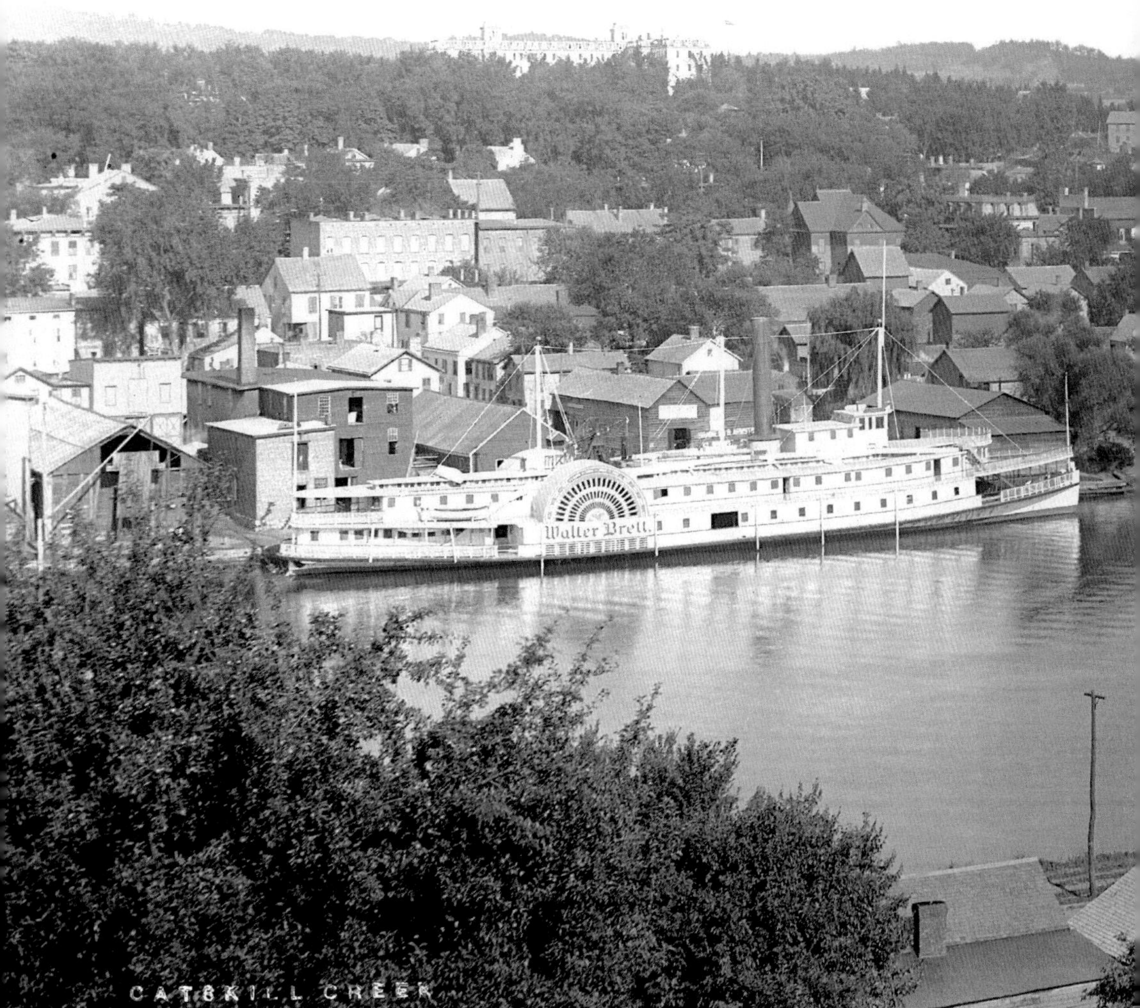


The paddle wheeler *Walter Brett* has pulled into port at the Water Street dock, which was used for sloops making local trips to nearby river towns such as Hudson, Athens, and Saugerties. The first steamboat sailing out of Catskill was the *Frank*, which began its first of many twice-weekly runs in 1836 between Catskill and New York City. Eventually, on busy days, several thousand people might pass through Catskill Village headed for nearby hostelries, such as the upscale

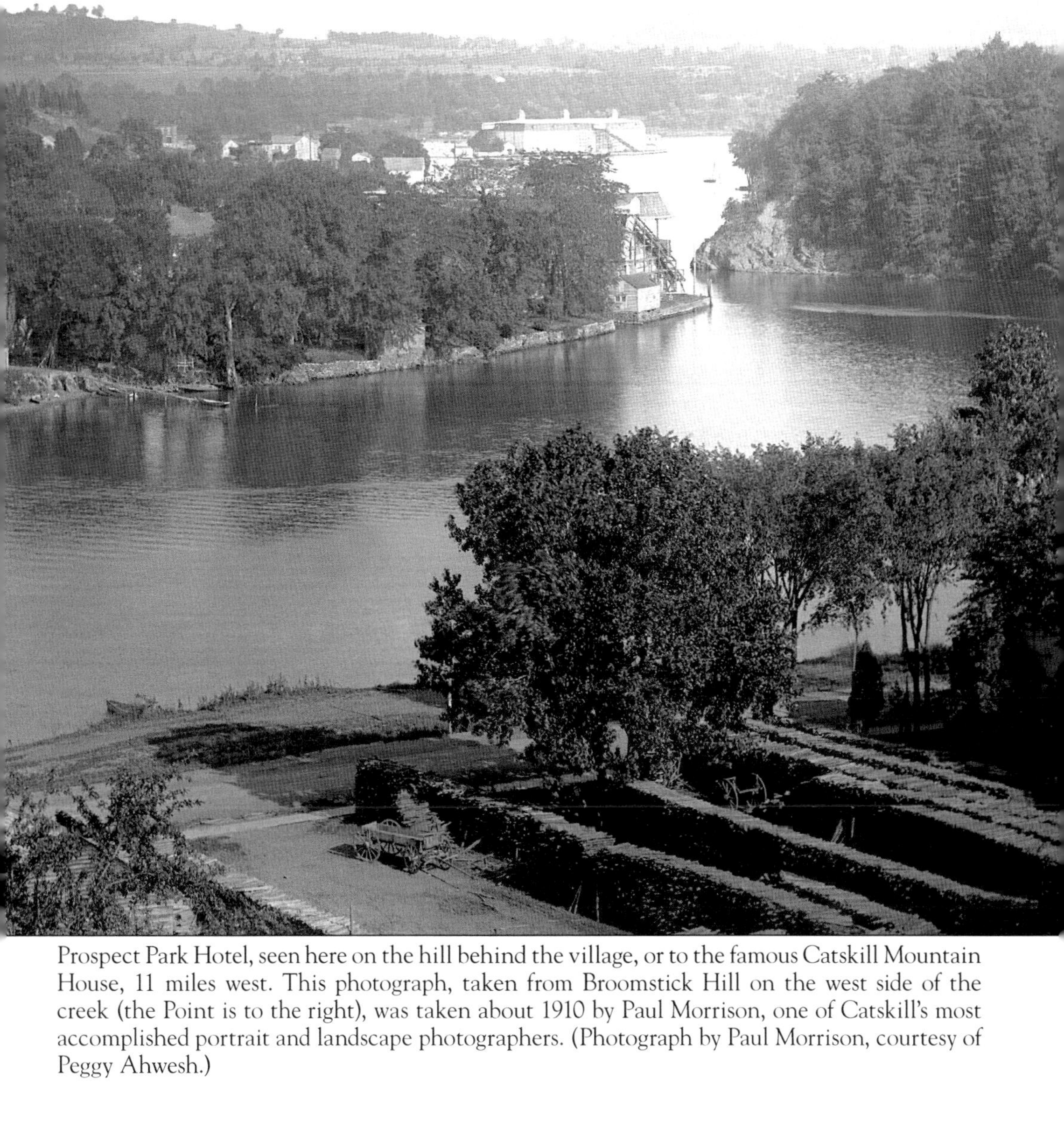

Prospect Park Hotel, seen here on the hill behind the village, or to the famous Catskill Mountain House, 11 miles west. This photograph, taken from Broomstick Hill on the west side of the creek (the Point is to the right), was taken about 1910 by Paul Morrison, one of Catskill's most accomplished portrait and landscape photographers. (Photograph by Paul Morrison, courtesy of Peggy Ahwesh.)

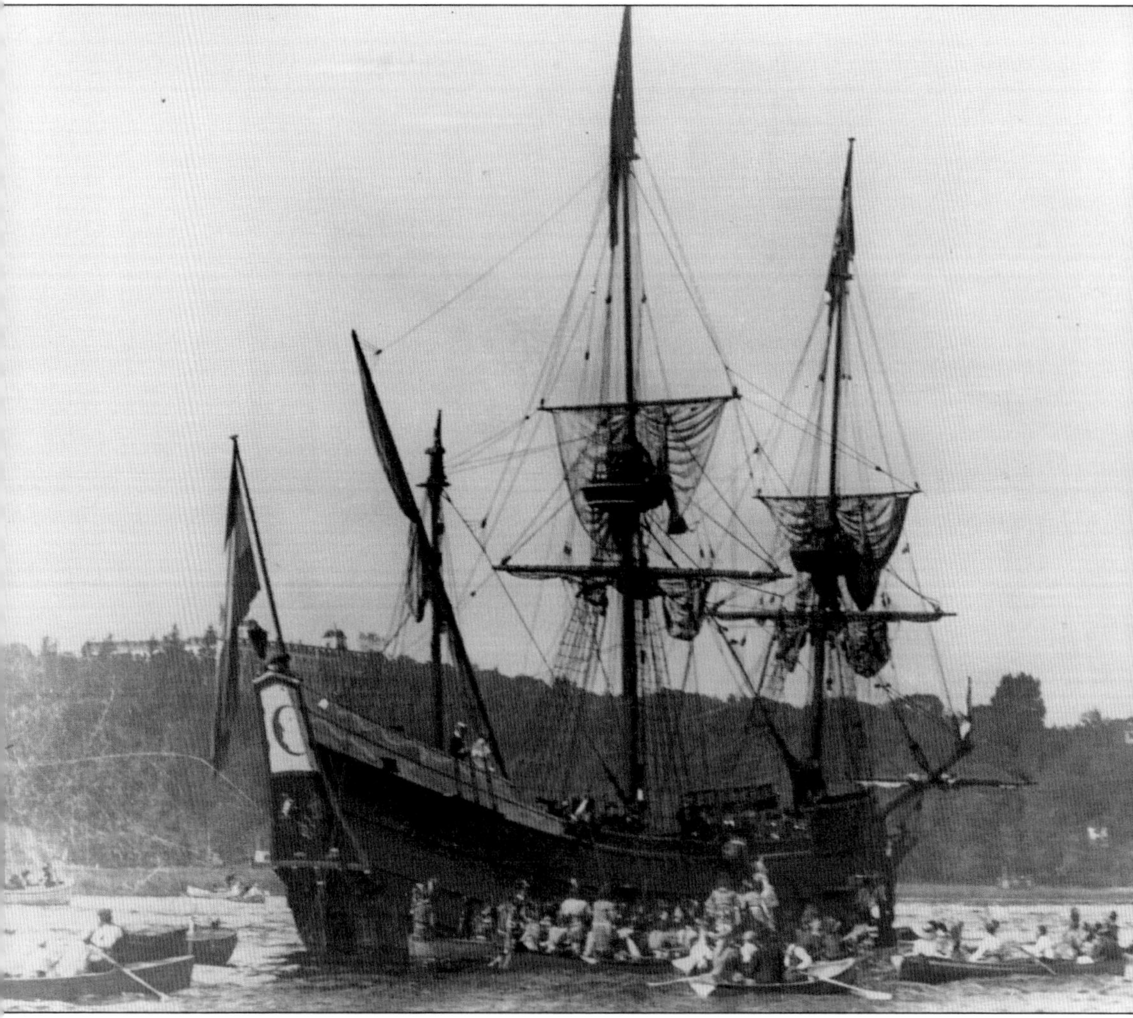

Henry Hudson was an English adventurer who worked for the Dutch East India Company, which underwrote his voyage in 1609 to find the mythical Northwest Passage. Instead, Hudson laid claim for the Dutch to what became one of their most valuable outposts, the area he called New Netherland that encompassed territory from today's Delaware to Upstate New York. In celebration of Hudson's accomplishment, a full-scale replica of his ship, the *Half Moon*, was built by the Dutch and given to America for its 300th anniversary (in 1909) of Hudson's 1609 journey to the New World, including the Hudson River landings at which the explorer was supposed to have stopped. Here is the *Half Moon* in 1909 in the river just to the north of Catskill's Point. The luxurious Prospect Park Hotel can be seen on the hill above. (Courtesy of Robert Meo.)

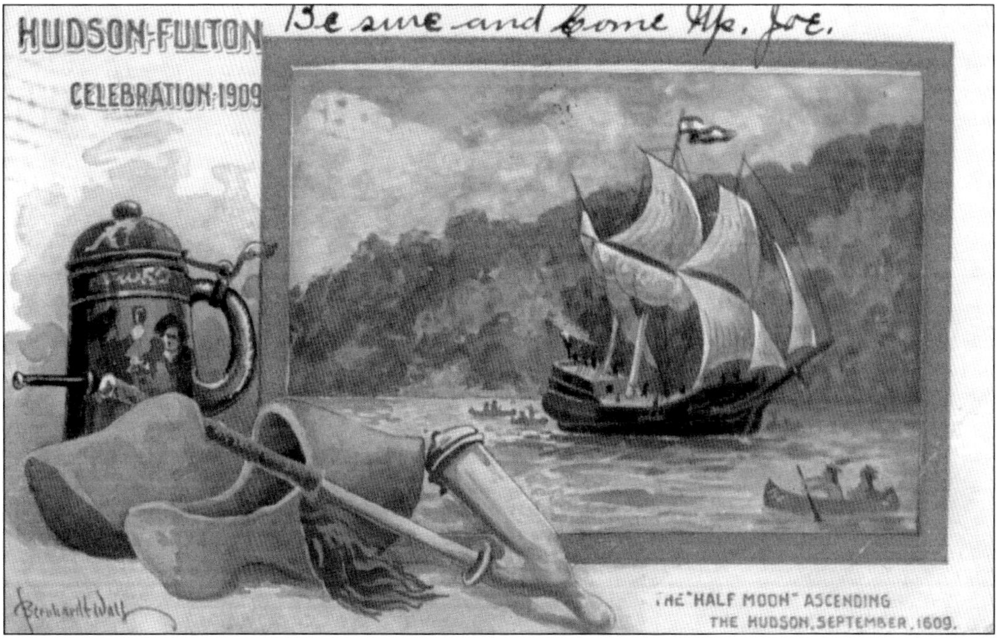


In these fanciful illustrations, Hudson's *Half Moon*, above, is probably being greeted by friendly local Mohican Indians. At right, Hudson is posed in front of an American flag. These whimsical trading cards, the work of Bernhardt Wall, were mass-produced in honor of the 300th anniversary of Hudson's trip. For many years, based on a misreading of Hudson's chronicler Robert Juet's journal, it was believed that Hudson cast anchor at the mouth of the Catskill Creek. Hudson did cast anchor at the mouth of a creek somewhere but most likely at today's Saugerties, and there he was greeted by "a loving people," who were curious and innocent. The Europeans were soon misbehaving—kidnapping, stealing from, and murdering their Native American hosts—but without Native American help, European colonization would have been impossible. (Courtesy of the Arthur Hamm collection.)

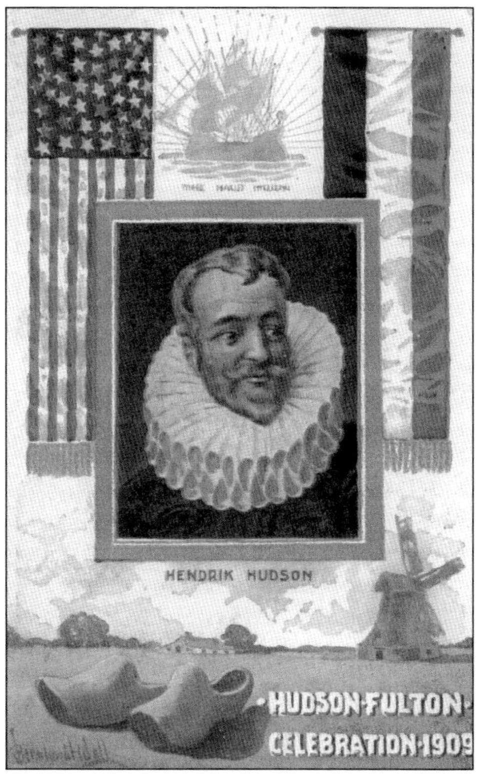

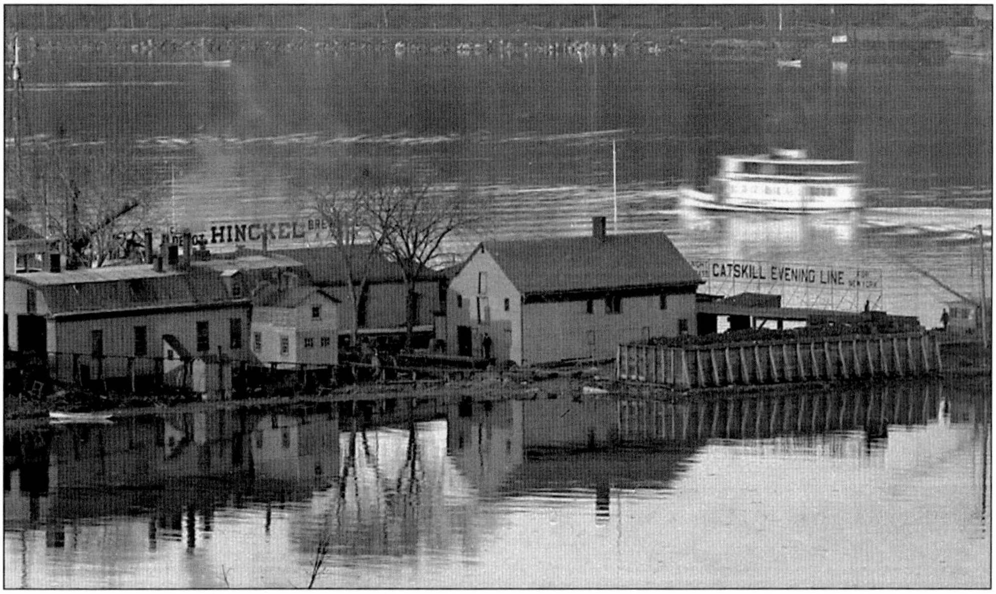


Paul Morrison's photograph of the Point was taken around the dawn of the 20th century and shows the landing used by both the Hudson River Day Line and the Catskill Evening Line. The picture below dates to about 1860 and shows the Point not too many years after the construction of the Long Dock, seen here as a strip of built-up roadway just wide enough for two horse-drawn wagons to pass each other. The Prospect Park Hotel is the imposing structure in the distance. (Above, photograph by Paul Morrison, courtesy of Peggy Ahwesh; below, courtesy of Robert Carl.)

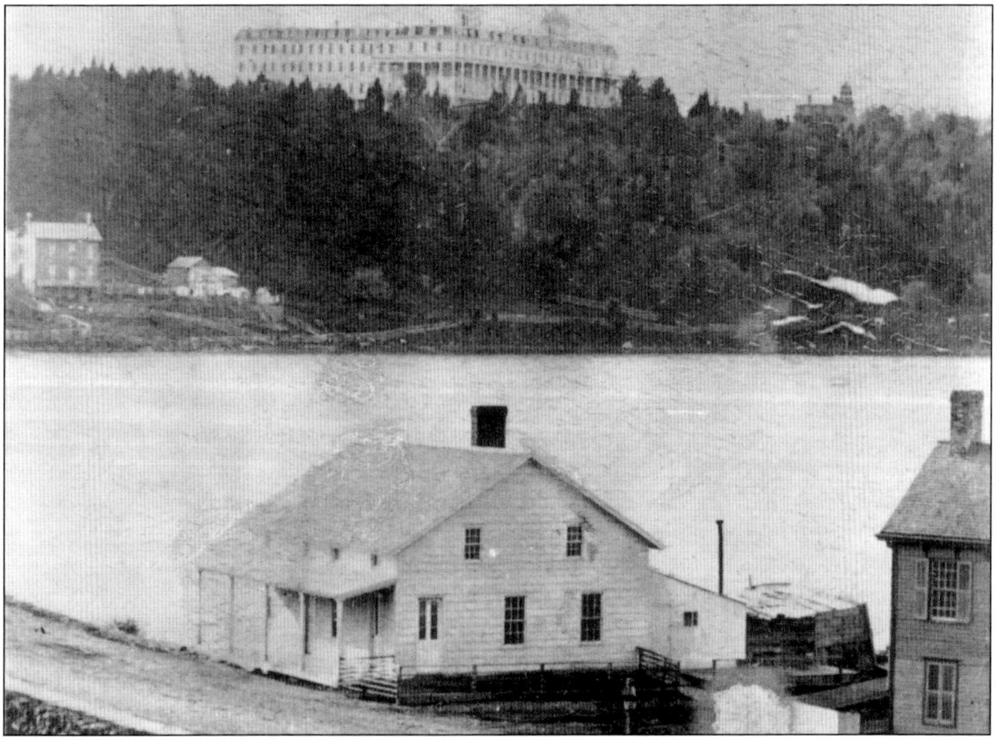

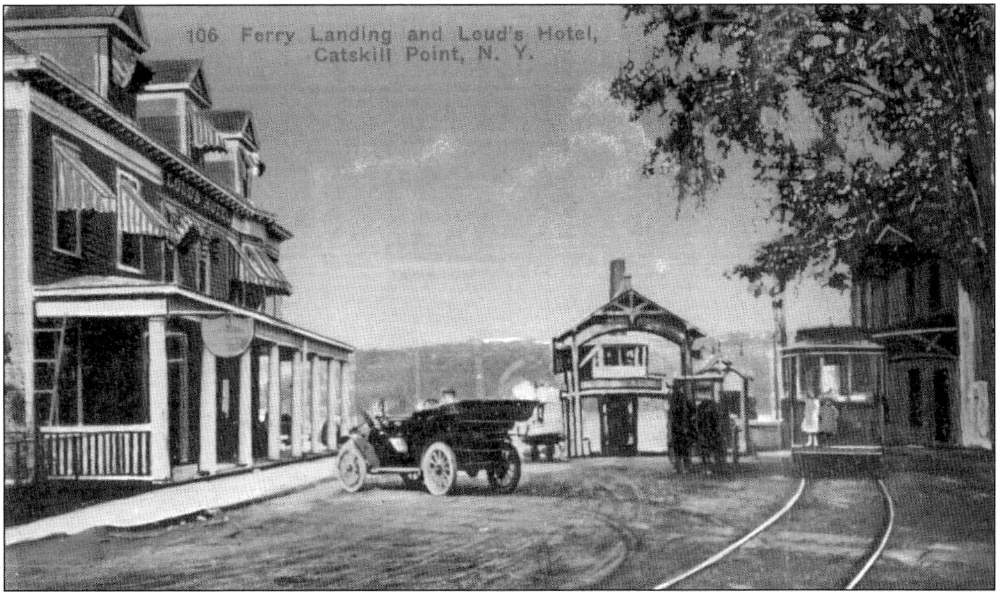


Loud's Hotel at the Point offered comfortable services for the weary traveler who might chose to rest before going onward by horse-drawn carriage into the Catskill Mountains 11 miles distant. In this photograph taken around 1915, there is a choice of transportation: automobile, horse, or trolley. This was an important landing for both night and day line boats until the final day line sailing in 1953. (Author's collection.)

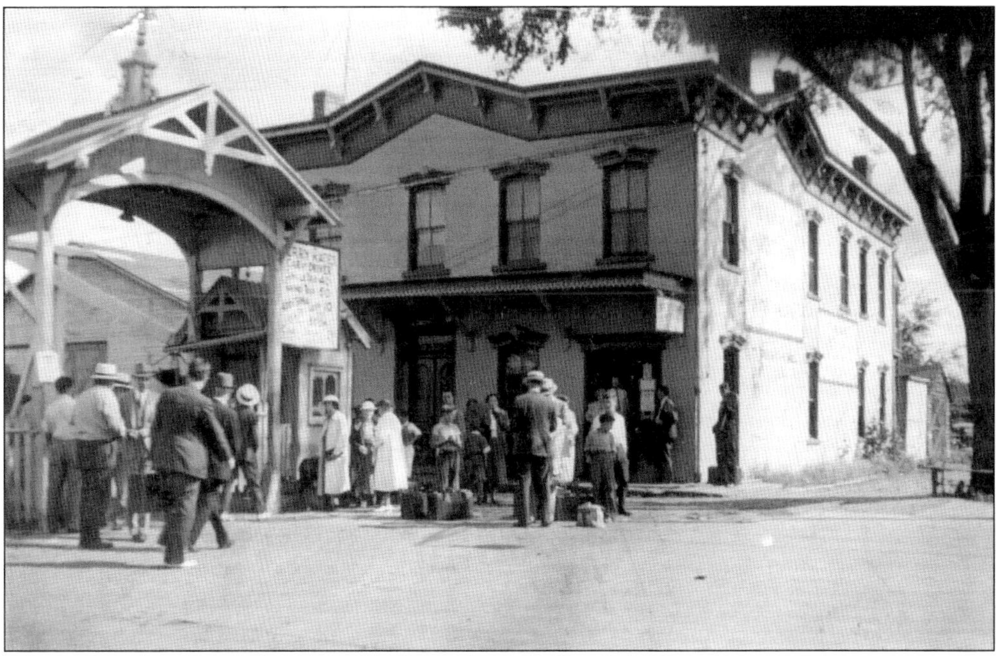

Opposite Loud's Hotel on the Point was the freight master's building, originally constructed in 1880 as the Union Hotel. The wetlands along the river to the north of this landing were filled in during the 19th century and are today the site of the public park and launch called Dutchmen's Landing. The freight master's building has very successfully been rescued and retooled as a museum of local history. (Courtesy of Robert Carl.)

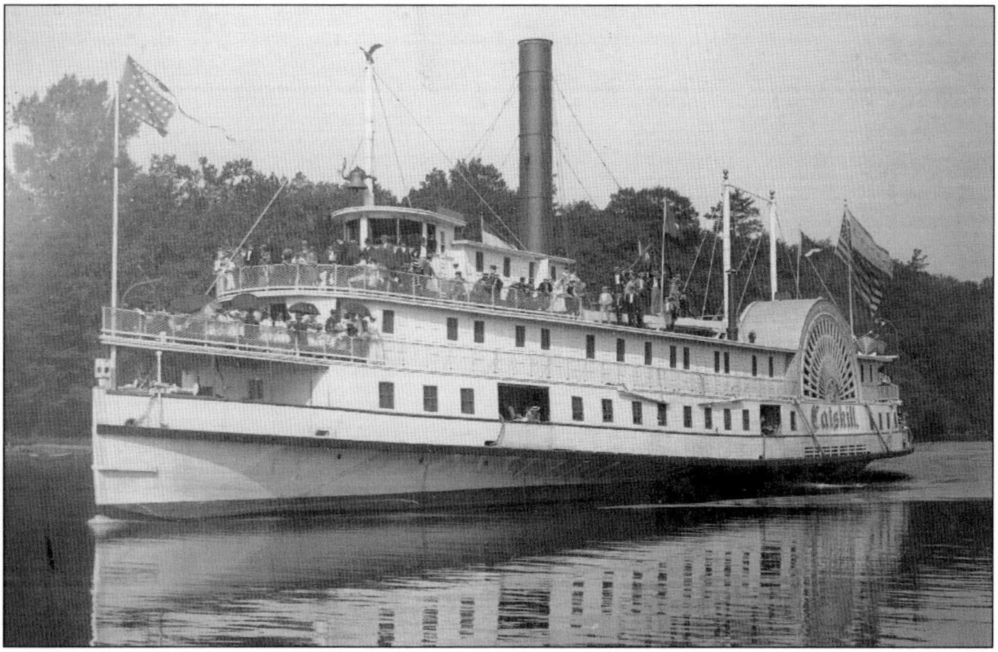

A round-trip to New York City from Catskill by steamer in 1920 left the Point at 6:00 a.m. and was back in Catskill at 8:00 p.m. It cost $1.25. The fastest steamer on the river, the *Onteora*, could make the trip from Catskill to New York City in six hours. The steel-hulled side-wheeler *Catskill* (above) was discontinued in 1929. (Courtesy of Robert Carl.)

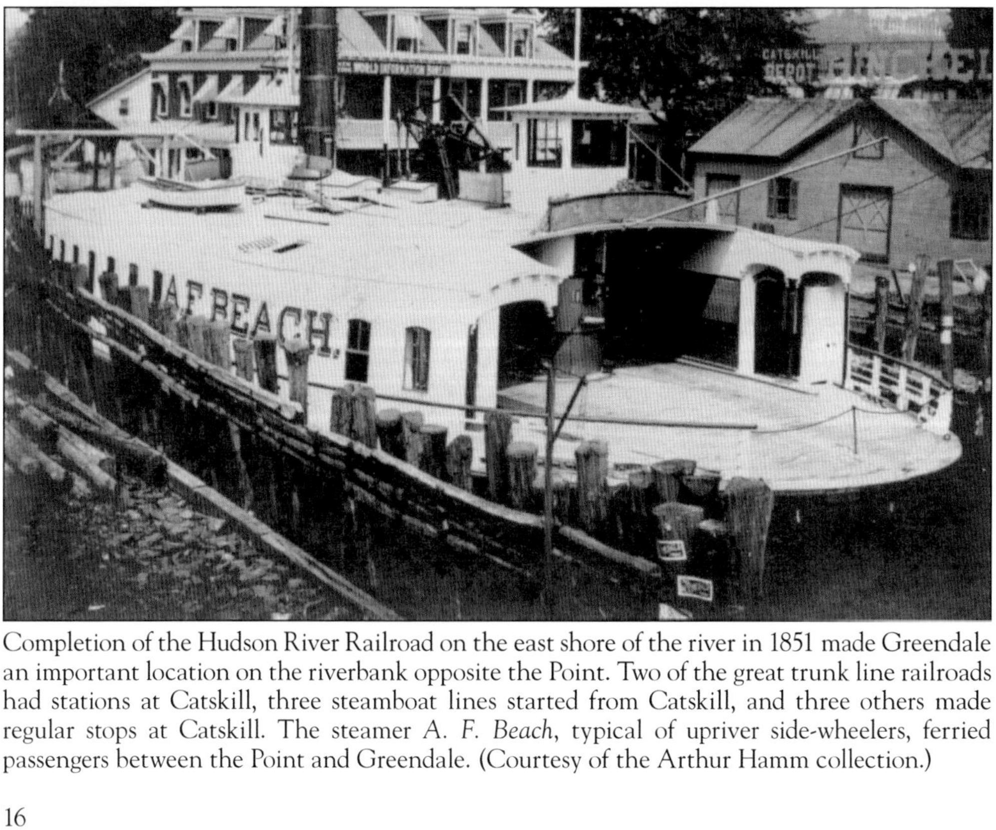


Completion of the Hudson River Railroad on the east shore of the river in 1851 made Greendale an important location on the riverbank opposite the Point. Two of the great trunk line railroads had stations at Catskill, three steamboat lines started from Catskill, and three others made regular stops at Catskill. The steamer A. F. *Beach*, typical of upriver side-wheelers, ferried passengers between the Point and Greendale. (Courtesy of the Arthur Hamm collection.)

# *Two*

# THE CREEK

The Catskill Creek rises to the west in Schoharie County, winds through rich farmland past summer resort areas such as Oak Hill, East Durham, Freehold, South Cairo, and Leeds, and joins up with the Kaaterskill Creek—one of the wildest and most romantic water courses in the entire area—west of the village at a junction that is the long-abandoned site of an ancient once-populous Native American settlement. The village grew up along both the east and west sides of the creek and is crossed by three bridges, the most heavily traveled being the Uncle Sam Bridge, dating to 1801, at the foot of Bridge Street in the center of the village. In a memoir, Catskill-born journalist Thurlow Weed writes of events taking place about 1807, when the Long Dock had not yet been filled in. He writes, in order to get a better look at the "first steamboat," a half-dozen boys put their clothes in their hats, their hats upon boards, and swam from the mainland out to the island to await the approach of Robert Fulton's steamboat the *Clermont*, the first on the Hudson River to take on commercial traffic, in 1807.

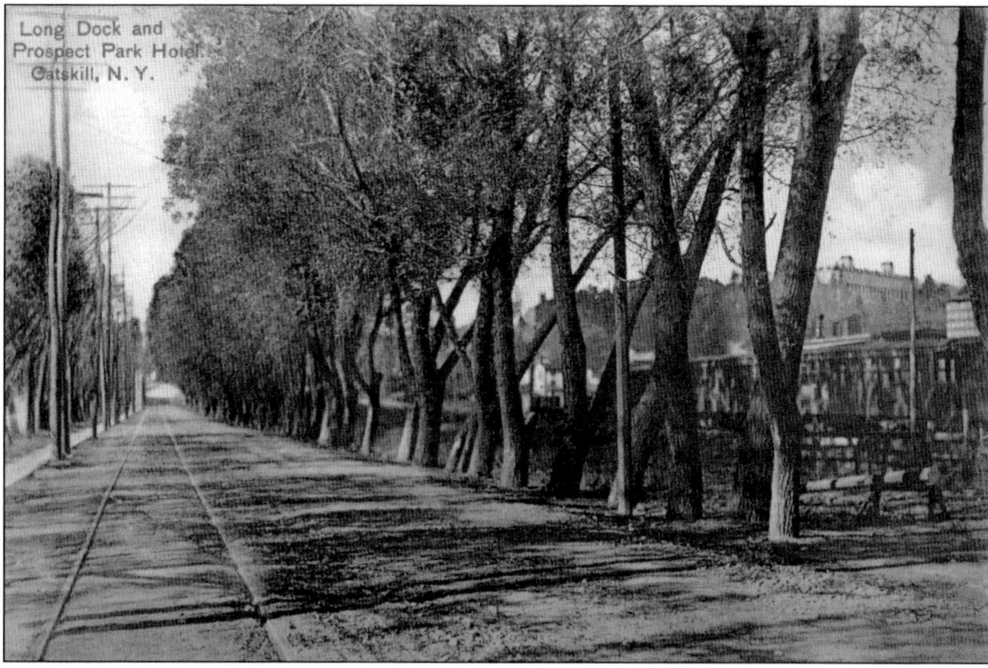


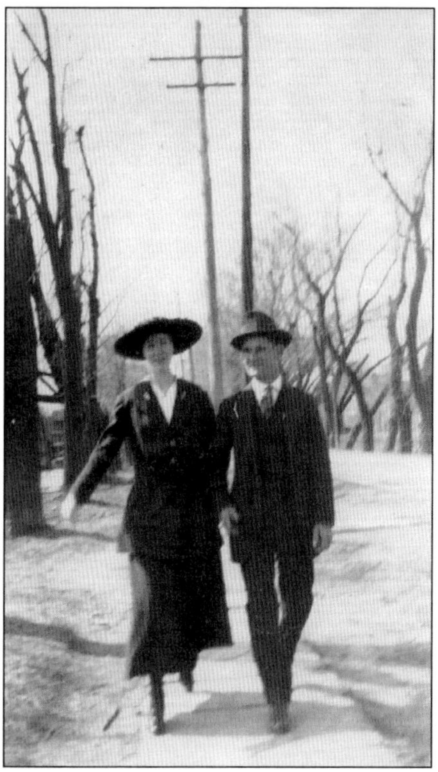

The Long Dock is a causeway from the point of solid land at the mouth of the Catskill Creek out to what were once two islands that had been joined by landfill in the 18th century. The photograph above shows the Long Dock in the early 20th century with trolley tracks, the Catskill Mountain Railroad at right, and on the hill the Prospect Park Hotel. A couple (at left) is strolling in the spring along the footpath to the Point. (Above, courtesy of the Arthur Hamm collection; left, author's collection.)

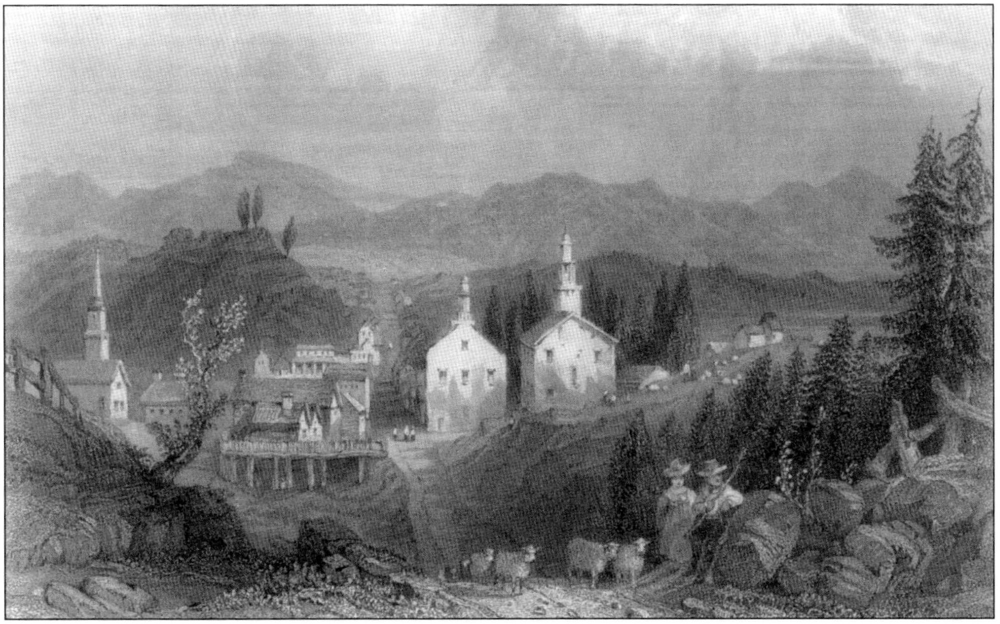

This view of Catskill from the top of Bridge Street around 1838 first appeared in *American Scenery*, which had steel-plate engravings based on drawings by English illustrator W. H. Bartlett. Visible are the steeples of the Dutch Reformed church and the Presbyterian church, the 1813 courthouse, and the Catskill Mountains in the distance. These buildings can still be found in the village today. (Author's collection.)

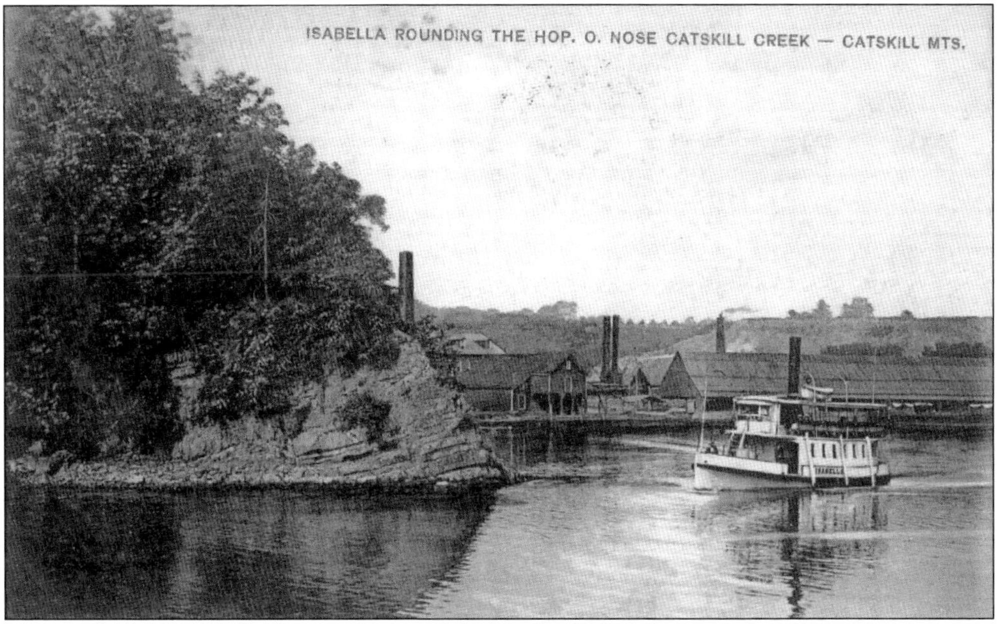


The steamer *Isabella* rounds the rocky promontory in the creek called Hop O' Nose, site of the first Dutch settlement in the 1630s and probably the site of a prehistoric Native American village. The *Isabella* made the four-mile journey between Catskill and Hudson. Remodeled several times, it was kept in use until the new Rip Van Winkle Bridge opened in 1935, putting the ferry service out of business. (Courtesy of Joan Jacobs.)

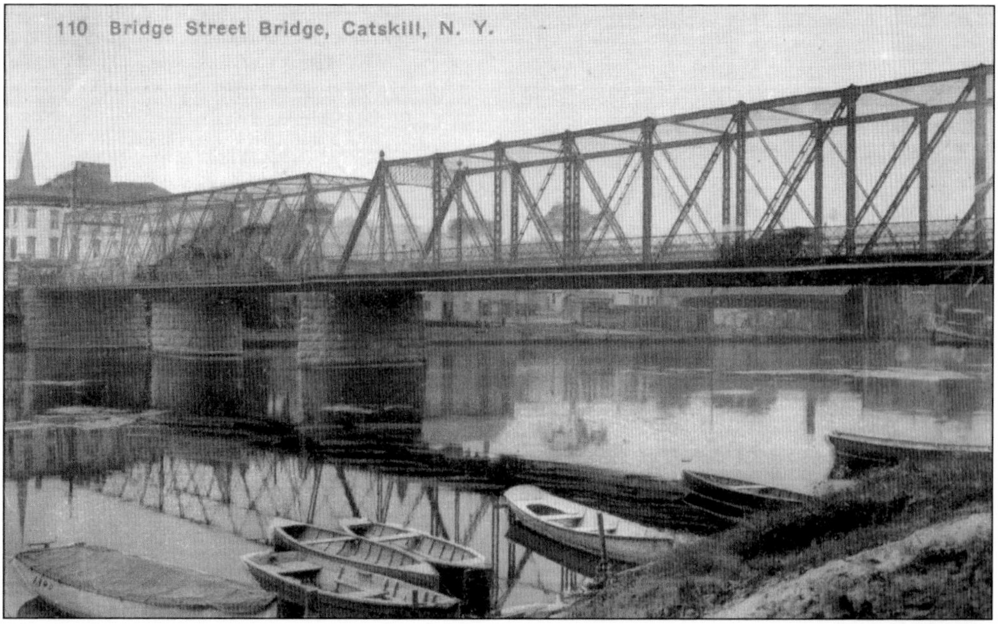


The Bridge Street bridge connects the two parts of the village, east and west. This is the old iron bridge, the second in this location since 1801 (the first was a wooden drawbridge). The bridge today is called the Uncle Sam Bridge after local man Sam Wilson, the Civil War–era grocer who was the original Uncle Sam of recruiting poster fame. (Courtesy of the Arthur Hamm collection.)

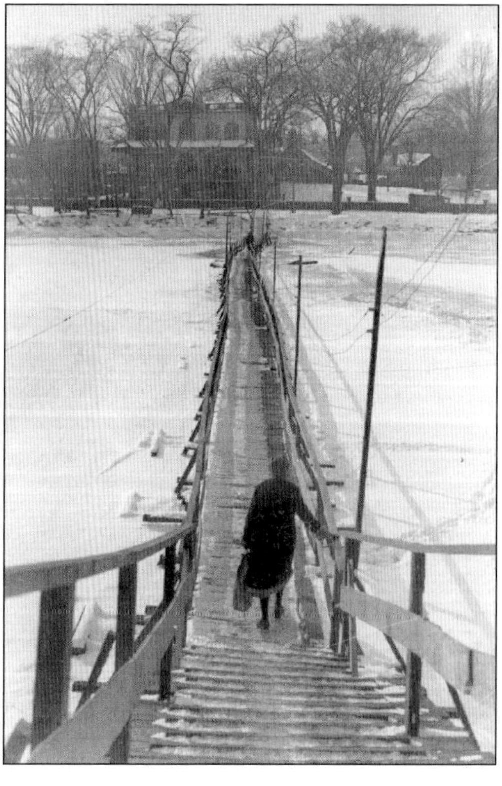

The Palmatiers' mansion on West Main Street is seen in the distance at the end of the temporary wooden bridge that crossed the creek after a disastrous maritime mishap in 1901 that destroyed the old iron bridge. A walkway was built on top of a pontoon arrangement made with empty oil barrels. The pedestrian appears to be hesitating before crossing the frozen creek. (Author's collection.)

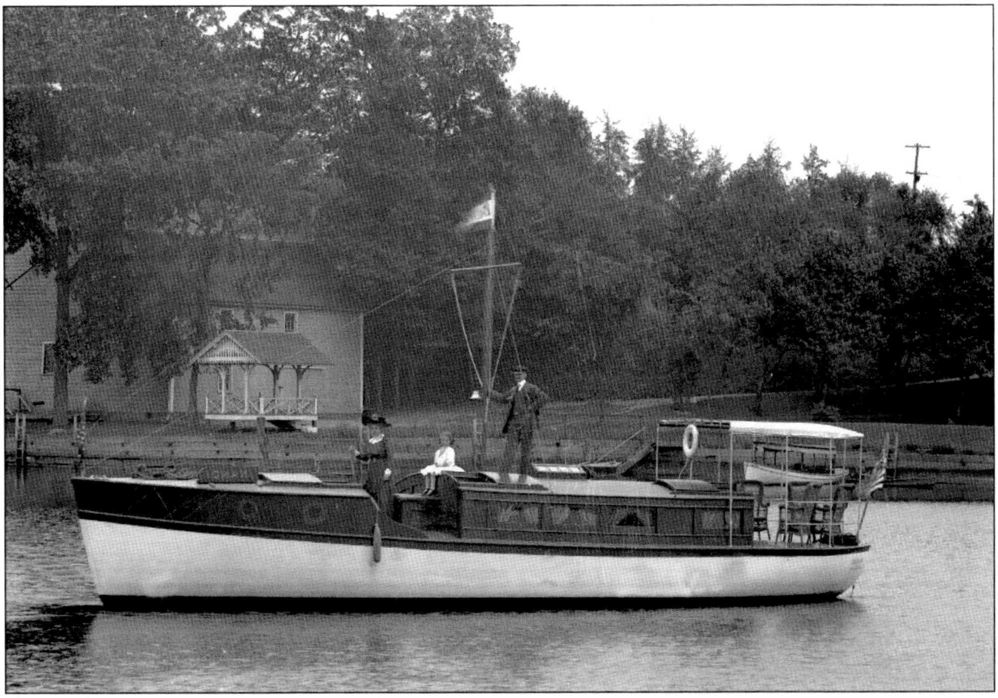

In Paul Morrison's photograph, an elegant Chris-Craft mahogany yacht from about 1920 is sailing up the creek past the Catskill marina. The natural harbor of the creek is an attractive port and recreational area with excellent facilities, restaurants, and shopping on nearby Main Street. (Photograph by Paul Morrison, courtesy of Peggy Ahwesh.)

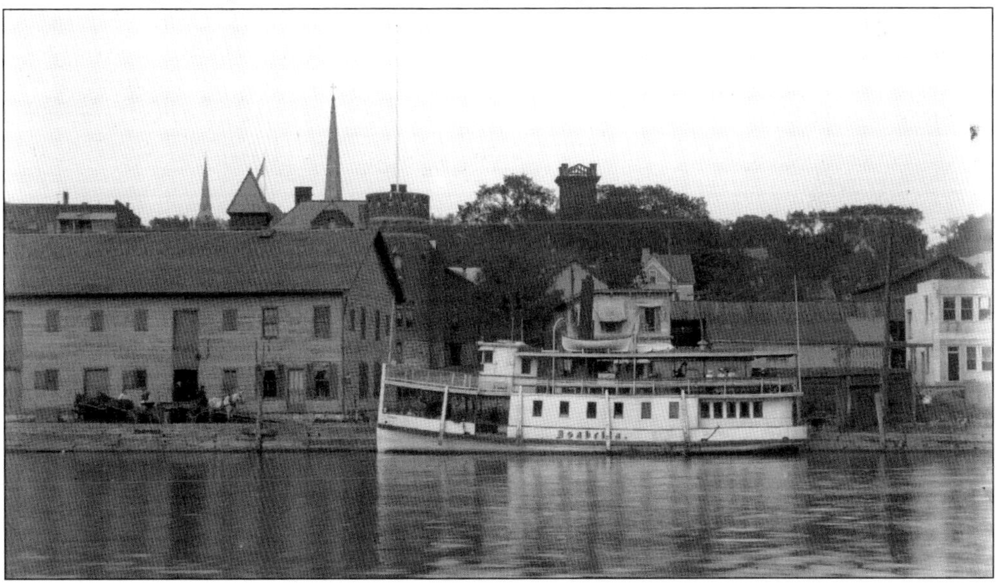

The *Isabella* docks around 1890 at the landing on the creek near midvillage. Directly in the background is the square tower of the Dutch Reformed church. To its left are the turrets of the elegant Richardsonian Romanesque armory, and above the turrets is the spire of the Presbyterian church, one of the great architectural treasures of the Hudson River valley. (Courtesy of Robert Carl.)

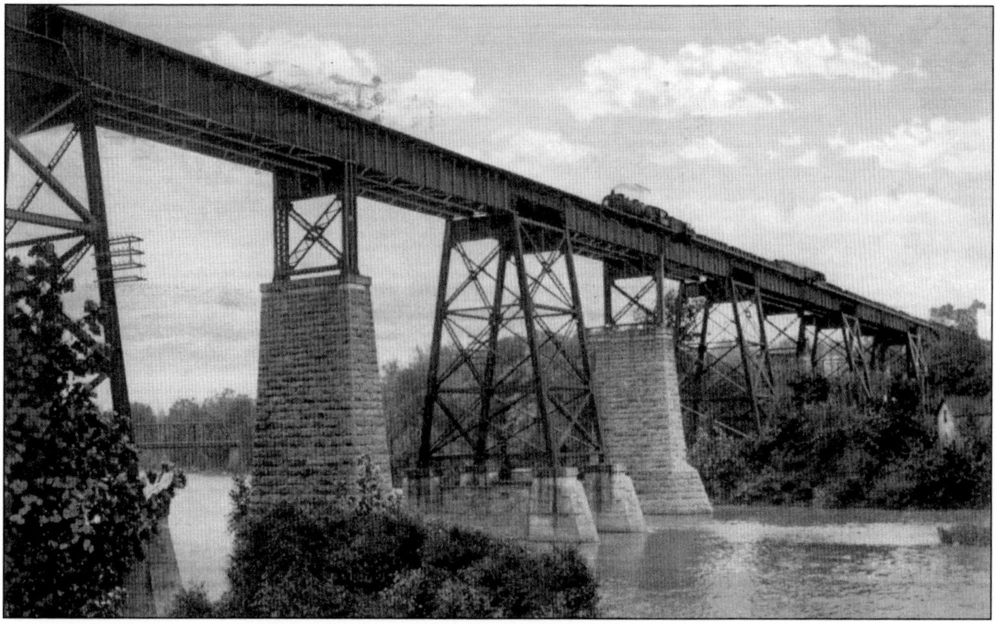

The West Shore Railroad bridge was praised in an article appearing in *Scientific American* in 1886 as one of the structural wonders of the modern world. Located up the creek from the Uncle Sam Bridge, it is still very much in use today. The train station is a short distance out of sight to the left; passenger service was discontinued in the 1950s. (Courtesy of the Arthur Hamm collection.)

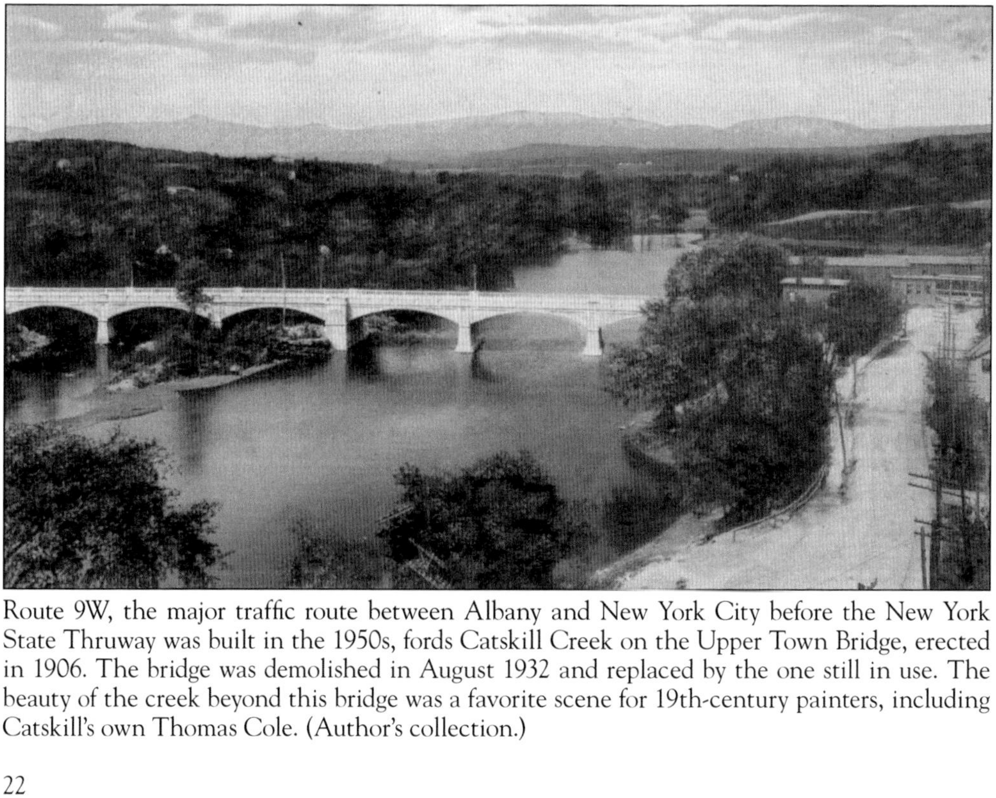

Route 9W, the major traffic route between Albany and New York City before the New York State Thruway was built in the 1950s, fords Catskill Creek on the Upper Town Bridge, erected in 1906. The bridge was demolished in August 1932 and replaced by the one still in use. The beauty of the creek beyond this bridge was a favorite scene for 19th-century painters, including Catskill's own Thomas Cole. (Author's collection.)

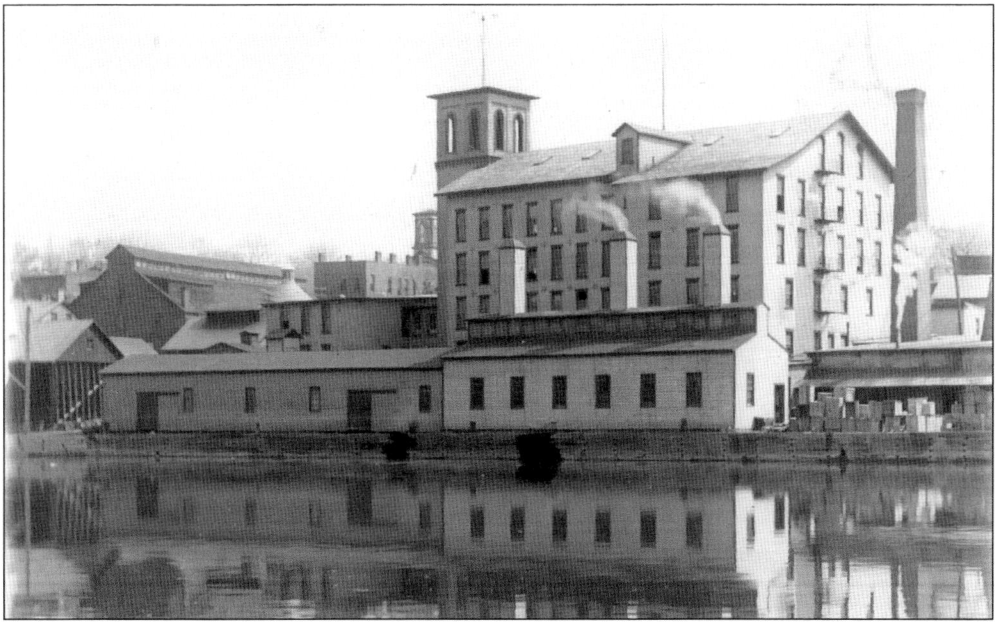

The Union Mills building, seen around 1910, was constructed in the 1840s to take advantage of ready creek transportation. It has served many uses, including a flour mill, a factory where uniforms for Union troops in the Civil War were made, a temporary high school, and a furniture storage building, and today it has been renovated into loft-style condominiums. (Courtesy of Robert Carl.)

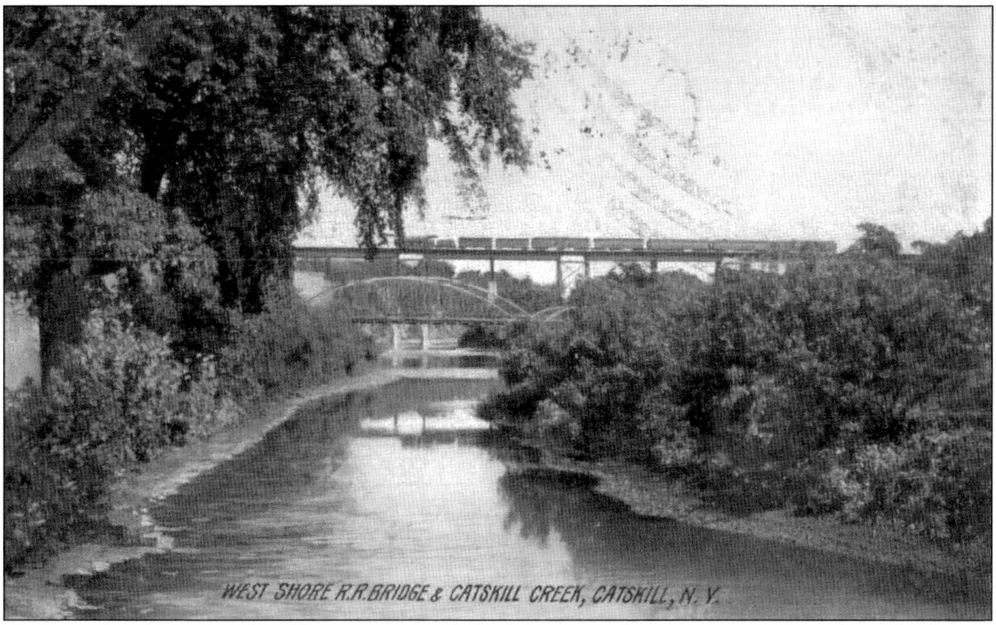


In the distance is the West Shore Railroad bridge, and below that is the Black Bridge over which narrow-gauge trains of the Catskill-Canojoherie Railroad ran regularly between Catskill's Point and tourist enclaves to the west. Commercial marine traffic, of which there was a great deal before the creek silted up, sailed up the creek on the other side of the island at the right in this photograph from 1910. (Courtesy of Joan Jacobs.)

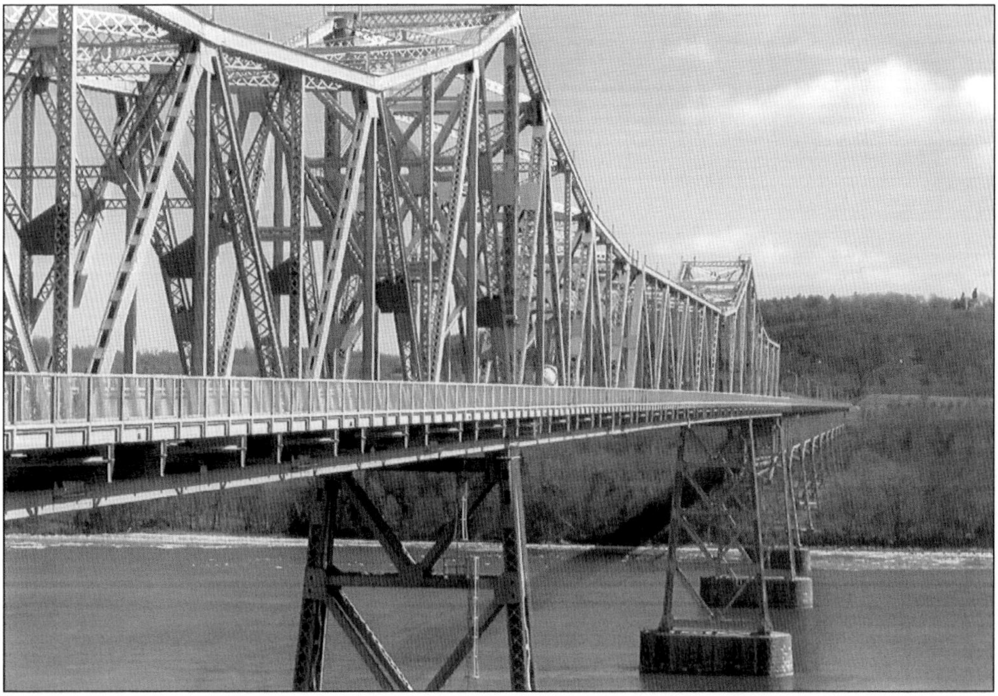

Completed in 1936, the Rip Van Winkle Bridge connects Catskill Village in Greene County with Columbia County. The bridge crosses over Rogers Island, which was the scene of the famous slaughter of the Mohican Indians in a territorial power struggle with the Mohawk Indians in the 16th century that James Fenimore Cooper wrote about in his historical novel *The Last of the Mohicans*. (Author's collection.)

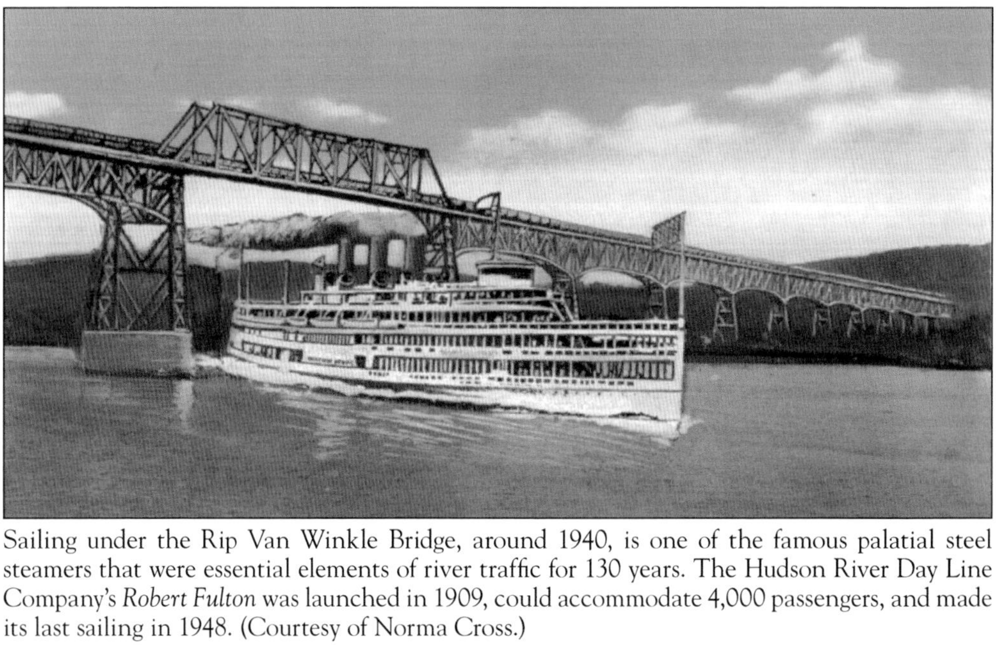

Sailing under the Rip Van Winkle Bridge, around 1940, is one of the famous palatial steel steamers that were essential elements of river traffic for 130 years. The Hudson River Day Line Company's *Robert Fulton* was launched in 1909, could accommodate 4,000 passengers, and made its last sailing in 1948. (Courtesy of Norma Cross.)

# *Three*

# MAIN STREET

Historic Main Street begins at the Point and runs parallel to the creek through the village's commercial strip, which dates to the 18th century and is, architecturally speaking, one of Catskill's most attractive and valuable visual assets. The route may have been an ancient track for Native Americans going to the river, and archaeological digs nearby have unearthed the remains of substantial settlements occupied over millennia before the arrival of Europeans. In 1801, the main street was incorporated into the Susquehanna Turnpike, the toll road that opened western lands for commerce and made Catskill one of the most important upriver ports. Main Street was Catskill's commercial center, and with the village also being the county seat, people came from many miles out in the country to handle legal matters, taxes, and licensing—just about anything that required professional services. An impressive list of services was available in the village, but none perhaps held a closer place to the hearts of many than the old general store. General stores at the dawn of the 20th century carried basics, including flour, sugar, crackers, candy, canned goods, and patent medicines, as well as dry goods such fabric, ready-mades, and thread. The general store also served as a center for exchanging local news and gossip.

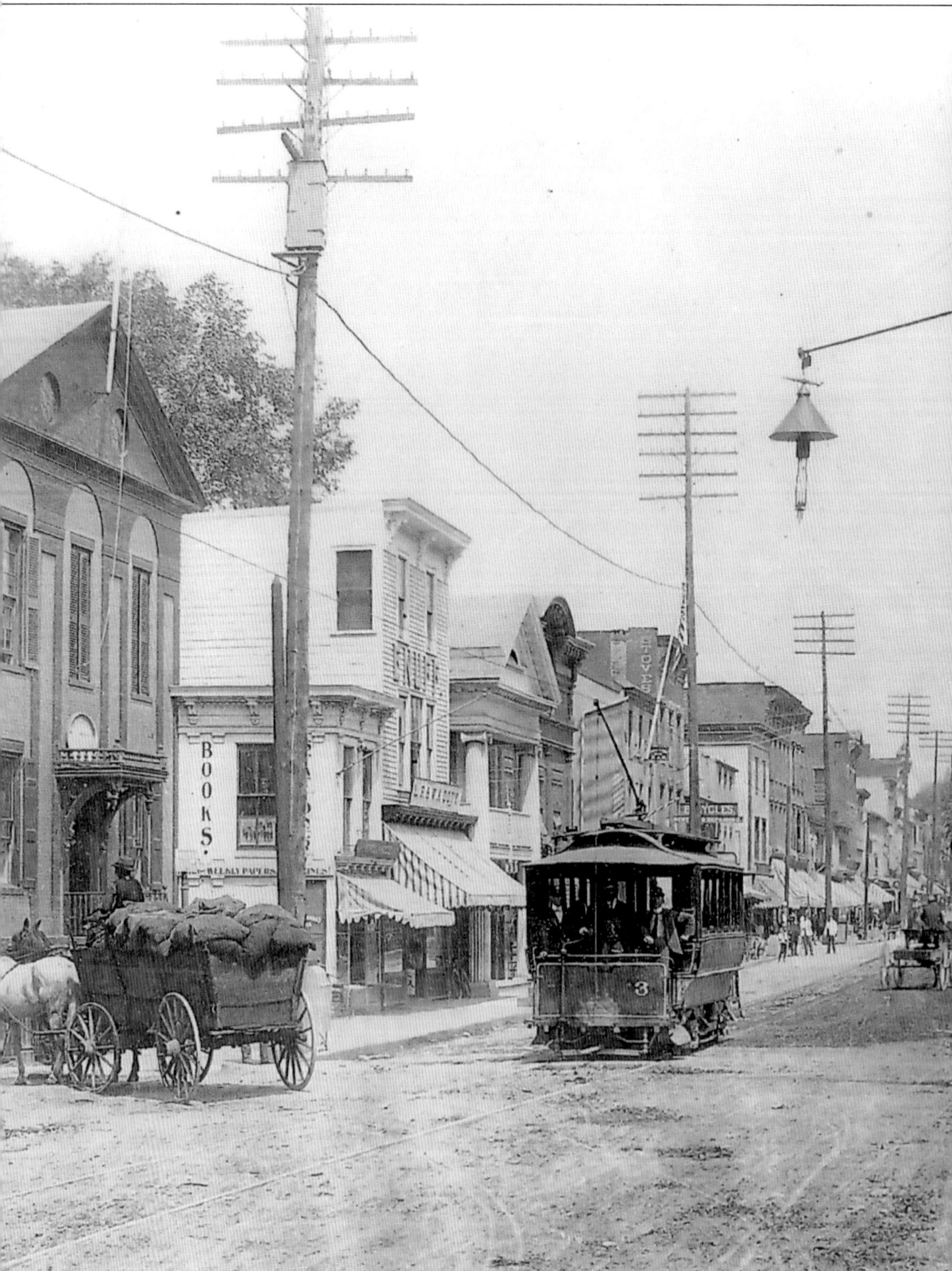
BOOKS.

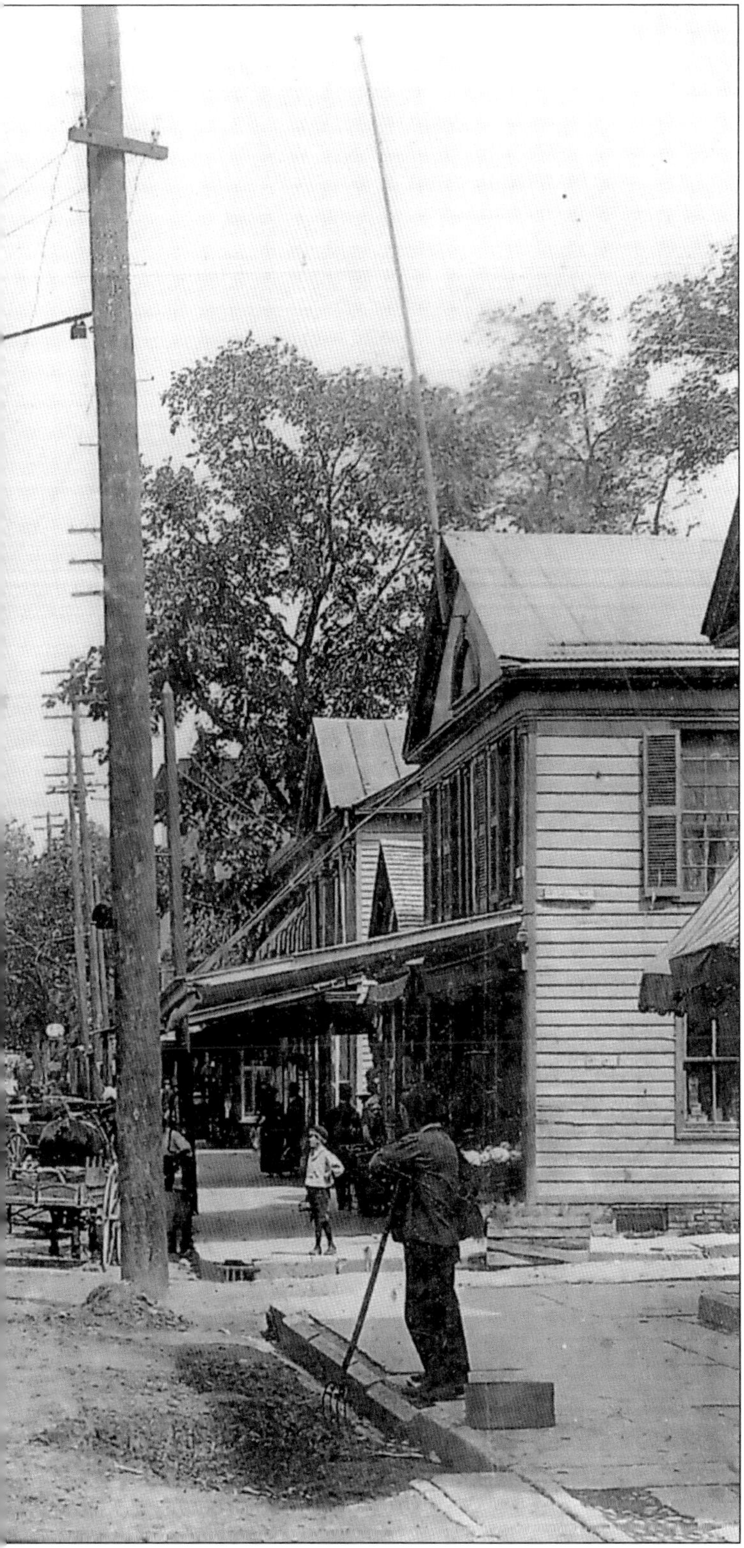

This view of Catskill taken at the intersection of Bridge and Main Streets about 1900 reflects the general air of prosperity of the village. With a population around 5,000, the village had modern electric trolleys, streetlamps, telephones, storm sewers, sidewalks, three banks, and shops that sold books and newspapers. The village was the county seat, served by two railroads, was one of the few major stops on the river between New York City and Albany, was a commercial manufacturing and farming center, and was the gateway to one of America's most desirable tourist regions, the Catskill Mountains. Main Street could still be a muddy thoroughfare in bad weather, however, and streets had yet to be paved, and pedestrians had to be wary of wagons and horses and ever-present piles of horse manure. (Author's collection.)

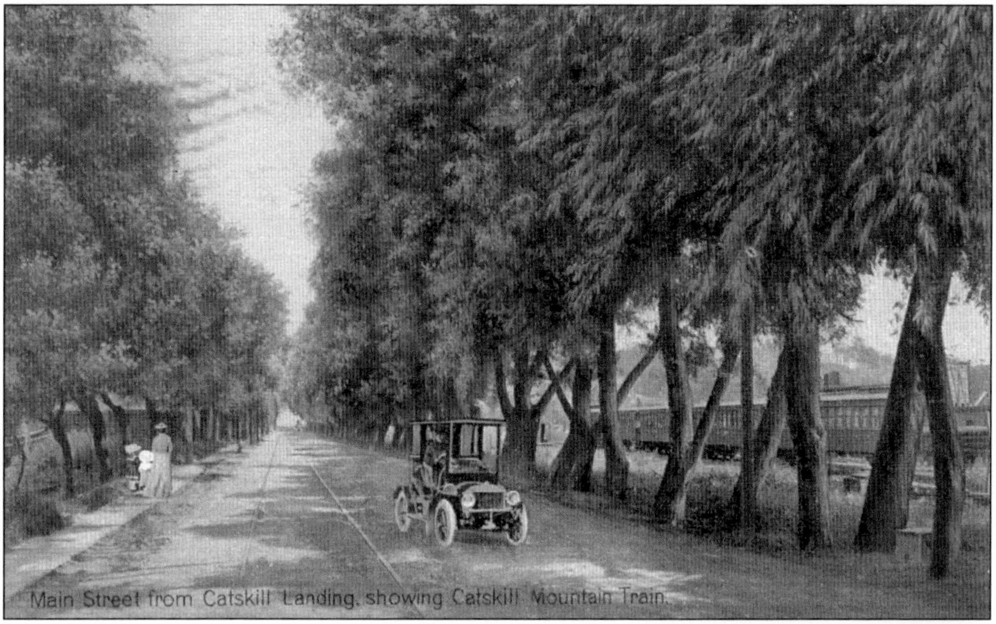


An undoubtedly emancipated lady drives a fashionable Franklin Steamer along Main Street toward the Point. Suffrage was a hot topic at the time this postcard photograph was taken around 1910, and driving one's own new horseless carriage was a valiant sign of independence. The Catskill Mountain Railroad (seen at the right) is probably filled with passengers who recently disembarked at the Point. (Courtesy of Joan Jacobs.)

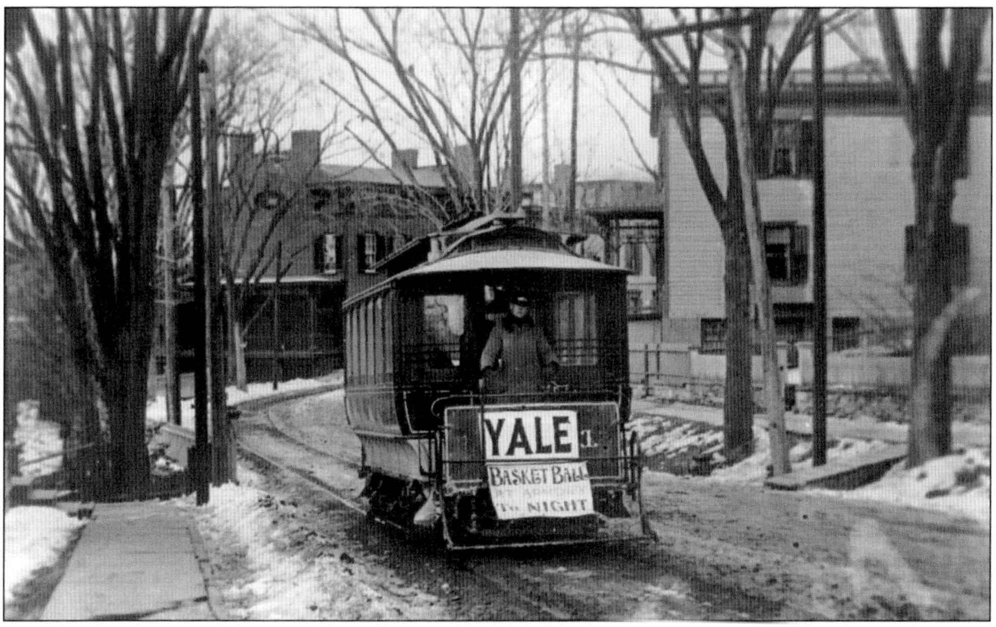


According to an item in the *Catskill Examiner and Recorder* in 1905, "Since the trolley line was allowed to wind its eccentric course through our village, Main Street (at all times bad in the winter) has become a positive menace. Accidents are of daily occurrence, and it is only by the utmost vigilance that a skilled driver can survive its perils." The Catskill basketball team had championship status; watch out, Yale. (Courtesy of Nancy Ursprung.)

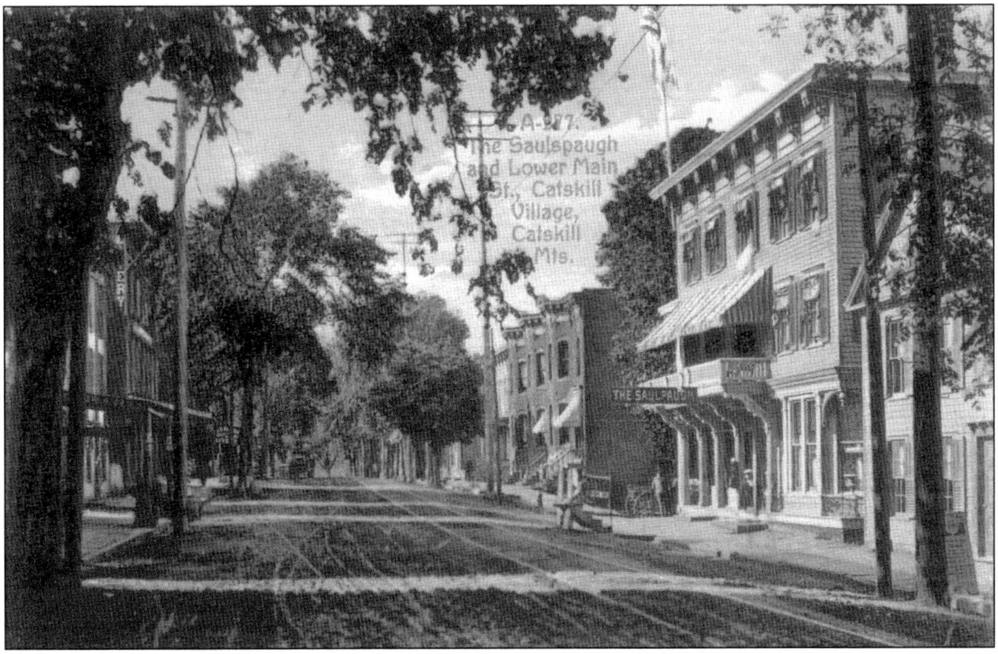


This Main Street view from about 1900 was from a location approximately where the post office is today. Looking spiffy with its striped canvas awning, the Saulpaugh Hotel, built in 1863 as the Windsor Hotel, was renovated several times and renamed under the management of Lambert and Samuel Saulpaugh. It had a popular lounge and a decent restaurant and was a great favorite with drummers hawking their wares along the valley. (Author's collection.)

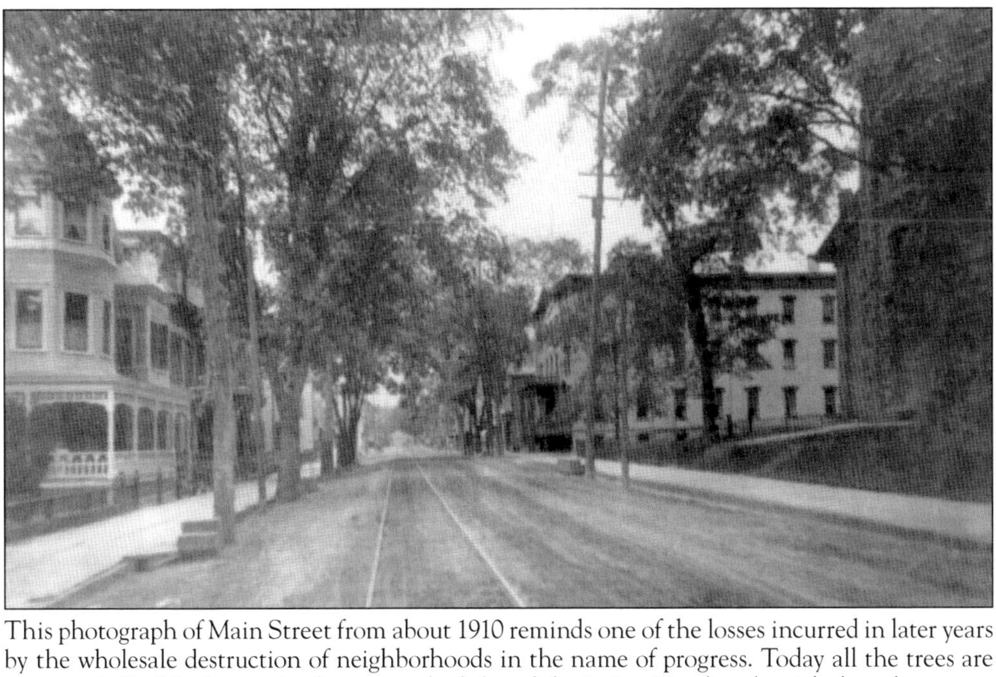

This photograph of Main Street from about 1910 reminds one of the losses incurred in later years by the wholesale destruction of neighborhoods in the name of progress. Today all the trees are gone, and all of the houses in the row to the left and the Irving Hotel to the right have been torn down. The Dutch Reformed church at right is all that remains. (Author's collection.)

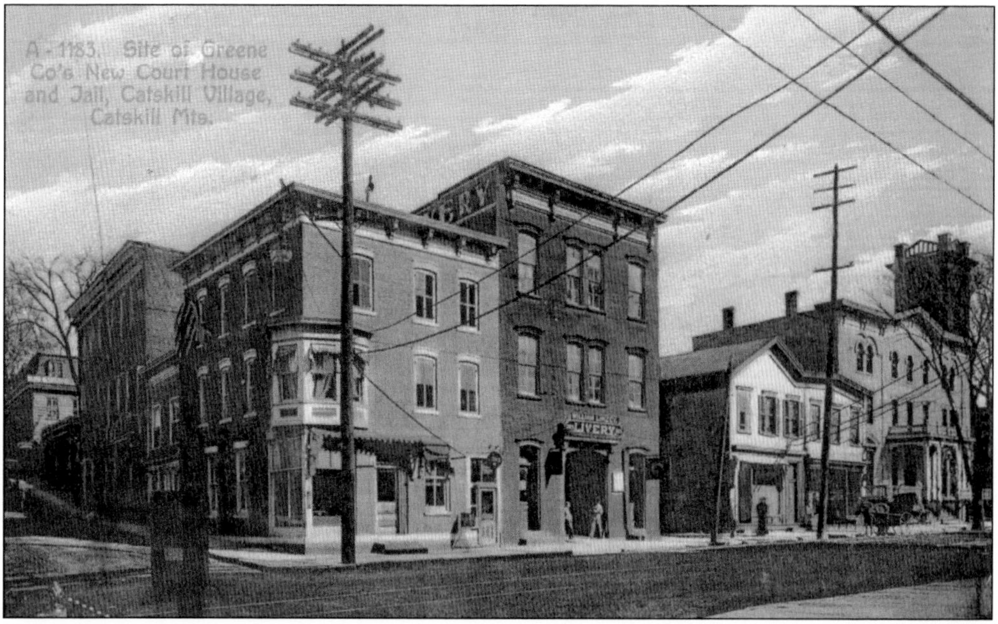

The southeast corner of Bridge and Main Streets, pictured here around 1900, once housed the popular Oyster Bay House saloon and restaurant, the Western Union Telegraph and Cable office, and William Linzey's livery. The village's first automobile sales office, established by Charles Wardel, was located in the corner building. This row of buildings was torn down in 1908 to clear land for the new courthouse. (Courtesy of the Arthur Hamm collection.)

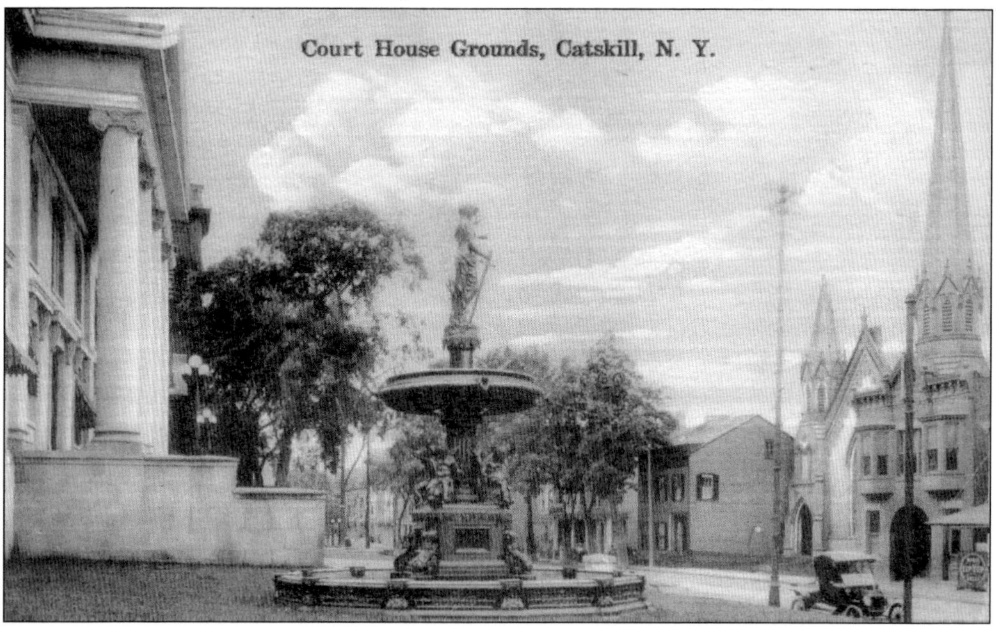

On the grounds of the 1910 courthouse was a classically themed water fountain, a gift to Greene County from one of its most prosperous sons, the Honorable Sen. William P. Fiero. Fiero and his family, descendants of Palatines, had a substantial impact on the development of the county. The fountain succumbed to rust and water shortages and was replaced in 1985 with some marble slabs. (Courtesy of Robert Carl.)

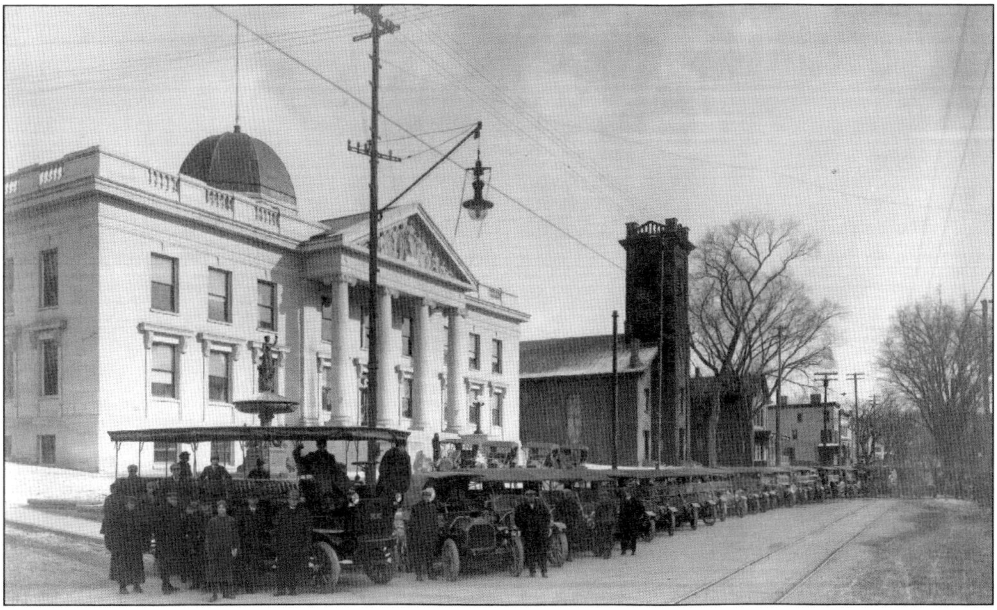

The new neoclassical Greene County Courthouse was built in 1908 and 1909 and in its day was said to be "the finest county building in the state." It was supposed to be fireproof, an important consideration in light of the long history of fire devastation in the village. Garage owner Amos Post has staged a parade of new Cadillacs to increase interest and sales. (Courtesy of Stephanie Walsh.)

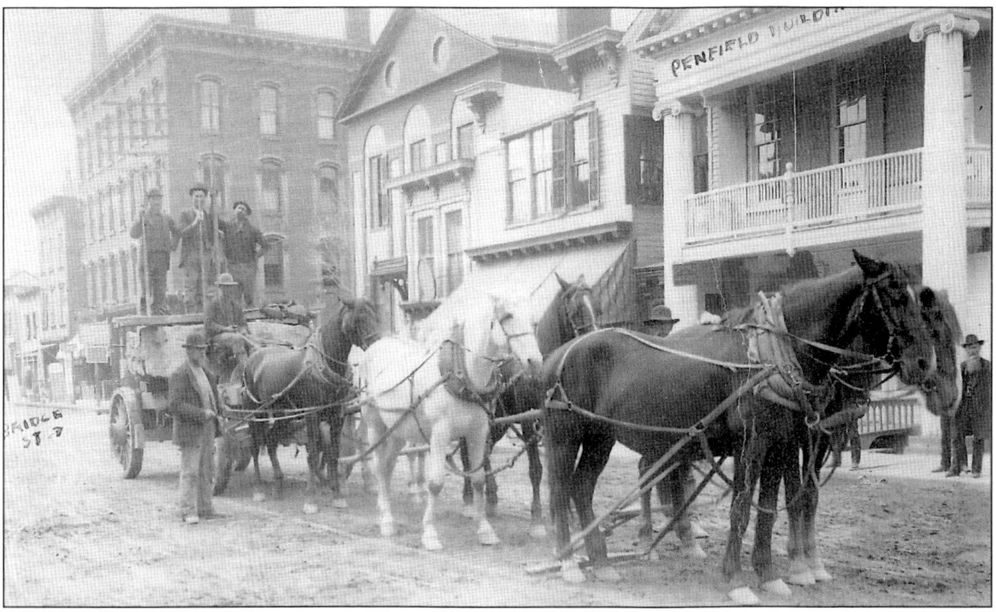


Drovers pose on Main Street in front of the Greek Revival Penfield Building that was soon torn down to make room for the Catskill Savings Bank, one of three banks that earned the local nickname "Little Wall Street." Behind the workmen in this 1898 photograph is the three-story "opera house" that was neither a house nor a theater for opera but served as a community center and a hotel and housed a billiard hall and popular restaurant serving German food. (Courtesy of Robert Carl.)

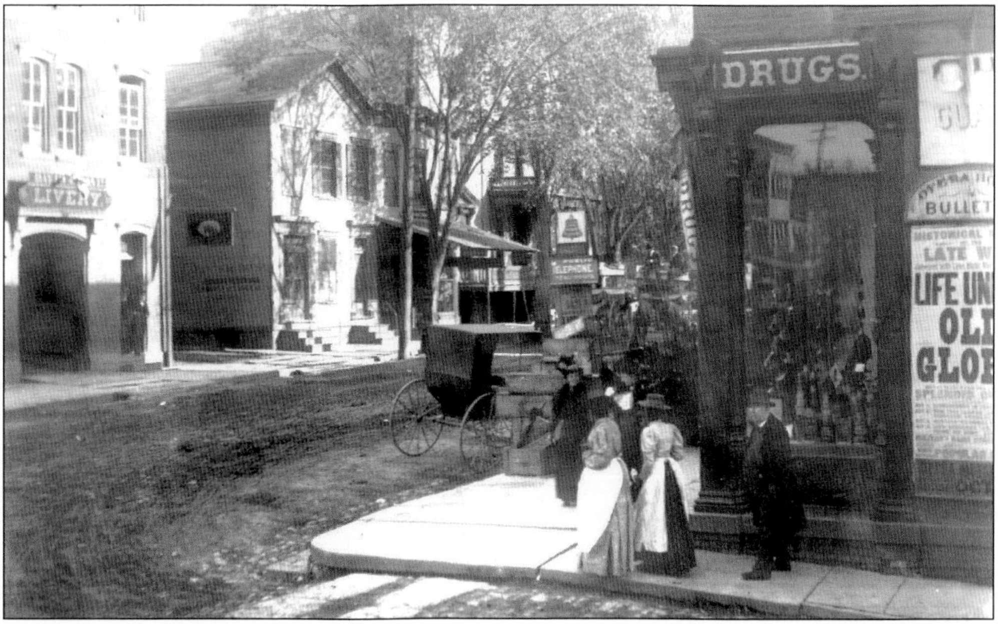


Pictured here around 1900 at the corner of Bridge and Main Streets is one of several village drugstores, the most famous of which was in the Dubois family many years and in business since the 1790s. It claimed to be the oldest continuously operated drugstore in New York State. A long-forgotten play called *Life Under Old Glory* is coming to the Nelida Theatre a half block up Main Street. (Courtesy of Robert Carl.)

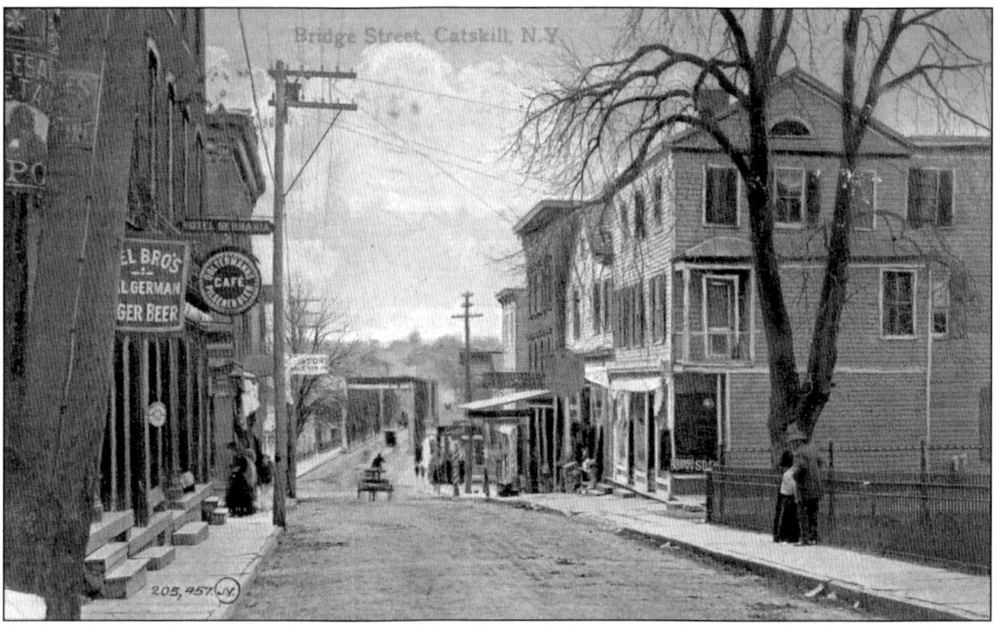


This postcard view from about 1900 of the section of Bridge Street between Main Street and the creek shows a stretch of unpaved road with Colterman's Café and the Hotel Germania on the left, the 1871 iron bridge ahead, and a row of commercial buildings that housed a popular bakery and photographer Paul Morrison's studio on the right. This dirt road was a portion of the principal route between Albany and New York City. (Author's collection.)

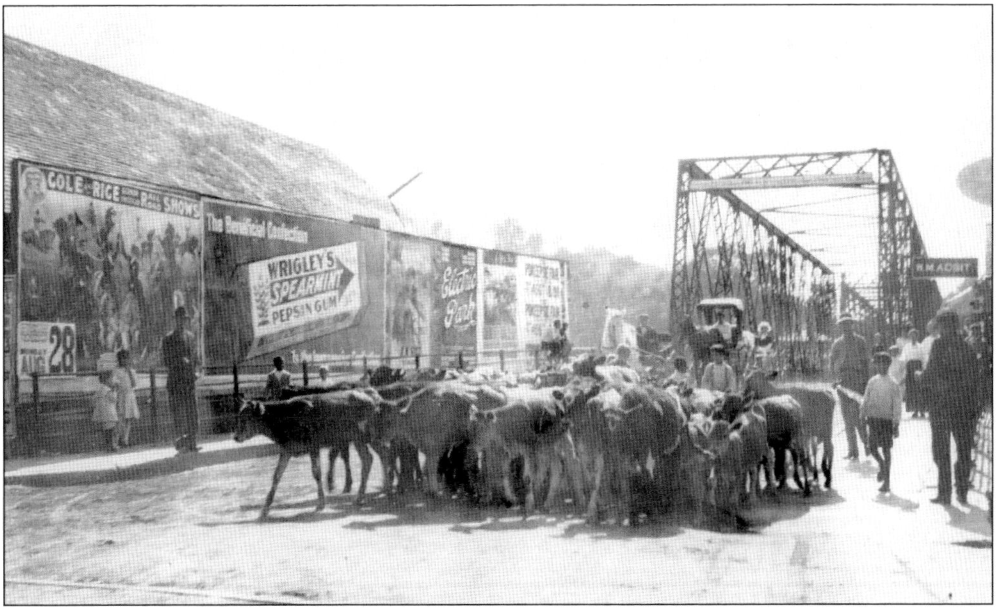


Traffic jams caused by herds of cattle having to share the road with wagons, carriages, and eventually automobiles were not uncommon. Here, around 1900, the cows are heading up Bridge Street toward the center of town. What happened then is unknown. The billboards are advertising a fair in Poughkeepsie, an "electric park," "the Beneficial Confection Wrigley's Spearmint Pepsin Gum," and a rodeo opening on August 28. (Courtesy of Robert Carl.)

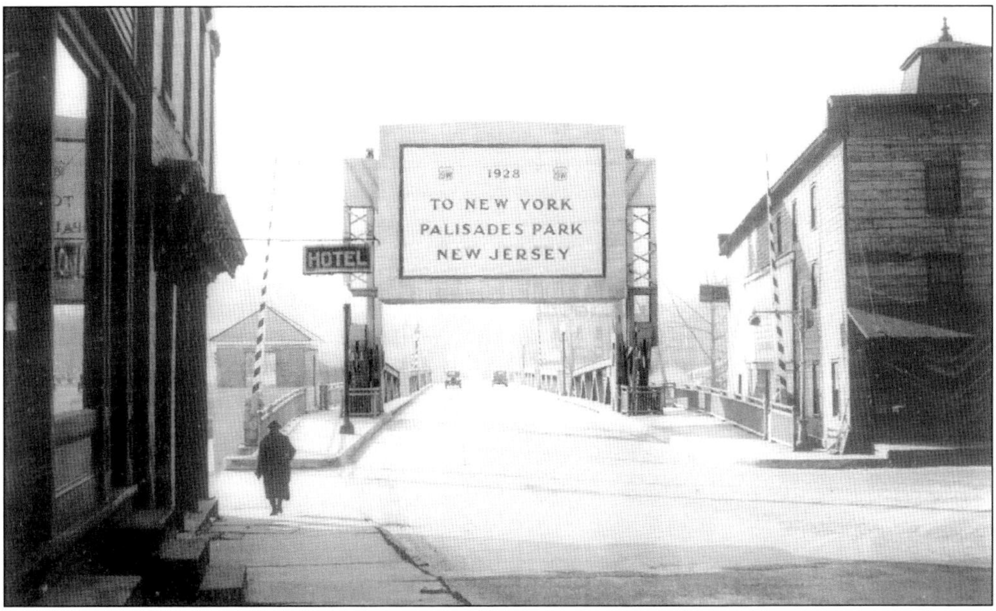


The third bridge across the Catskill Creek since 1801 was a drawbridge operated by a counterweight, evident here from the foot of Bridge Street, although it has been said that nobody ever saw the drawbridge actually working. The writing on the 1928 counterweight reads, "To New York Palisades Park New Jersey." This roadway was today's Route 9W, from Albany through Catskill to New York City. (Courtesy of Robert Meo.)

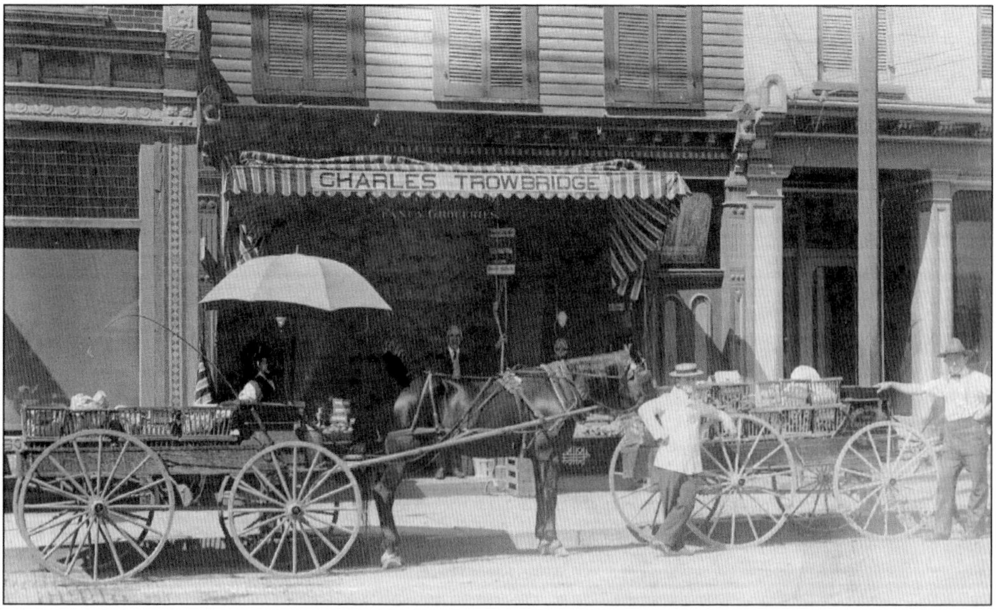


The two delivery wagons above are filled and ready to go with supplies from Charles Trowbridge's grocery in this post-1900 photograph. Could that be Charles Trowbridge Sr. at right and Charles Trowbridge Jr. next to him, both wearing straw boaters on what must have been a summer day? The Trowbridge family ran this market for almost half a century, living above it, as did so many other Main Street merchants. (Courtesy of Robert Carl.)

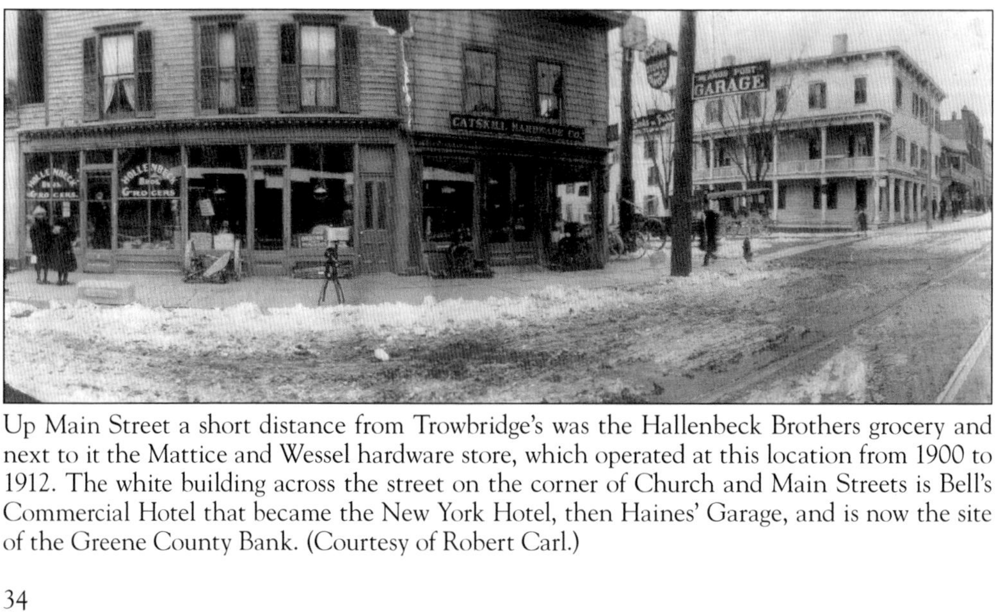


Up Main Street a short distance from Trowbridge's was the Hallenbeck Brothers grocery and next to it the Mattice and Wessel hardware store, which operated at this location from 1900 to 1912. The white building across the street on the corner of Church and Main Streets is Bell's Commercial Hotel that became the New York Hotel, then Haines' Garage, and is now the site of the Greene County Bank. (Courtesy of Robert Carl.)

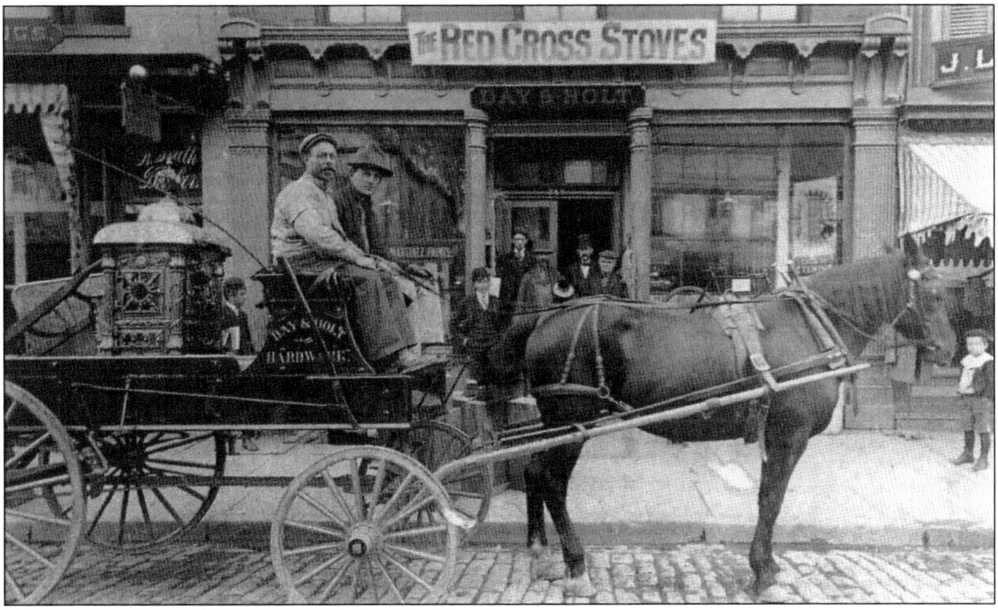


For many years, one of Catskill's most prosperous businesses on Main Street was owned and run by generations of the same family. The Day and Holt general hardware store dated to the early 19th century and is seen in the photograph above taken around 1890. Day and Holt was the primary vendor of Red Cross Stoves, advertised as "efficient" and "sure to save money on your coal bills." There were two public water fountains on Main Street for the villagers. The one below was watched over by an unidentified iron woman who must have vouched for the purity of her product. Water was first piped down in wooden troughs in the late 18th century to Main Street from a Spring Street pond that is still there, although it is no longer the source of sweet water for any creatures except a few brave ducks. (Above, courtesy of Pat Walsh; below, courtesy of Robert Carl.)

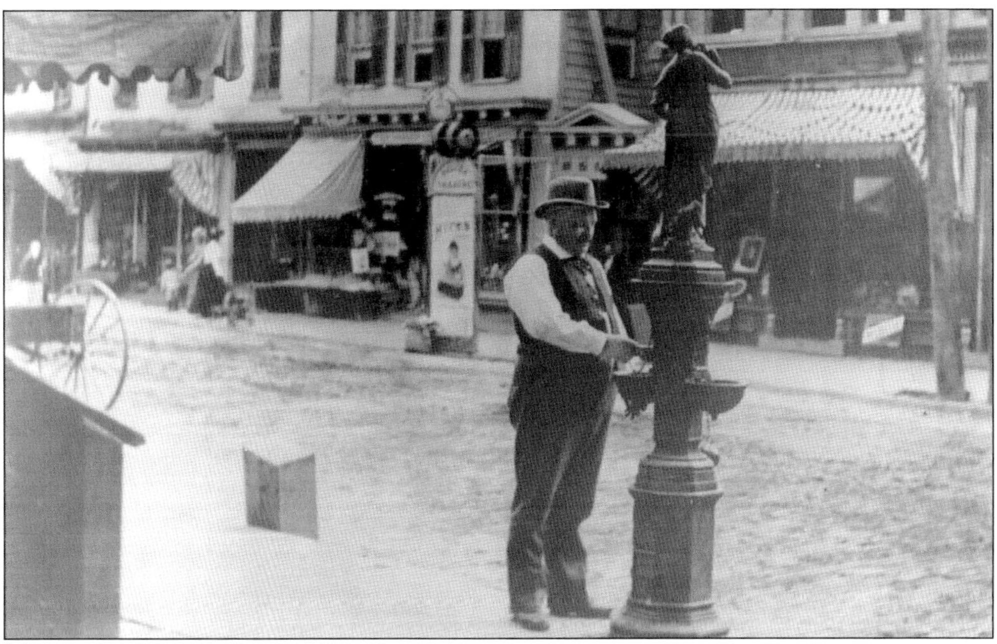

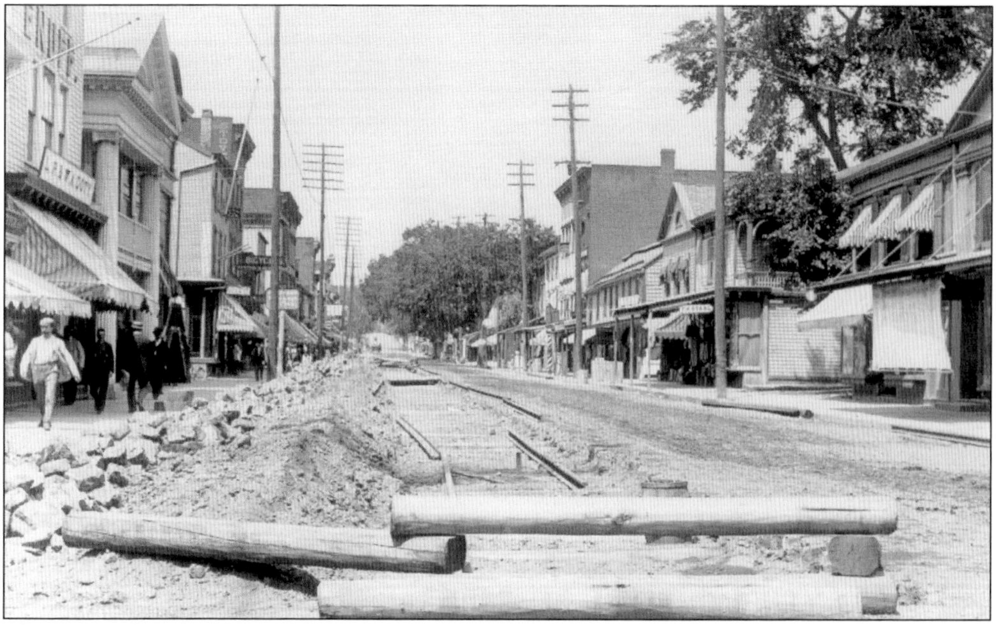

The pace of improvements in the village transportation system accelerated substantially at the dawn of the 20th century. Main Street was torn up in 1901, when the photograph above was taken, to lay tracks for a new electric trolley that in addition to two railroad lines gave a progressive cosmopolitan air to the village. The trolley tracks began at the Point and ended at Leeds, four miles distant. It cost a nickel to ride in the village and 15¢ to go one way to the end. Below, another photographic view of Main Street, taken a few years later, is a record of the changing times. Seeming to vie for the same space are a 1903 four-passenger Ford, a two-passenger runabout buggy, a four-passenger phaeton carriage, and the electric trolley. (Courtesy of Robert Carl.)

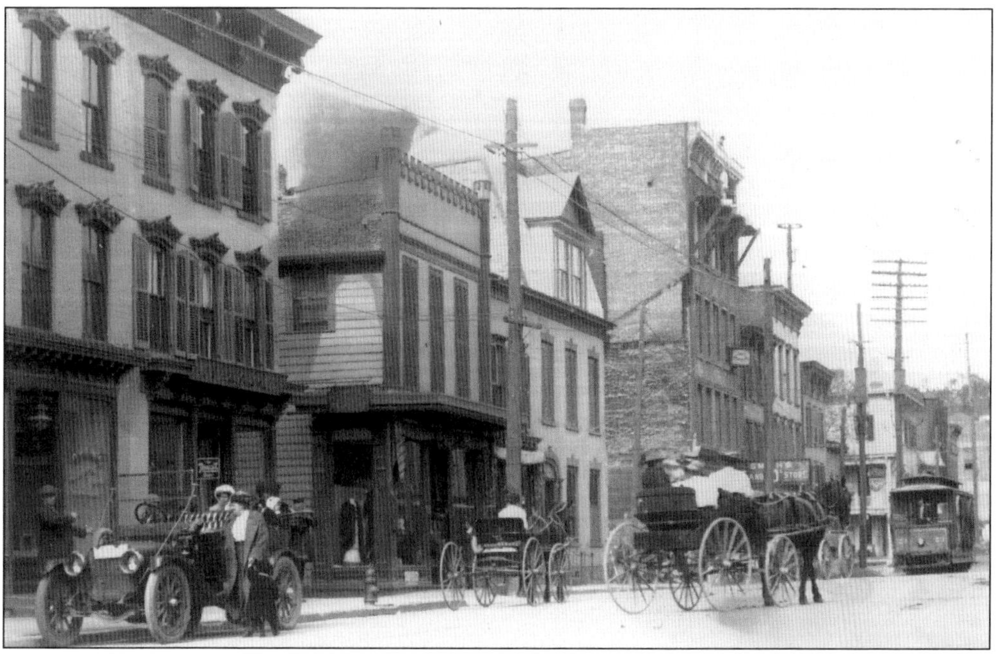

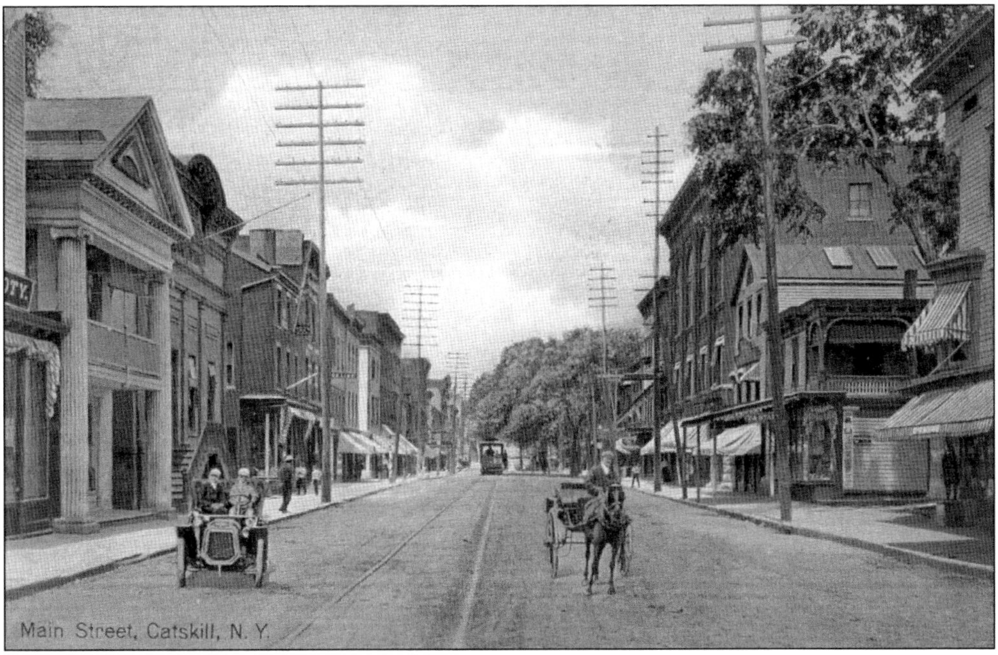


If villagers could not go somewhere, they might travel vicariously to other worlds through postcards, some in surprisingly accurate and glorious full color and some in black and white, as is evidenced from these two views of Main Street about 1908. Shifting eras from the horse-drawn runabout to the horseless carriage are the subject of the view above, although automobiles were still relatively rare, frequently unreliable mechanically, and prohibitively expensive (until Henry Ford introduced his Model T for about $700 in 1908). A lone bicyclist (below) rides fearlessly down the middle of the street past the Catskill Village building (home to the Francis N. Wilson fire company on the first floor) and Bell's Commercial Hotel and may even overtake the electric trolley on its wobbling way to the Point. (Courtesy of the Arthur Hamm collection.)

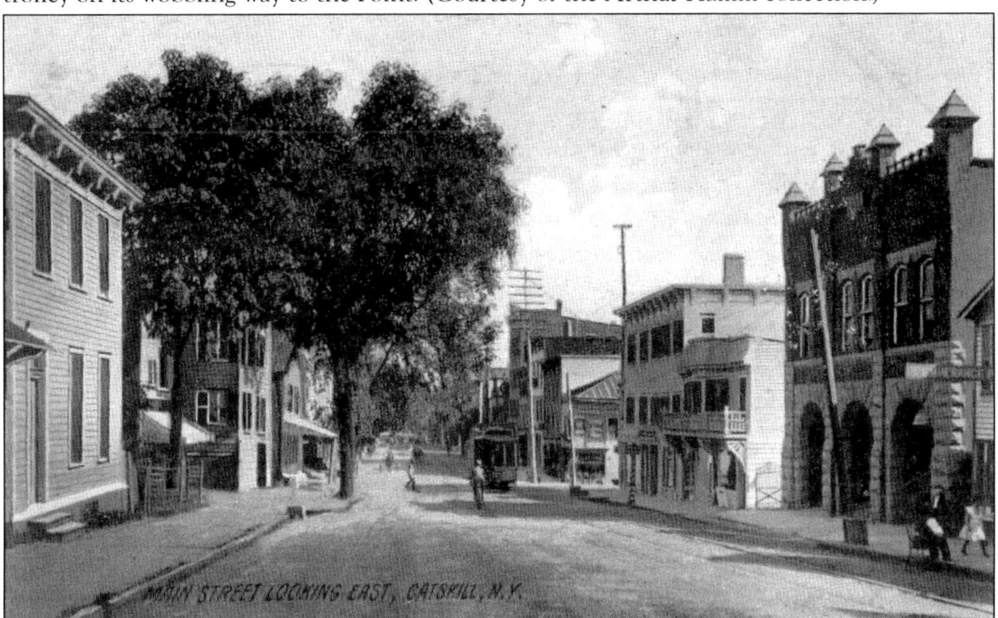

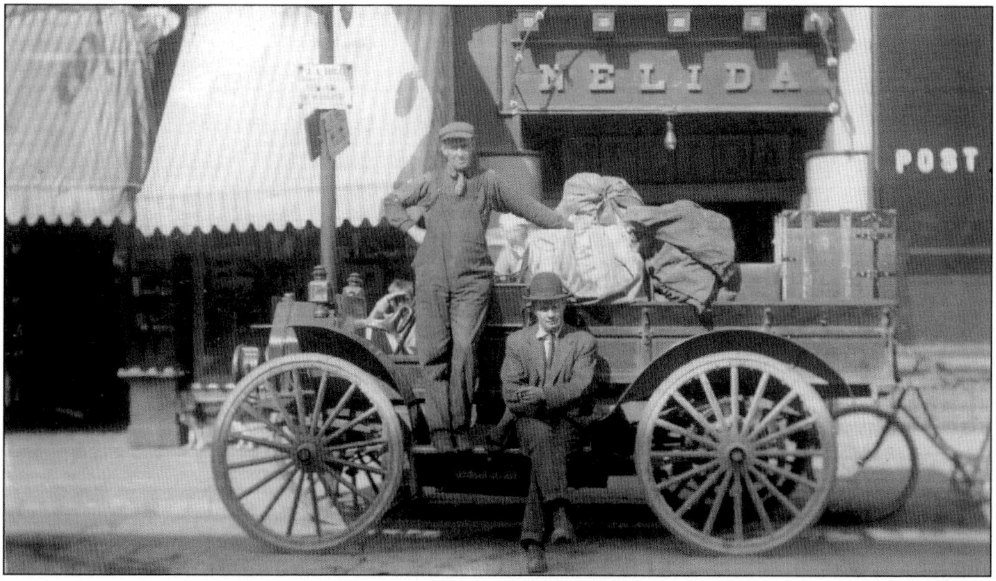


An early wooden-wheeled delivery truck (above around 1905) is parked outside Catskill's Nelida Theatre, originally built in 1880 as a roller rink, converted to a vaudeville house, and opened as a legitimate theater with a touring production of Joseph Jefferson's enduring dramatization *Rip Van Winkle* in 1888. The Nelida stage drew stars such as Jack Dempsey, Ethel Barrymore, and John Drew Barrymore. Around the corner from the Nelida was the Mackey Building (below, around 1900) that was at various times a rooming house, a dry goods store, a saloon, a mattress factory, and the post office. It was torn down to make room for a parking lot. The Nelida burned in 1918 and was replaced by today's Community Theatre, equipped for stage productions but used as a movie house. (Above, courtesy of the Arthur Hamm collection; below, courtesy of Robert Carl.)

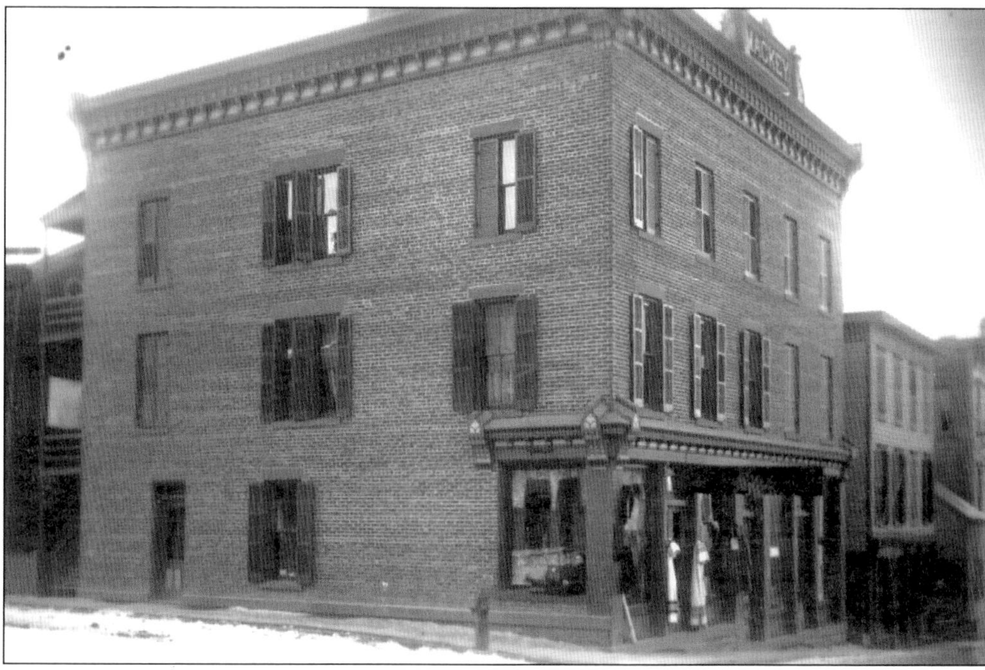

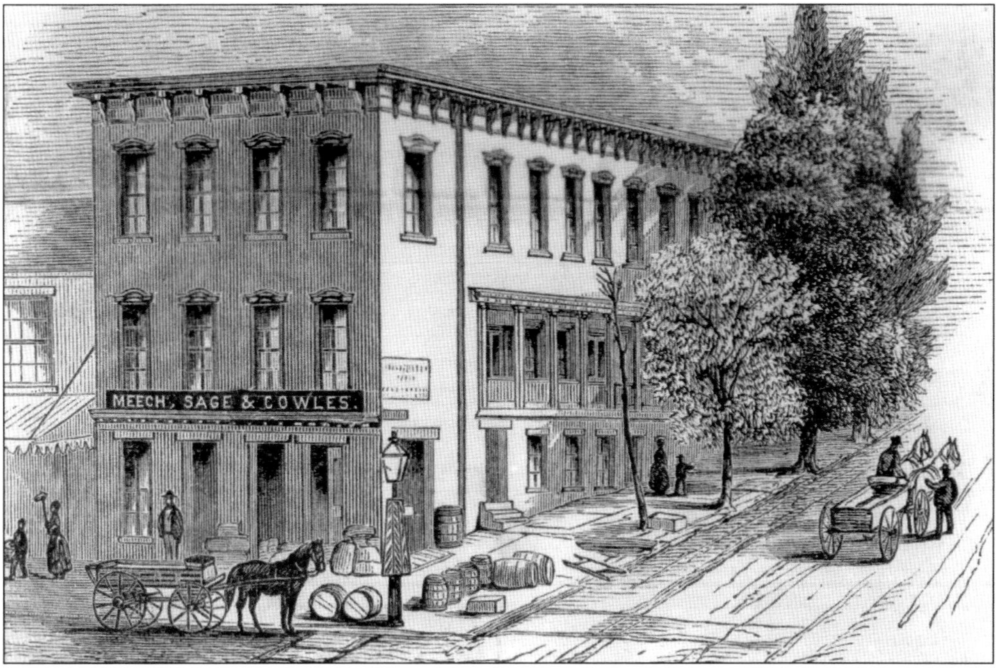


This elegant office building known first as Meech's Hall on the corner of William and Main Streets was built in 1867 in the then-popular Victorian Italianate style. It became the Express Office, headquarters for Sage Coal and Harness Shop, and the warehouse and grocery of Catskill merchant Noble Pitt Cowles, who made his fortune in land development and shipping Greene County groceries to the Union army. (Author's collection.)

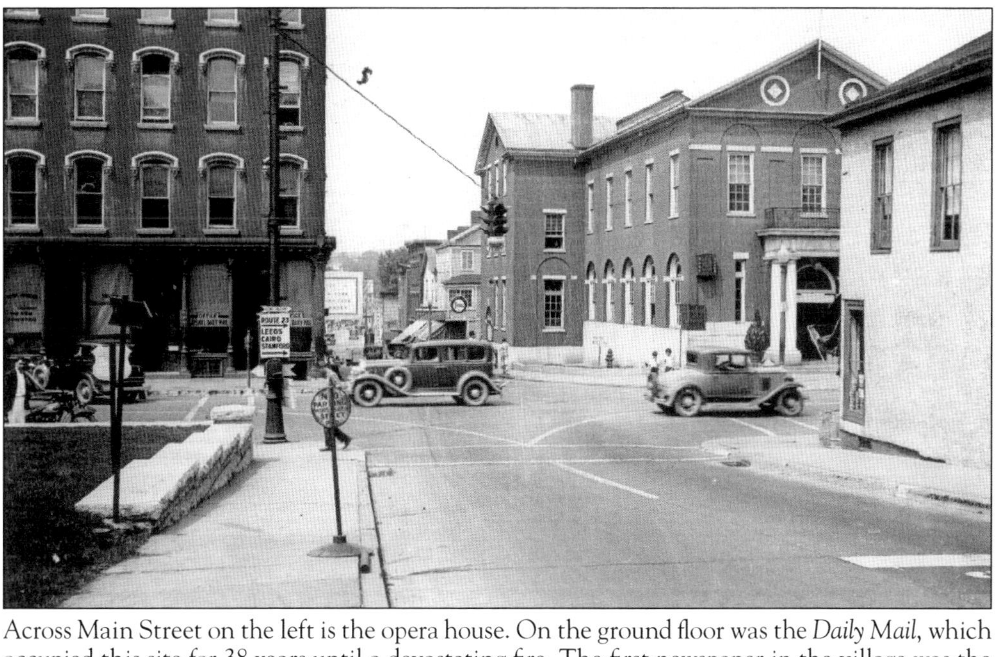

Across Main Street on the left is the opera house. On the ground floor was the *Daily Mail*, which occupied this site for 38 years until a devastating fire. The first newspaper in the village was the *Catskill Packet* in 1792, published by Mackey Croswel, whose brother A. H. Croswel was the first postmaster, appointed by George Washington. (Author's collection.)

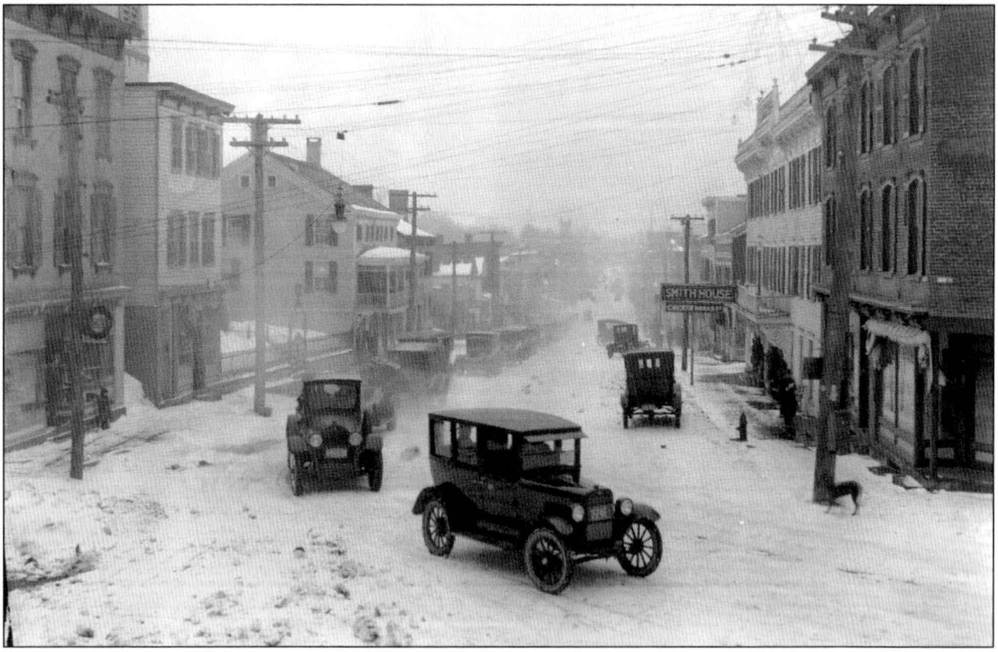


Amos Post's funeral cortege in February 1923 makes its way up an icy, snow-slick Main Street and out to the Jefferson Heights rural cemetery two miles away. For many years, Post was the agent for Overland and Franklin Motor Cars. The lead car in the procession, however, appears to be a 1922 Ford Model T. (Courtesy of Stephanie Walsh.)

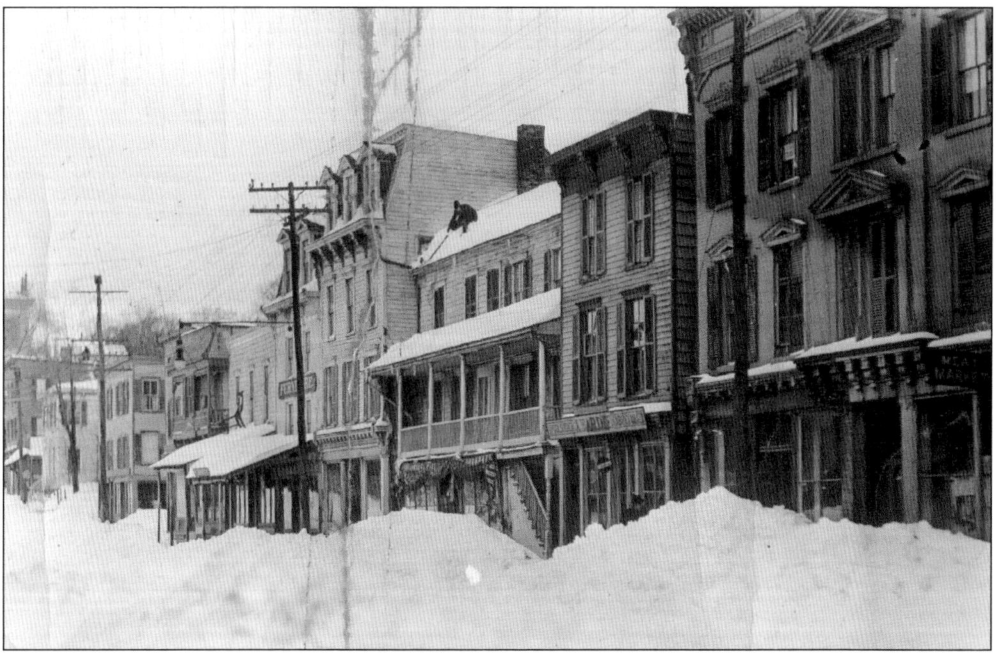

The blizzard that began on March 12, 1888, dumped a record five feet of snow on Catskill Village over 24 hours, with drifts as high as 30 feet. Snowplows as they are known today did not exist, and when the snow eventually began to melt, the valley was inundated with floods. This photograph of upper Main Street is undated. (Courtesy of the Arthur Hamm collection.)

# *Four*

# ACCOMMODATIONS

Among its many successful industries, including fishing, brick making, tanning, boatbuilding, milling, textiles, transportation, farming, ice, beef, potash, wheat, and timber, Catskill is most remembered today for having once been able to accommodate record numbers of tourists in the village and nearby in a remarkable choice of guest houses and hotel accommodations. The concept of weeklong vacations for workingmen and workingwomen came into vogue by the mid-19th century, and people with new time on their hands needed places to go, mostly near their homes in the area around New York City. Many visitors to the area in the 19th and early 20th centuries arrived by train, and waiting carriages took weary travelers to nearby lodgings for clean air, recreation, and rest. At the same time, there was a building boom as a result of the profitable trades, business ventures, and industries that were flourishing, especially along the creek and Main Street. Domestic dwellings were being built to advertise the eclectic tastes of Catskill's newly rich. Many of these luxury accommodations still exist, having become the source of inspired restorations today and are among the most visible attractions in the village.

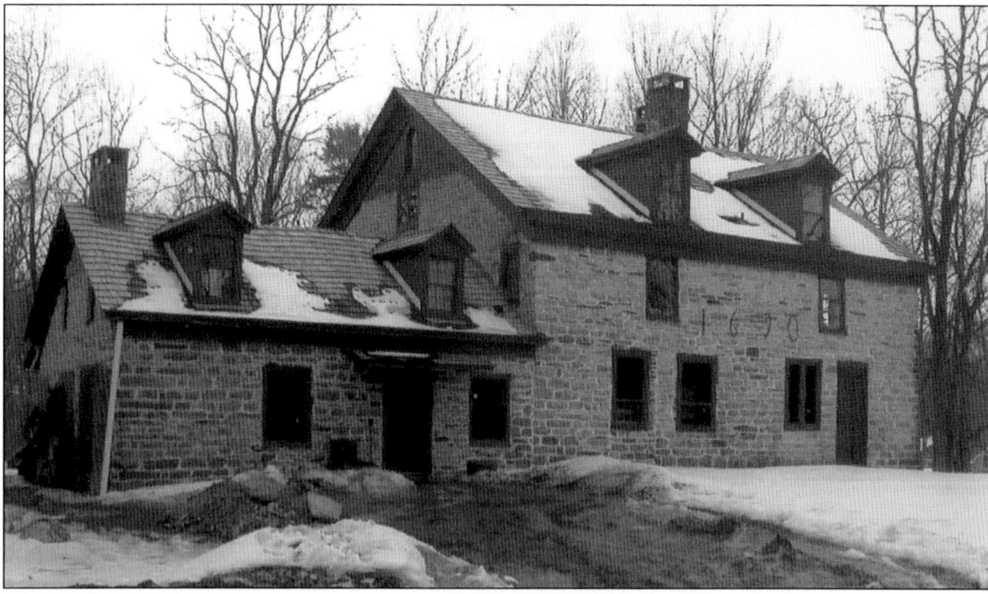

The Van Vechten House (above) was built by Dirck Thunesse Van Veghten near a Native American fort called Mawignack about 1690. Between 1681 and 1686, Van Veghten also built a sawmill and a gristmill on the nearby Hans Vosen Kill. The Van Vechtens lived in the homestead for nearly 200 years. This photograph was taken in 2007 when the "1690 House" was undergoing major renovations. (Author's collection.)

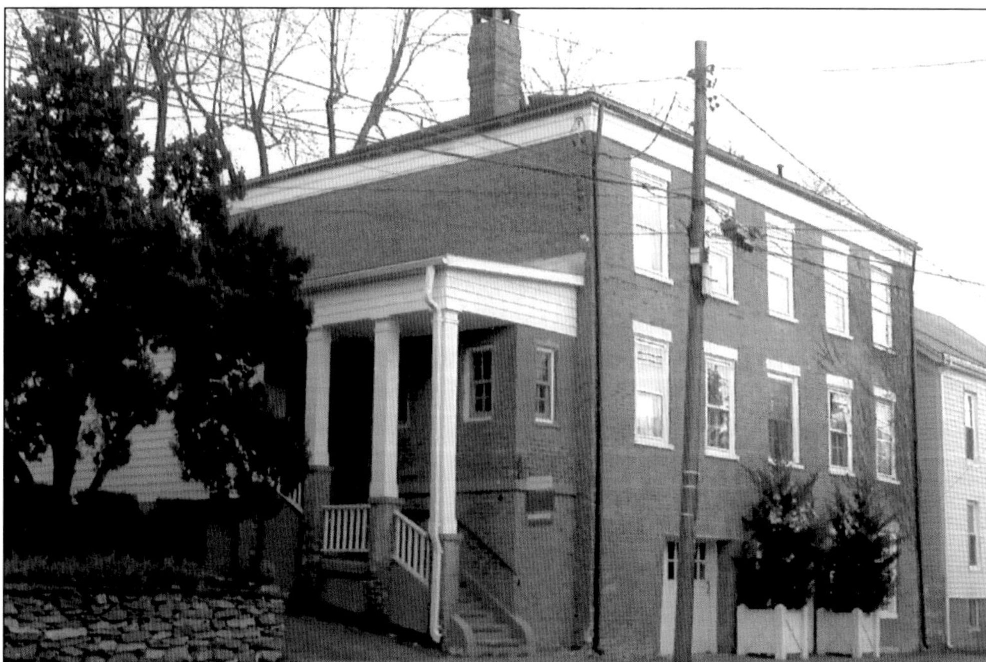

Facing on the oldest section of Main Street is the home of Stephen Day, one of the village's most successful early businessmen and community leaders. The seat of Catskill's Day family from 1791 to 1925, the house is run today as a bed-and-breakfast, and its ground floor, the site of Catskill's first commercial bank in the 1790s, is a designer's studio. (Author's collection.)

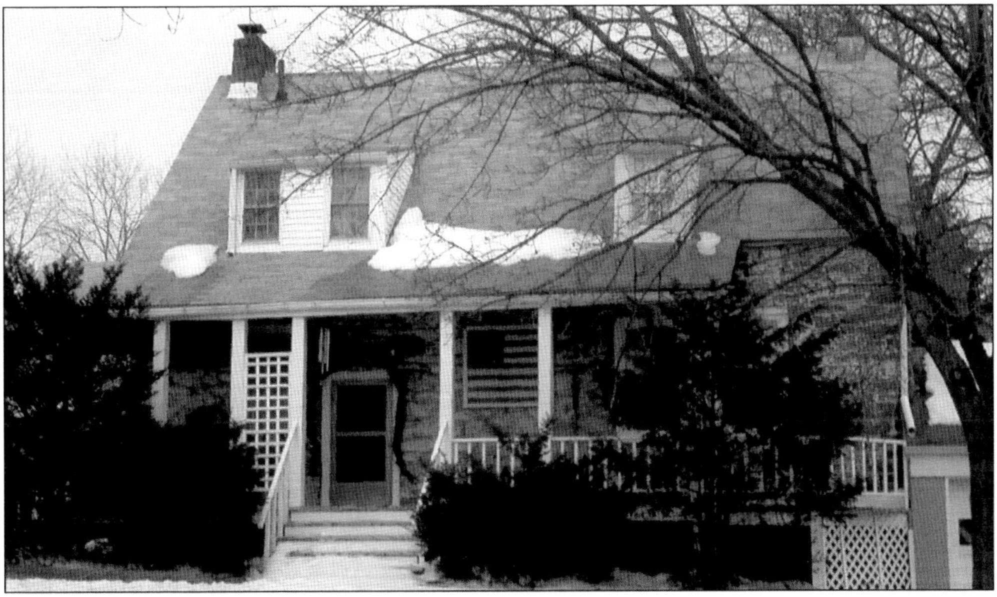

The Dubois family of Catskill are descendants of Huguenots who came to New Netherland in 1660. Cornelius Dubois inherited from his father a 600-acre farm along the Catskill Creek that included today's entire village, and here in 1762 he built a stone house (above). An ardent supporter of the American Revolution, Dubois served as a lieutenant colonel in the New York militia and, as the 1932 historic marker on West Main Street notes, the "Surrender of [the British commander] Cornwallis [was] celebrated here in 1781." West of Dubois's home and part of the Middle School Historical Complex is the gray stone house that his son Benjamin built in 1774; today it is used by the school administration. These two stone houses are fine examples of the Dutch-style vernacular architecture found in the Hudson River valley in the 18th century. (Author's collection.)

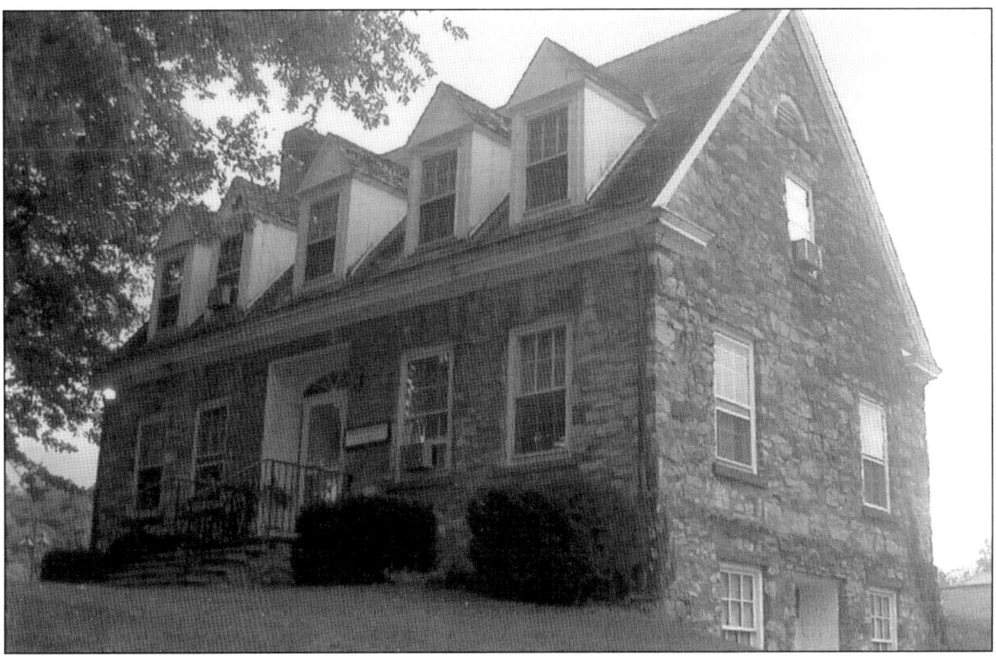

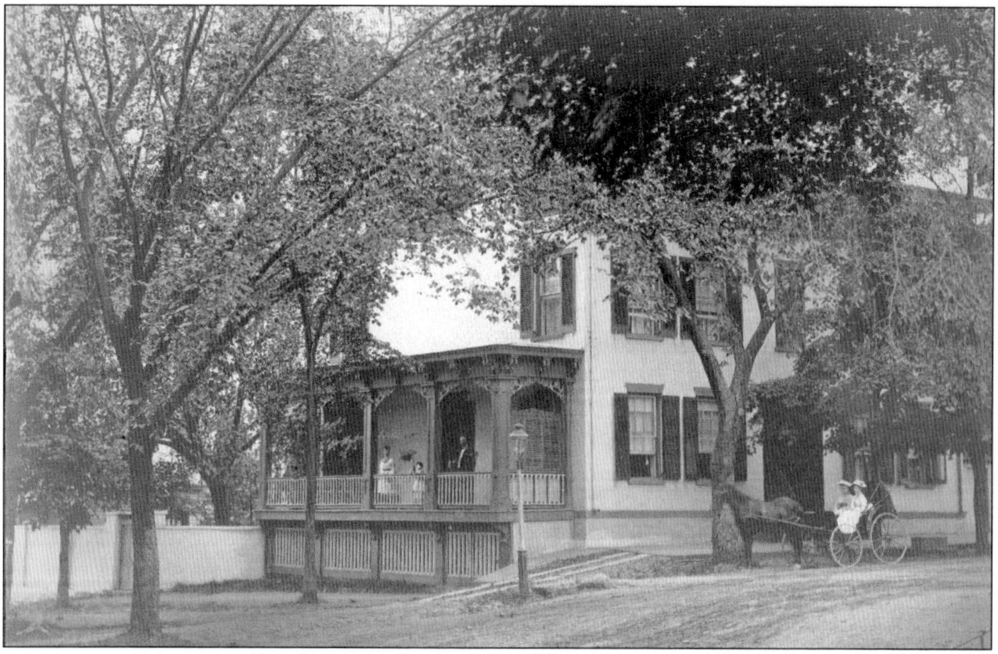

The handsomely proportioned Georgian residence (above) on Main Street at Greene Street was built by Lyman Hall in 1811 on the site of a tavern that was owned and run in the late 18th century by the legendary Sybil Luddington, the "female Paul Revere." The earliest newspaper in the village, the *Catskill Packet*, was first published in 1792 in the stables behind the house. The Federal-style house (below) built in 1797 for Moses Cantine was subjected to a mid-Victorian-era makeover and is best known today as the home of Sam Wilson, the original Uncle Sam of army recruitment fame. A young local lawyer, Martin Van Buren, married Hanna Hoes, Wilson's cousin, here in 1807. Van Buren's long political career culminated in 1836 when he was elected president. Today the house is a restaurant with a pirate theme. (Author's collection.)

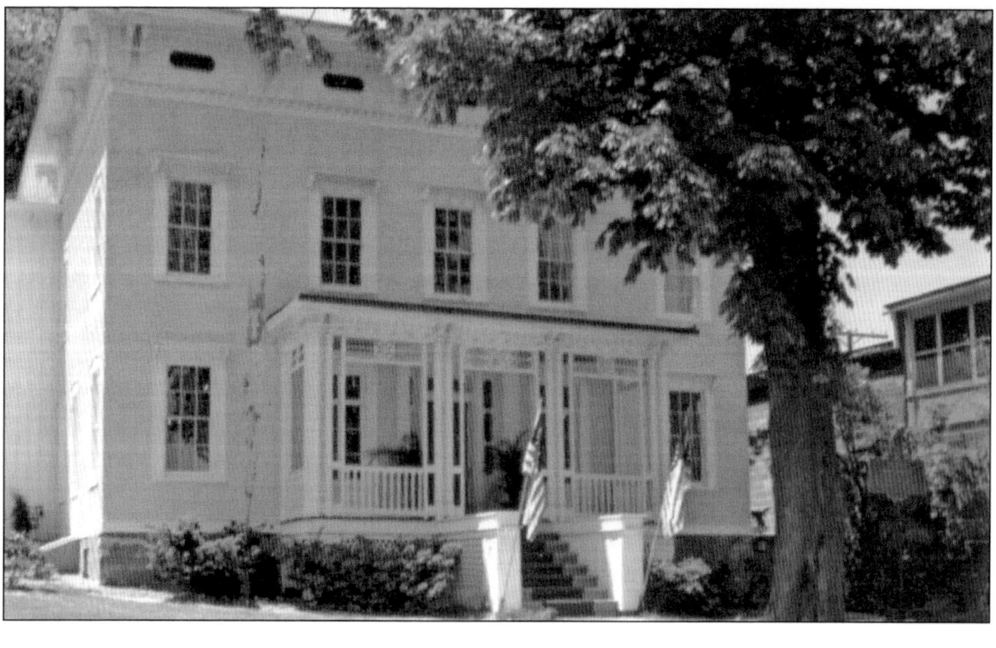

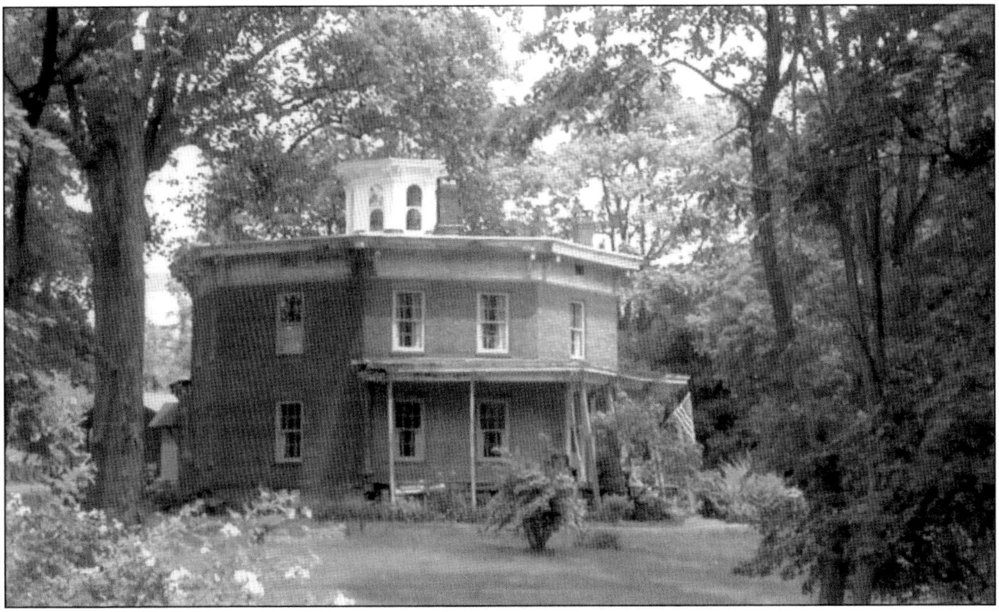

Cherry Hill was built in 1861 by David Van Gelder, a farmer and master builder whose specialty was covered bridges. Built in the octagonal style advocated by Orson Fowler, Cherry Hill is now the only structure of its kind left in Greene County. The Old Stone Jug (below), also known as Dies's Folly, was built in 1764 by Englishman John Dies and his wife, Jane Goelet Dies, both from socially prominent circles in New York City. Their home is said to have been one of the finest Georgian structures in the Hudson River valley. Converted into an academy for girls after Jane Goelet Dies's death in 1799 and eventually broken into tenement flats for indigent families, the house was dynamited in 1896 for a brick factory. Today the property is the location of a low-income housing project. (Author's collection.)

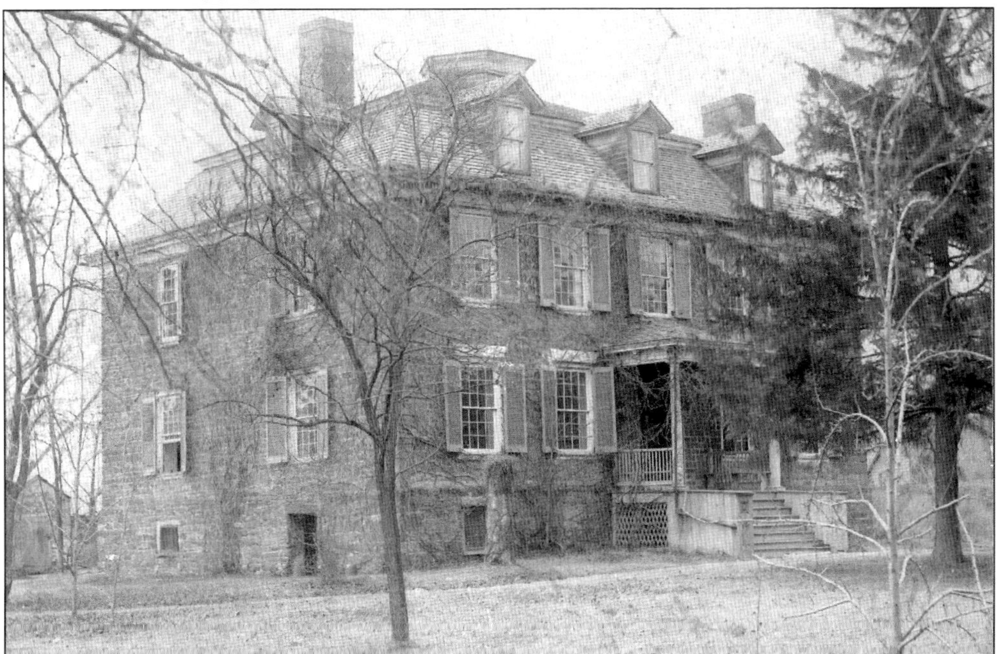

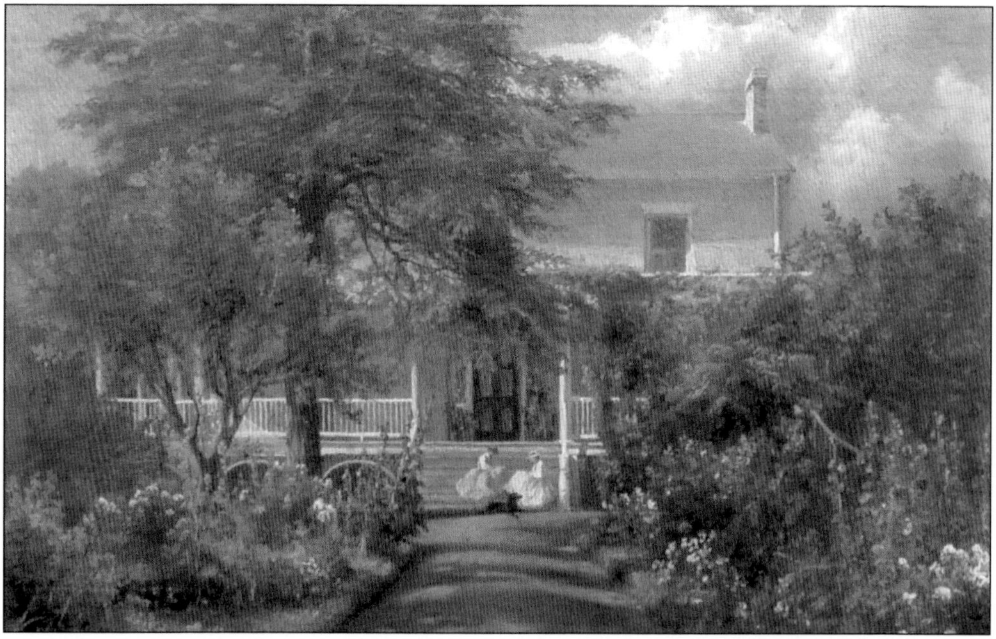

Cedar Grove, a fine Federal mansion at the edge of the village, was built in 1816 by two brothers, John Alexander Thomson, a successful local merchant, and Thomas Thomson, whose large fortune was made in trade in the West Indies. The two brothers adopted four young nieces when their mother died. The youngest of these, Maria, married landscape painter Thomas Cole in 1836 and, after being widowed in 1848 with four young children, lived on at Cedar Grove until her death in 1883. The painting (above) was done in 1868, 20 years after Cole's untimely death, by the American pre-Raphaelite painter Charles Herbert Moore. The photograph (below) was taken after the recent restoration. Cedar Grove was designated a national historic landmark in 1965. (Above, courtesy of Edith Cole Silberstein; below, author's collection.)

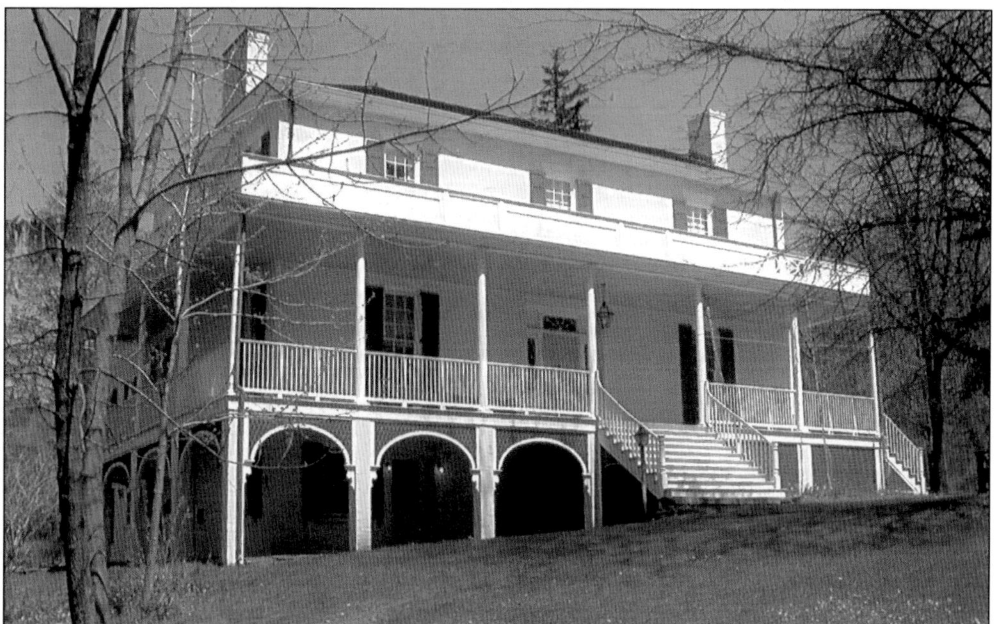

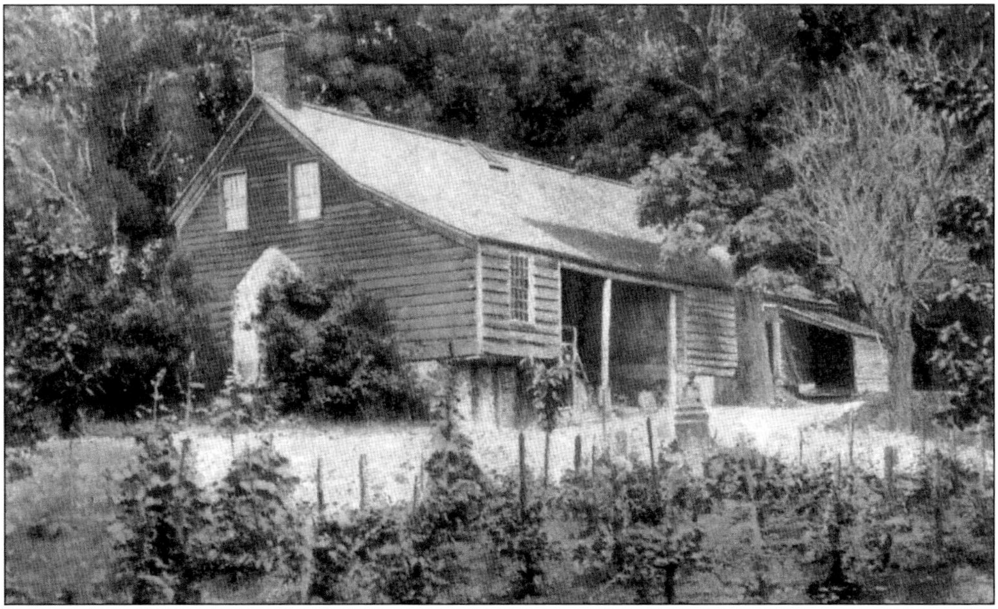

Cedar Grove was the home of Cole from 1836 until his death in 1848. The originator and preeminent painter of the Hudson River school of landscape painting, Cole first came to Catskill Village in 1825 and was deeply affected by the natural beauty of the Hudson River valley and the wild terrain of the nearby Catskill Mountains. In 1840, Cole created his famous four-canvas allegory *The Voyage of Life* in the so-called old studio (the photograph above, around 1890). The last years of his life, from 1846 to 1848, Cole painted in his new studio (below, around 1880). Cedar Grove remained in the family for six generations and then was sold and underwent the ravages of neglect. A local philanthropist purchased the property in 1998, overseeing the work of restoration, and the property was opened to the public in 2001, Cole's 200th birthday. (Author's collection.)

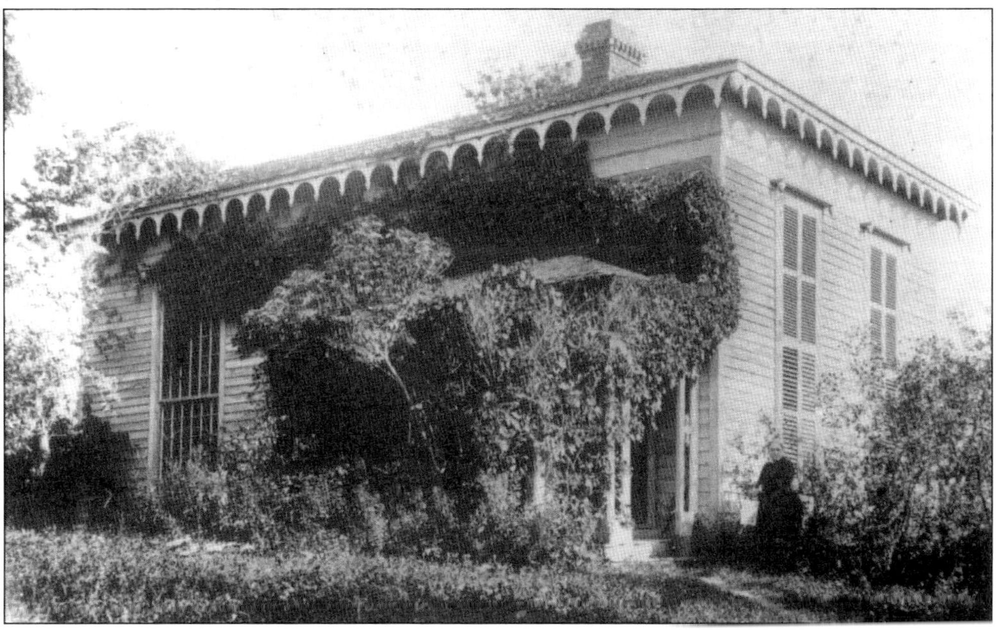

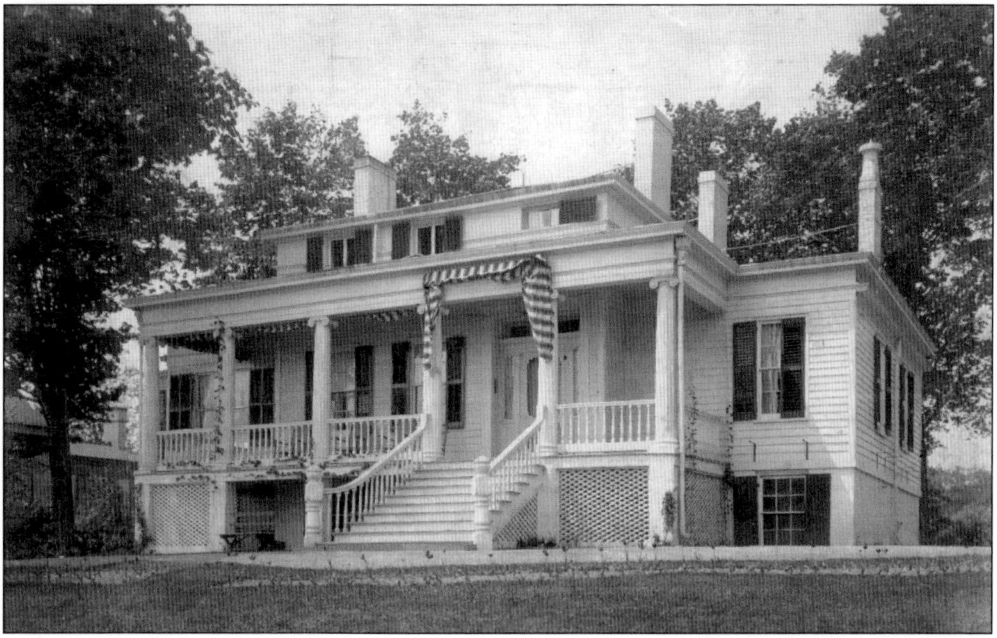

John Powers came to Catskill during the period known as "the Great Leap Forward" in the 1790s and established himself as a successful lawyer (one of his clients was Martin Van Buren), a politician, a gentleman farmer, and a land developer. He purchased a large tract of land that today comprises most of Catskill's East Side Historic District, and he built his impressive Greek Revival mansion (above, around 1900) overlooking a magnificent sweep of the Hudson River. His architecturally important residence was willed to the village and is managed by a volunteer group of friends. Extensive gardens were maintained for many years (below, around 1910) when it was possible to hire several gardeners full-time to maintain them. Changed over to mowed lawn, this area is used today as a car park for concerts in the house and other special events. (Author's collection.)

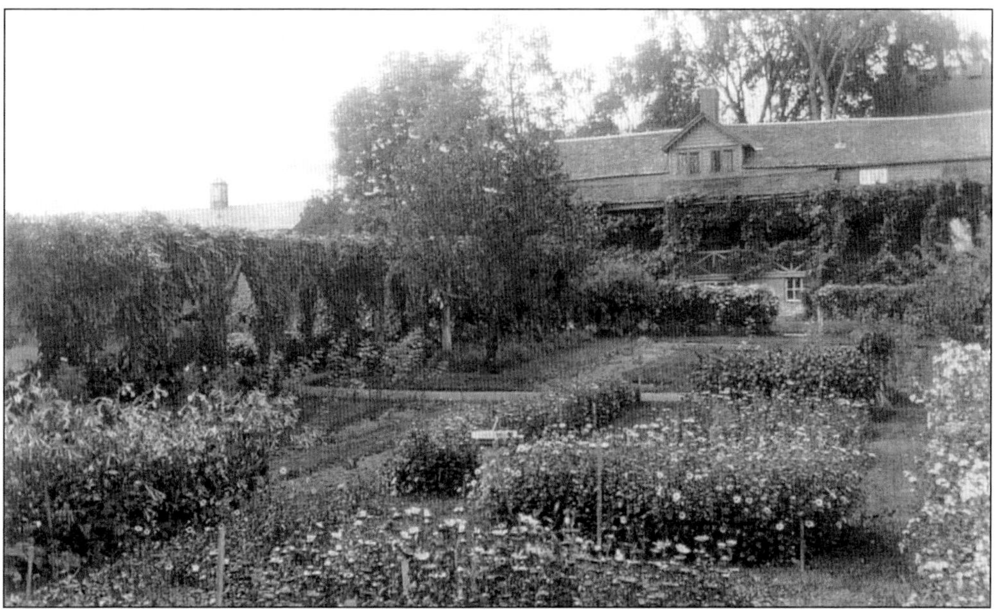

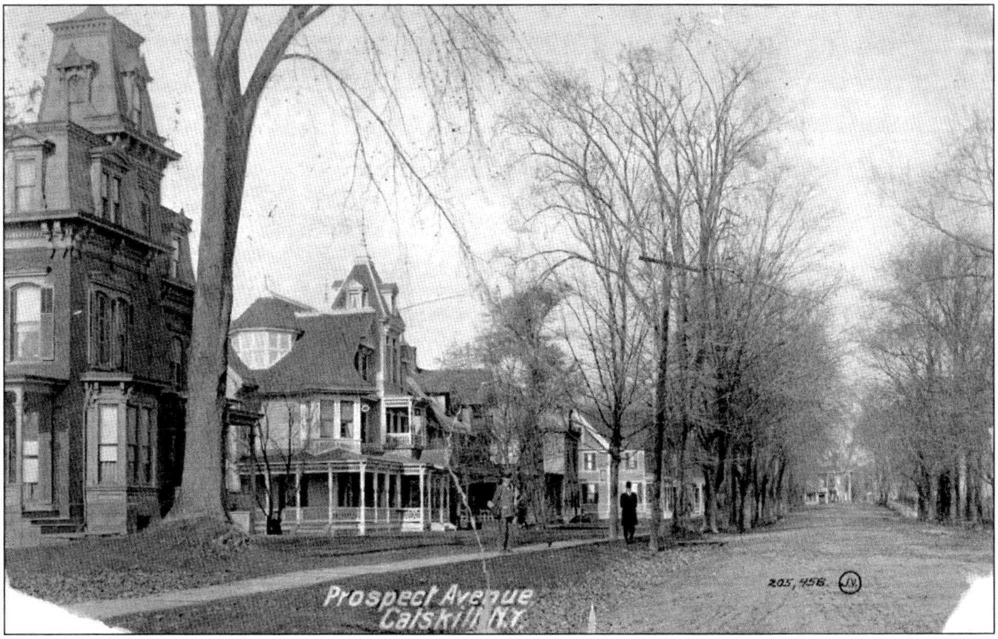


The streets along the top of the hill above the village Main Street form the nucleus of the registered East Side Historic District. Punctuated by large single-family homes that were built in the 19th century, the district today is remarkably well preserved. Seen on Prospect Avenue around 1900 (above, left) is the mansard mansion built in 1870 by the owner of the Union Mills along the creek. The fashionable stick-style mansion (below) on Prospect Avenue was the home for many years of Judge Emory A. Chase, a village champion of the new style of civil architecture (he is said to have been the prime promoter of the 1910 neoclassical courthouse) and one of the early collectors of village history. (Author's collection.)

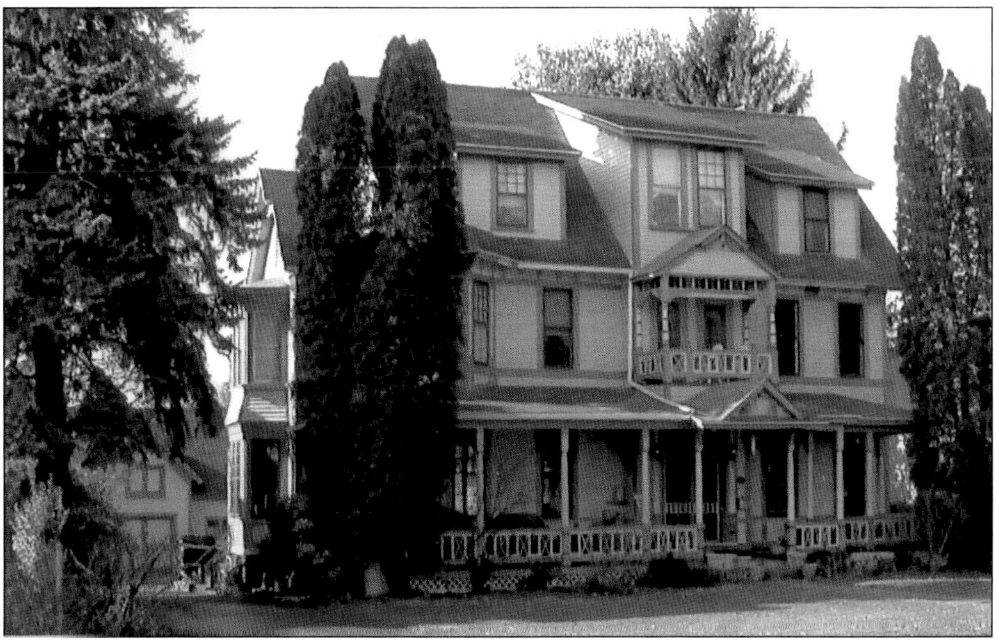

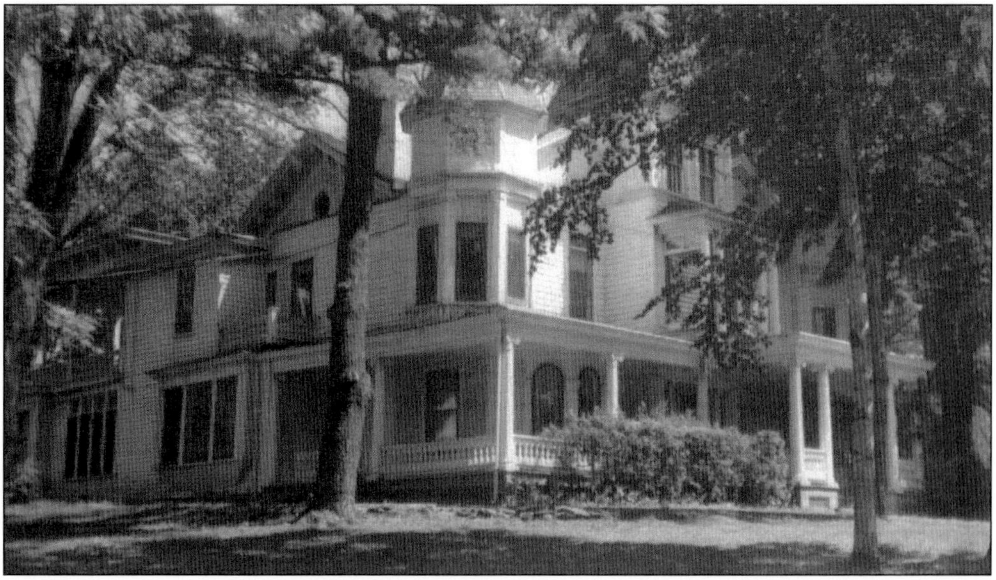

Several large estates were established on Spring Street, once an ancient Native American tract that became the main road into the village. It was appropriately named because of the number of sweet-water springs that percolated seasonally. In addition to the national historic landmark site Cedar Grove at what was once the far limits of the village, Spring Street was the location of Isaac Pruyn's appropriately named Springside (above). A pond on the estate provided the village below in the late 18th century with its supply of fresh drinking water through gravity-operated wooden conduits. The mansion (above, around 1920) was originally a simple farmhouse that, like Topsy, grew and grew again. In the early 1950s, the Haines family renovated Pruyn's mansion in the Georgian Colonial style (below, around 1995). (Author's collection.)

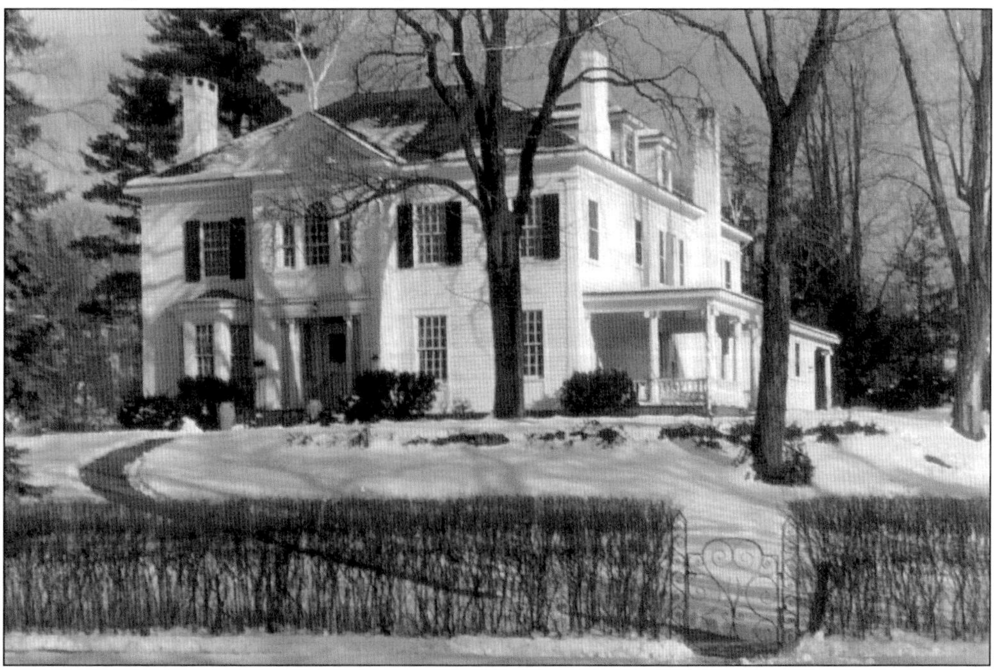

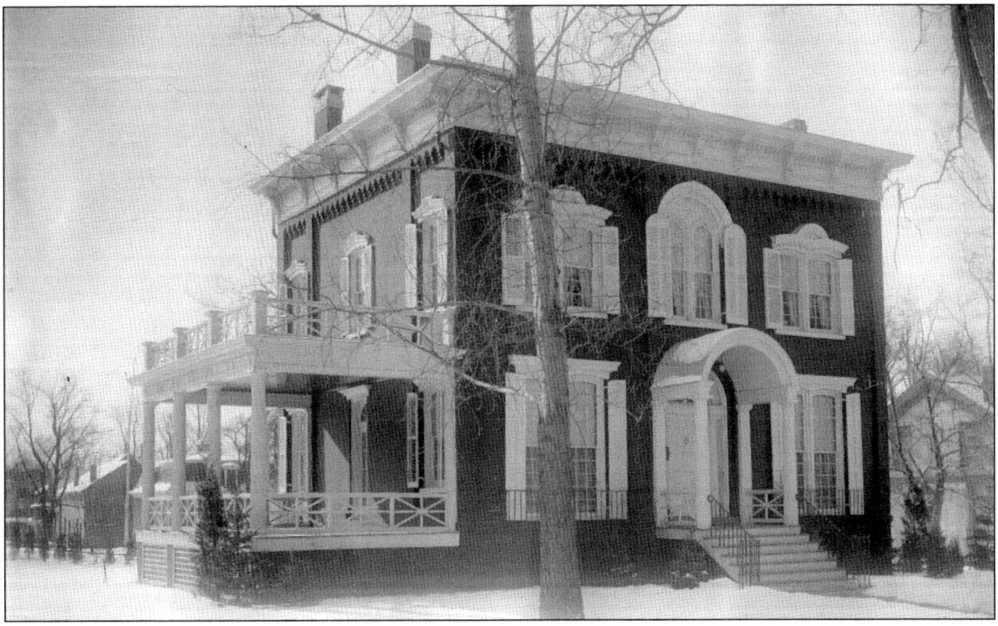

At the top of Bridge Street are homes built by Noble Pitt Cowles and Charles L. Beach. Cowles, who made his fortune as a grocer and land developer, built this Italianate Hudson River bracketed four-story home (above) in 1869. During the early 1900s, the house was partially updated in the compatible Colonial Revival style. The Beach house (below, around 1900, the day after a roof fire) was built in 1838. It was among the first on the hill and was the home of the entrepreneur who developed transportation in Greene County, Beach. He was the owner of the famous Catskill Mountain House (which he could see on the distant mountaintop from the second-story windows of his village home) and was principal investor and champion of the county railroad system. The Beach house was divided into apartments in the early 1980s. (Author's collection.)

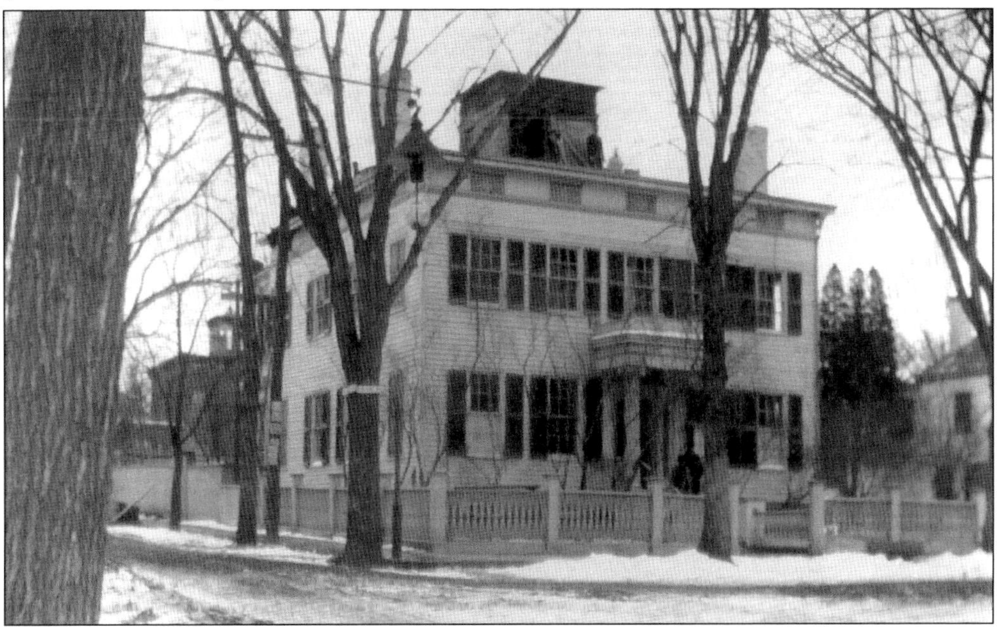

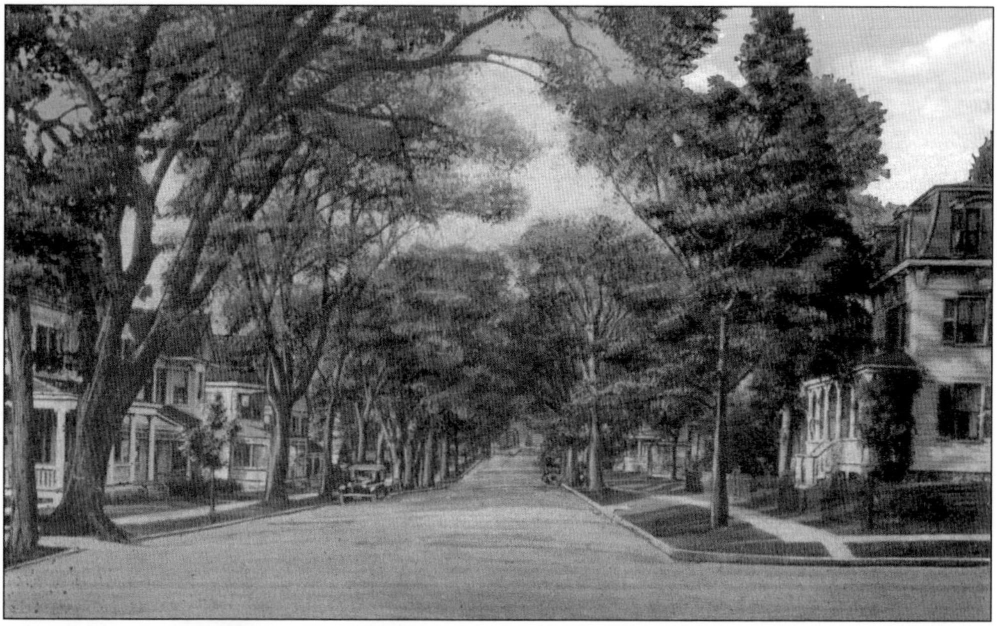

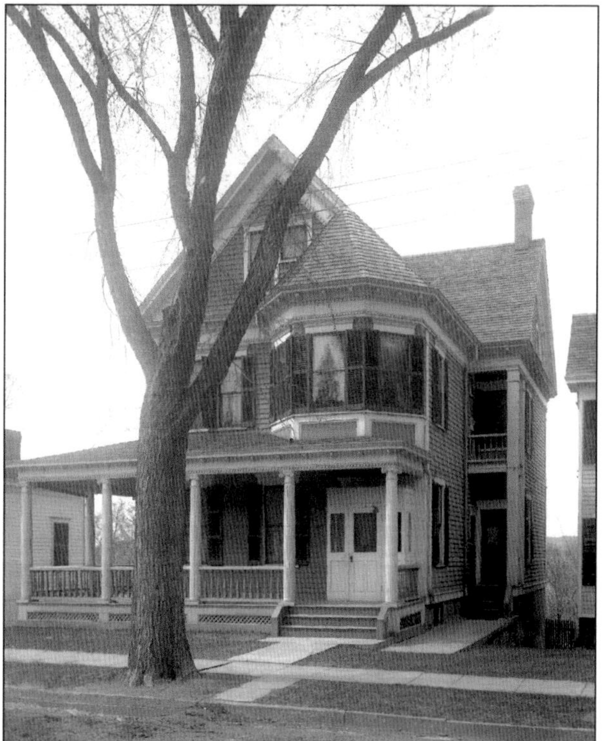

Judging from the parked three-door Ford Model T touring car, this photographic view (above) of Liberty Street, one of Catskill's most comfortable residential enclaves, was taken about 1914. Liberty Street was opened in the 1830s, and a number of residences from that period are still intact, having been maintained or restored over the changing years. At left is the home at 9 Liberty Street that was built by Charles A. Beach in 1902 with a second-story porch in the back that overlooked the 11-mile-distant South Mountain on which stood his family's acclaimed Catskill Mountain House. At the other end of Liberty Street is the home of his uncle Charles L. Beach, the son of liveryman Erastus Beach, who kick-started the family's transportation empire and its fortune in the 1820s. (Author's collection.)

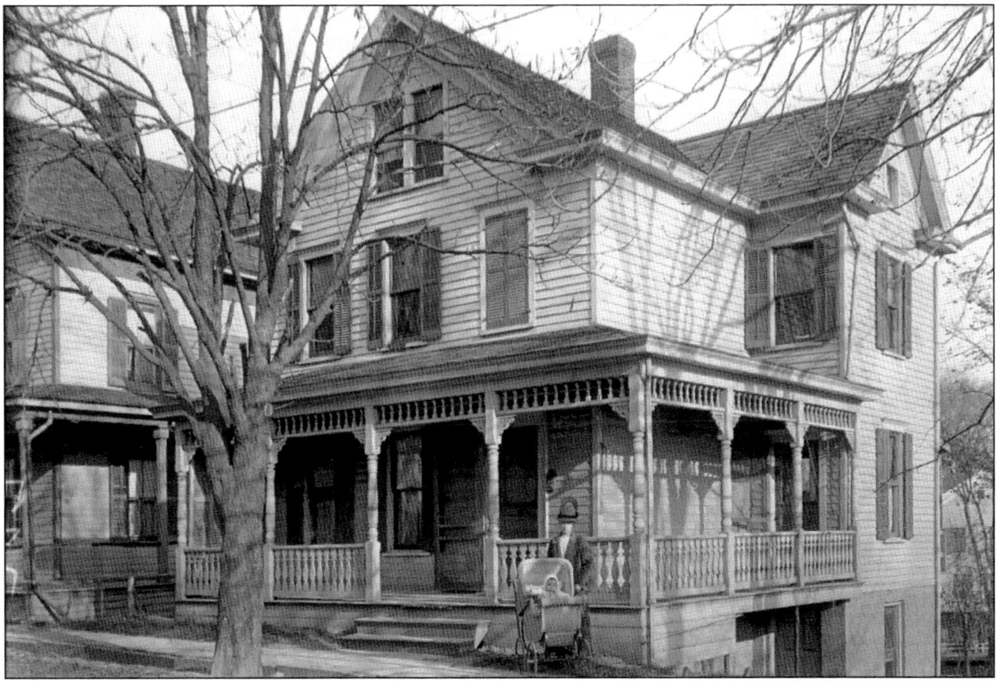

This tidy late-Victorian home at 90 Thompson Street (above) is characteristic in many ways of the comfortable family-friendly domestic dwellings that were built on speculation in the 1890s and were—and still are today—gracious reminders of Catskill's small-town ambience. There are a number of these houses in Catskill that follow a similar plan with slight variations—porch, front parlor, back parlor, dining room, and kitchen. A young mother is seen posing proudly with her newborn in front of a house that might be her new home. The porch photograph (below) by Paul Morrison shows an unidentified contented young woman with, perhaps, her daughter in a Catskill home around 1910. (Photographs by Paul Morrison, courtesy of Peggy Ahwesh.)

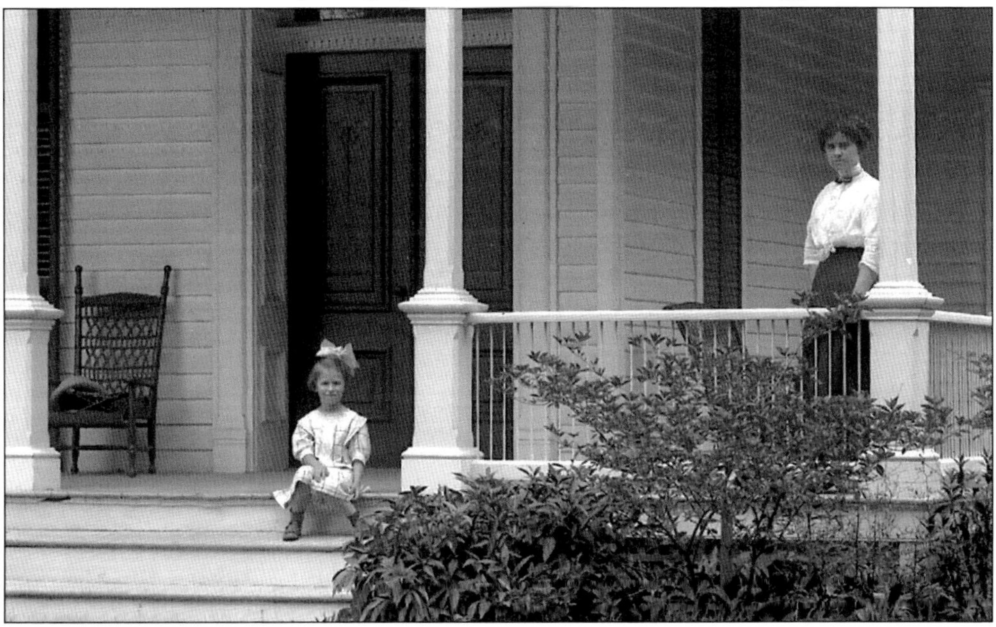

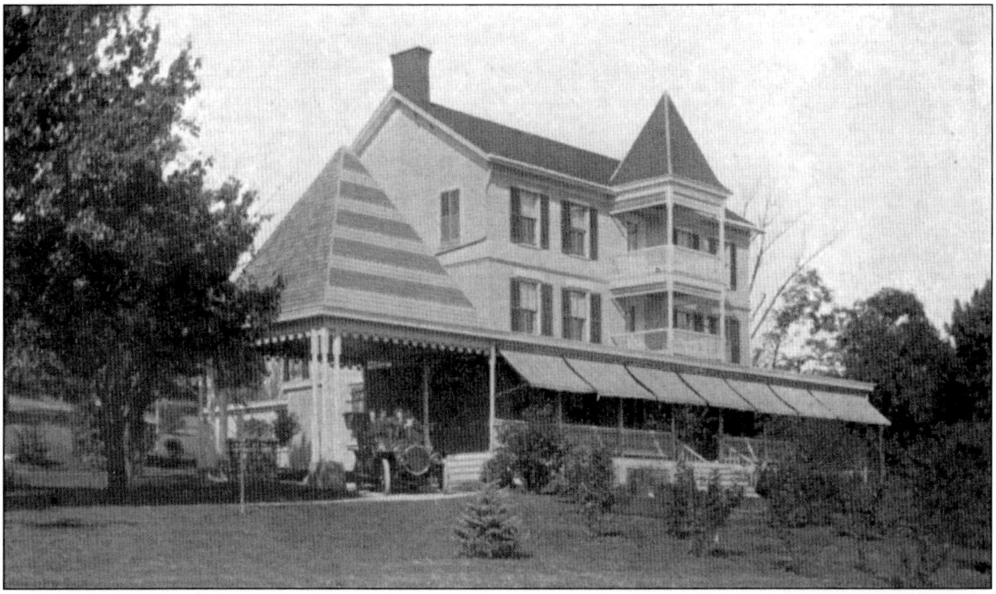

In the 19th century, Peter Dubois built a large house (above) in stages that eventually contained 19 bedrooms and was run as a summer boardinghouse. It is hard to believe today that preparations for three meals a day for 19 or more people might have taken place in the Dubois kitchen (below) when the boardinghouse was running at peak efficiency in the early years of the 20th century. The Littlefield Stove Company in Albany manufactured iron stoves that used coal or wood and had reservoirs like the one seen here. It advertised "strictly first-class stoves" that were "perfect in operation . . . with reservoir" and used "26-inch sticks." With those advantages, perhaps cooking for two dozen paying guests three times a day on this stove was not all that bad. Or was it? (Courtesy of Nancy Ursprung.)

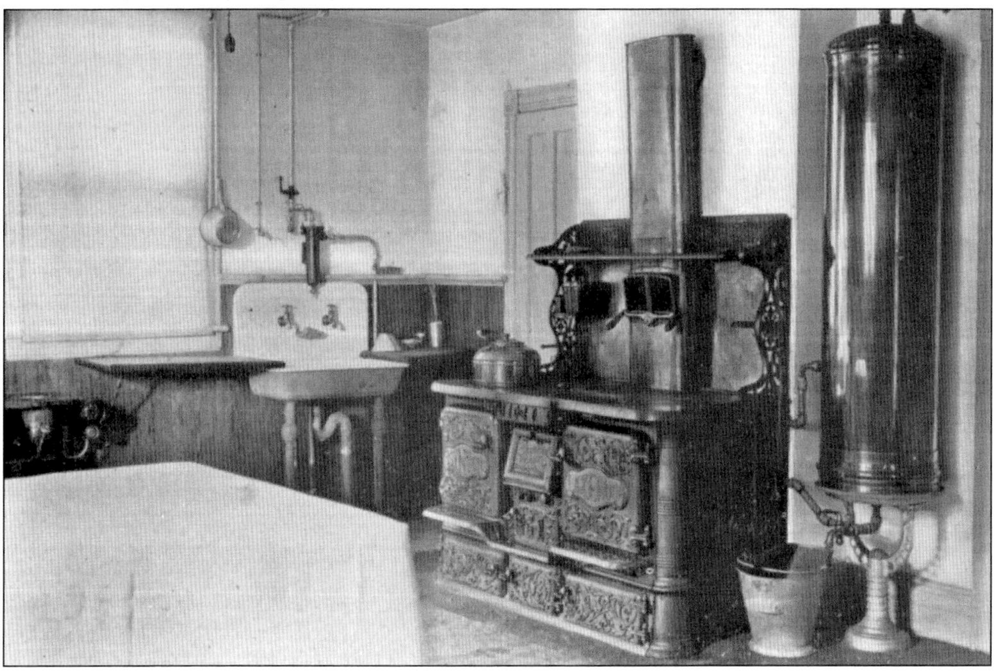

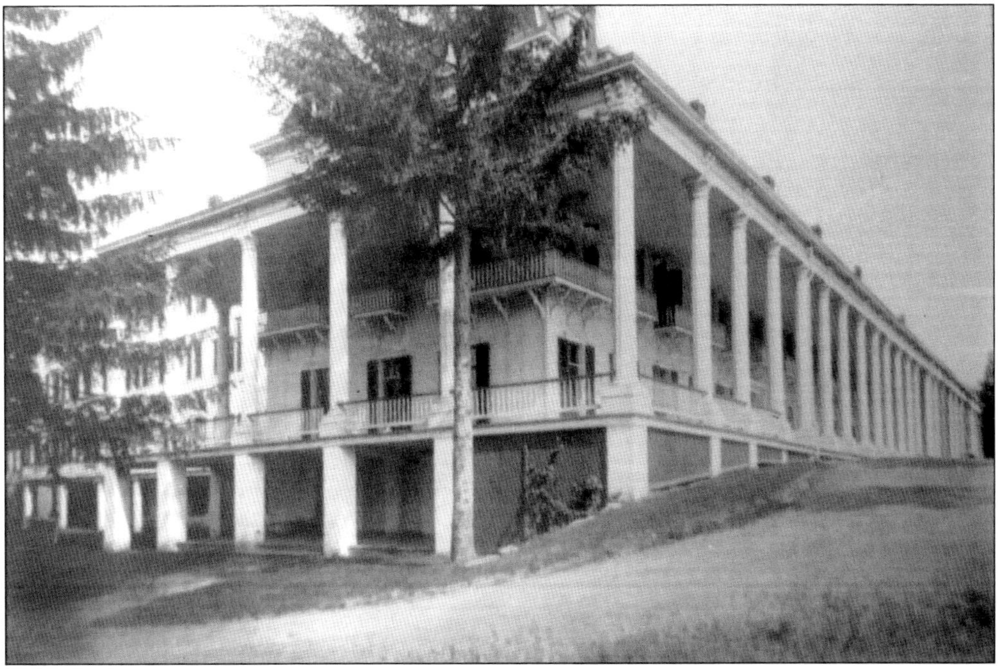

On a prominent bluff above Catskill Landing, the Prospect Park Hotel (above) was considered, according to its advertisements, to be the "pioneer among modern summer hostelries" where "wealth and fashion long held sway." The Prospect Park Hotel was sold to the Franciscans in 1908. It burned to the ground in 1914 and is today the site of St. Anthony's Friary. Another popular hostelry within the village was the Grant House Hotel (below), constructed in 1867 on Jefferson Heights and also considered to be one of the preeminent hostelries in the Hudson Valley in its day. Like so many of these large wooden structures, the Grant House Hotel was destroyed by fire in 1923. The property was sold to Greene County as a site for its newly organized Greene County Memorial Hospital. (Author's collection.)

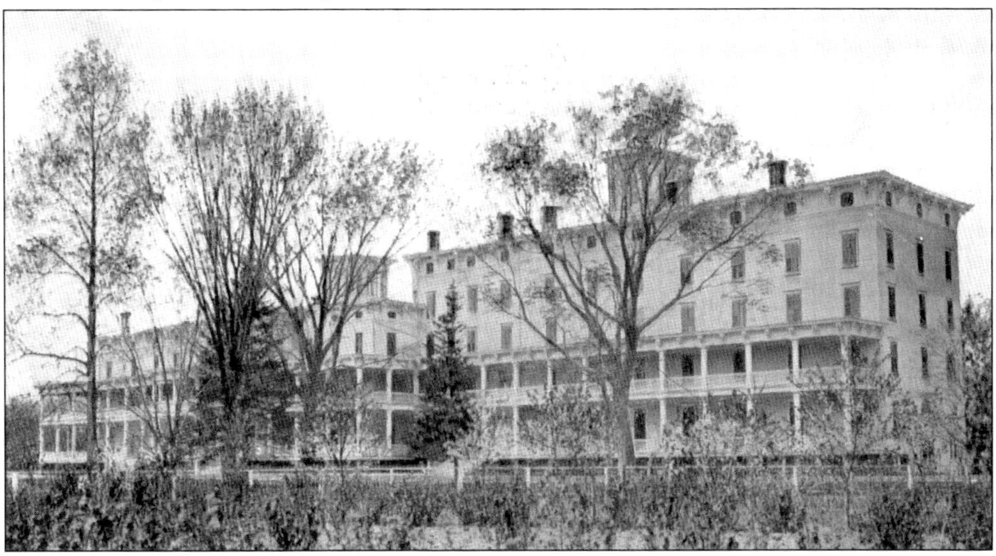

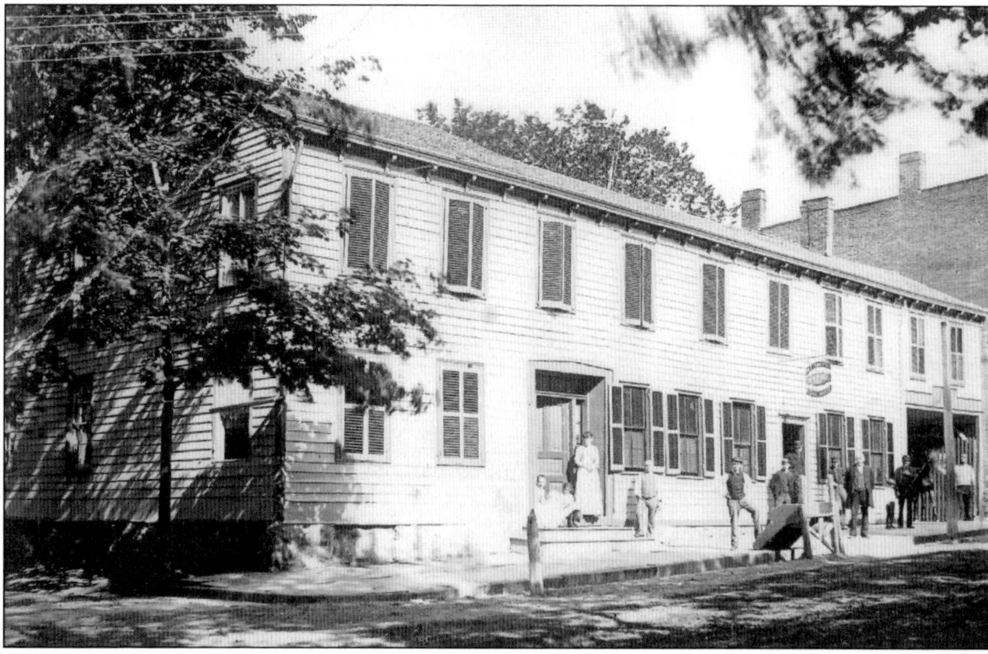

The Smith House was located on Main Street for more than 140 years. One of Catskill's oldest hotels, having opened in 1820, it was named after the three generations of Smiths who owned and ran it until 1922. The photograph above shows a two-story building shortly after the Civil War; it reached an apogee of elegance by the dawn of the 20th century (below) with its added third story and striped summer awnings. It was torn down for a parking lot in 1962 after years of decline. The Smith House is perhaps best remembered for a bit of promotional eccentricity: for many years an elm tree grew out of the floor in the dining room and sprouted up through the roof. (Author's collection.)

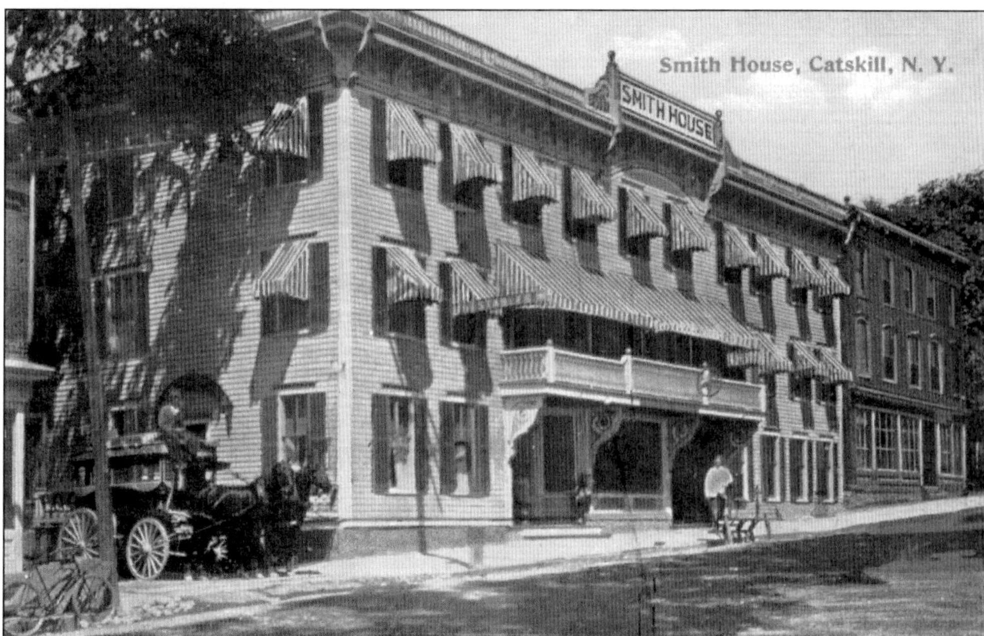

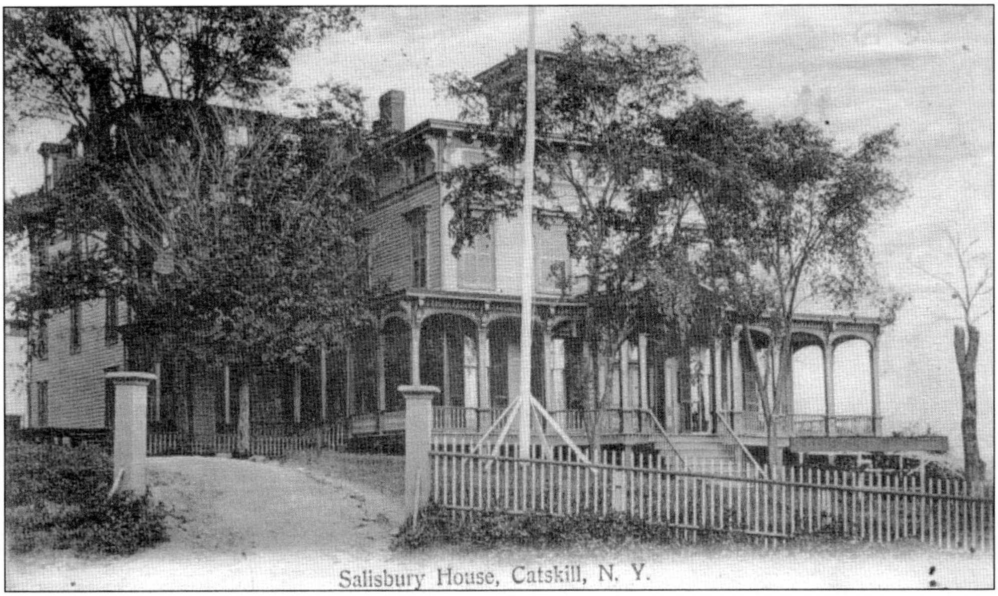


Two popular village hotels that thrived on the tourist and commercial trade were the Salisbury House, located on the Susquehanna Turnpike in Jefferson Heights, and the Irving House on Main Street at the corner of Clarke Street. Accommodating as many as 80 guests, the Salisbury House (above) burned in 1963, and its front lawn was turned into a car wash and transmission repair shop. The Irving House met with a somewhat less ignominious end. Said to have been the equivalent of any five-star hotel in its day, the Irving House was torn down in 1908 to clear its lot for the new Greene County Courthouse. (Author's collection.)

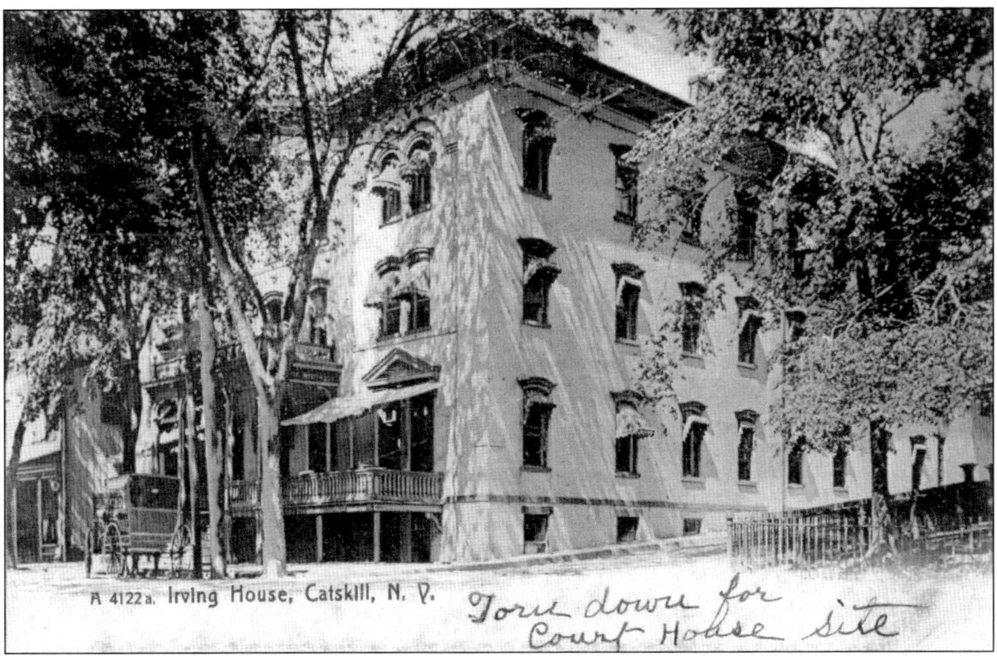

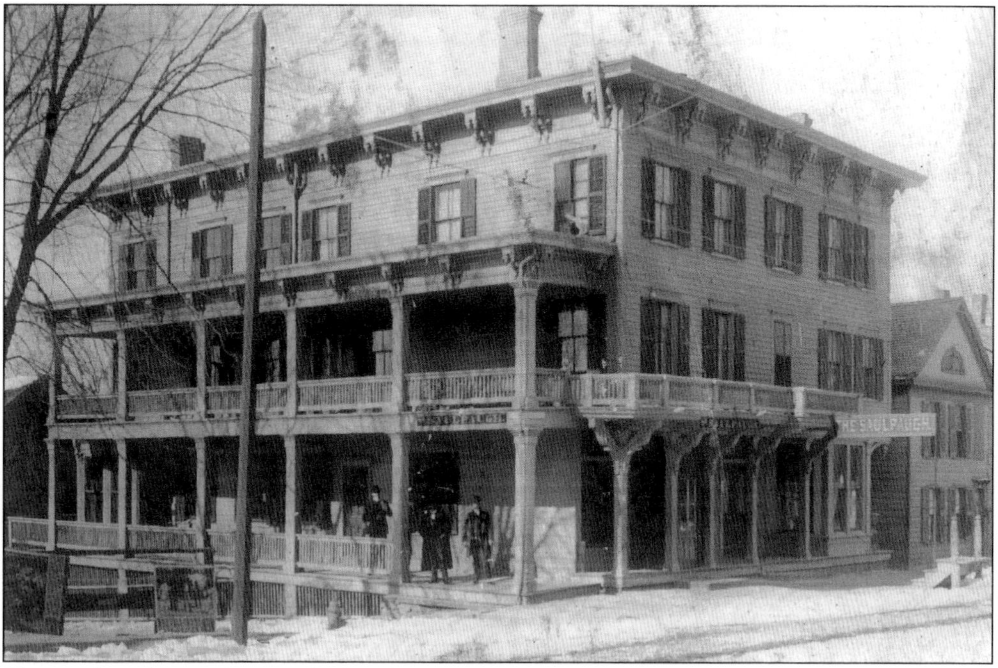

The Saulpaugh Hotel, named after the family that ran it for several generations, was located on Main Street diagonally across the road and convenient to the new 1910 county courthouse. Because of this advantageous location, exposing it to the patronage of politicians, lawyers, businessmen, commercial travelers, and tourists, the 60-room Saulpaugh survived into the 1970s and was the last hotel to operate in the village. It was built in 1863 as the Windsor Hotel, and toward its end, it had a popular restaurant and lounge. But it was finally bought by the county, torn down, and replaced with a parking lot. The photograph above shows the Saulpaugh around 1895, while the photograph below shows the hotel after one of its makeovers as the New Saulpaugh. (Author's collection.)

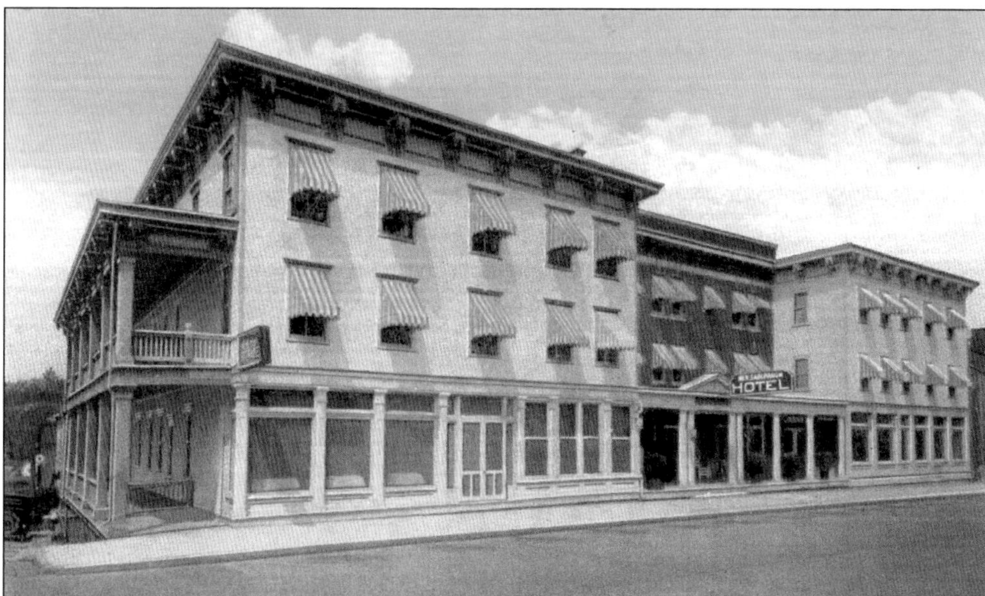

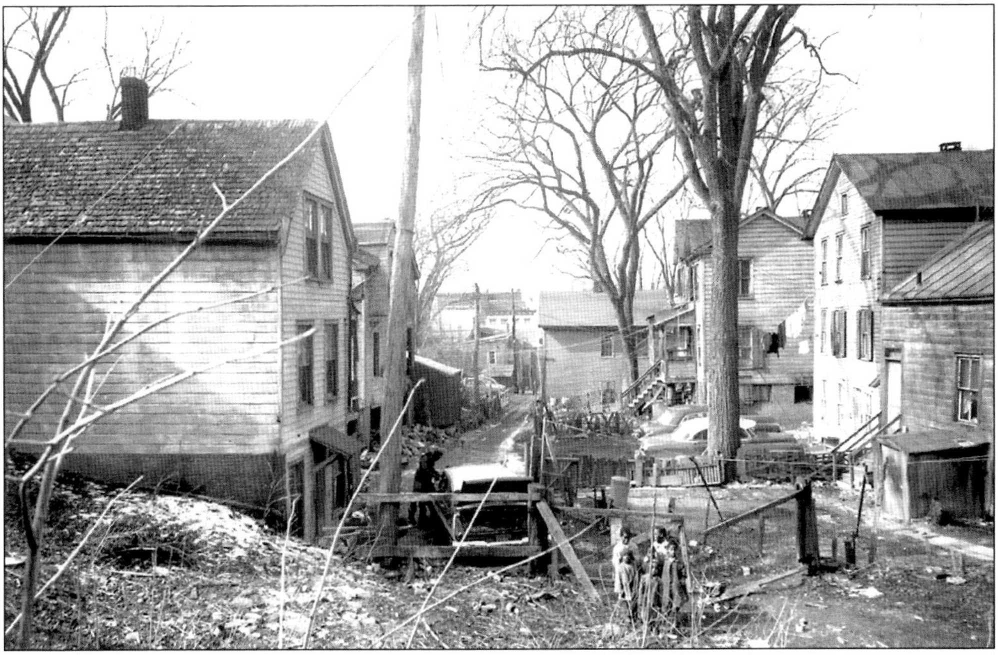

Willard Alley (above, around 1960) was occupied primarily by African Americans transplanted from the South to work in Catskill's brickyards and cement factories. It was demolished in order to create the municipal parking lot in an overzealous effort to "clean up" the community and encourage downtown parking. The perspective on Broad Street (below) is from south to north, looking up toward the intersection with Greene Street (around 1900). This area was one of the first to develop uphill from Main Street, but it was also the approximate site—long since lost to development—of an Esopus Indian village, one of several built on the hillsides on the east side of the creek. In 1684, the local Native Americans sold the land here to Dutch settler Gysbert Uyt de Bogart for a pittance, effectively ending their right to further occupation. (Courtesy of Robert Carl.)

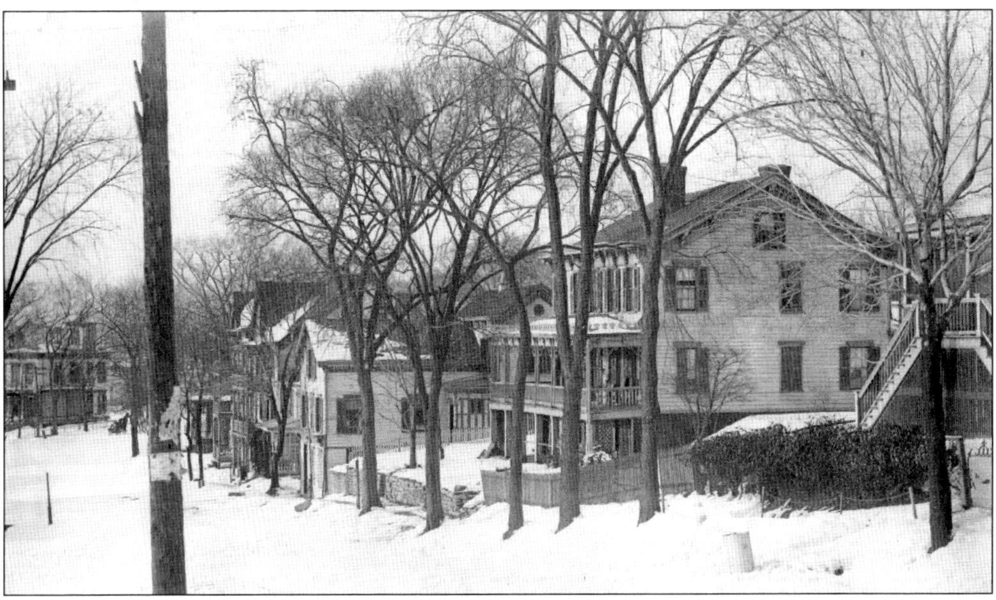

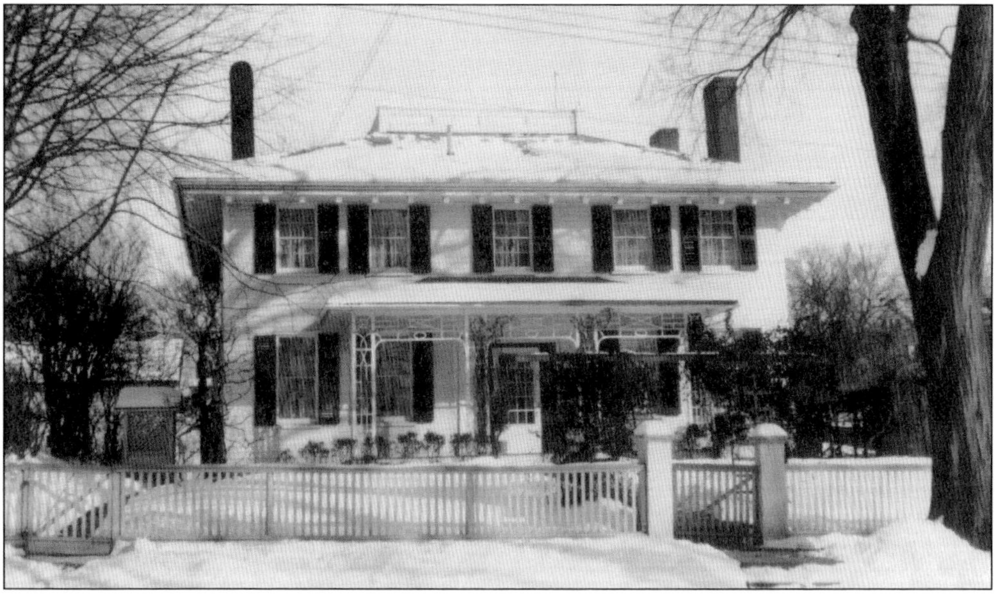

Frederick Hill built his imposing American Colonial–style home (above, seen around 1940) in 1844 on Broad Street, providing his young bride with numerous household luxuries, including wood-burning fireplaces in each of the 10 principal rooms. Two blocks up on Prospect Avenue (below, around 1940) is a Dubois-built home originally constructed with a fashionable mansard roof in the latter years of the 19th century. It was seriously damaged in a fire in the early 1930s and subsequently rebuilt in the Colonial Revival style that was—and still is—used so effectively by villagers with basically conservative tastes. (Above, author's collection; below, courtesy of Damon Pouyat.)

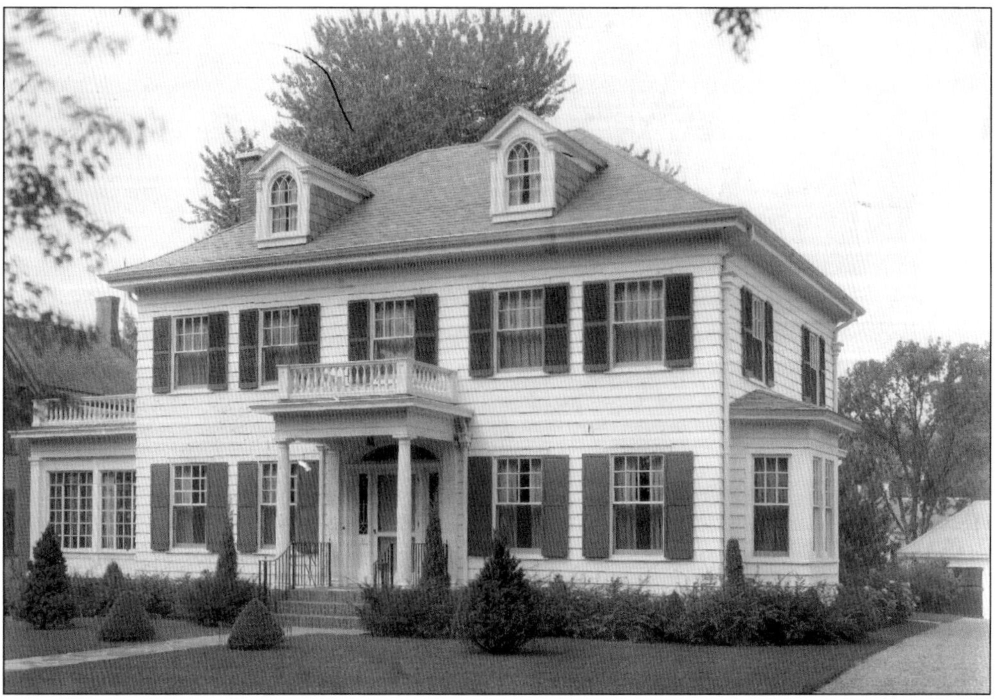

# Five

# MISHAPS

Although this is not always the case, some disasters can actually result in improvements. For example, in the days prior to 1852 when passenger steamboat racing on the river was not prohibited by law, the steamship *Henry Clay* overheated downriver in a race with the *Armenia*, the boiler exploded, and hundreds of hapless passengers drowned or were burned to death, including such notables as Andrew Jackson Downing and Nathaniel Hawthorne's sister. The good that came out of this was the enactment of the first rigid Steamboat Inspection Act by the New York State legislature that greatly reduced further similar disasters. The Catskill Village fires, although costly and destructive, often cleared land for new better-built, fireproofed, and more attractive buildings. The fire of 1851 was perhaps the worst in village history, sweeping up from Main to Broad Streets, reducing to ashes and rubble a substantial swath of developed land. Firefighting was ineffectual; only buckets of water were available. In 1863, the village passed new laws that included requirements for better organization and equipment, election of firemen, uniforms, firehouses, and fire prevention. These did not stop fiery conflagrations altogether, of course, but they did reduce their dire consequences as well as result in one of the great fraternal organizations of Catskill Village, the firefighters, who are still there today after approximately 160 years of volunteer service to the community. Included among the mishaps are some projects done in the names of progress and urban renewal, from the wanton and much lamented destruction in the 1890s of a Georgian mansion called the Old Stone Jug to the razing of a handsome and substantial armory and the demolition of Grandview School. There have been some recent victories against this kind of progress, and the overall effect on the community of saving its visual inheritance is greater than ever before.

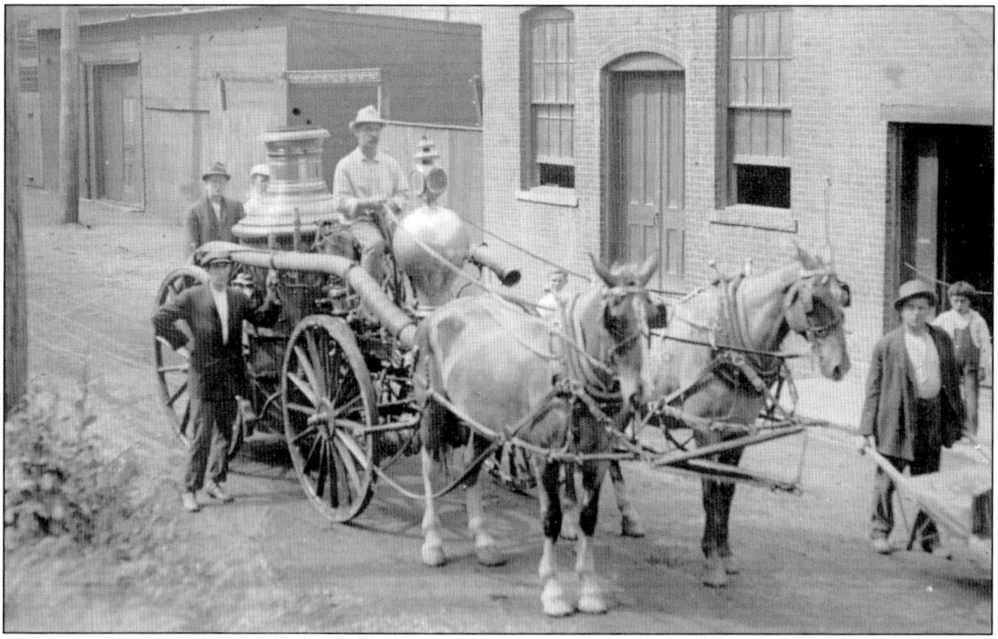

Catskill's earliest horse-drawn fire truck (above) consisted of a wagon on which a pump was mounted that drew water from one of seven underground cisterns built under Main Street in 1836. One of these mysterious cisterns (some of them still exist) has been described as "100 feet long, 15 feet wide, and eight or nine feet deep, completely lined with brick, with domed ceiling, and partitioned into two chambers by a brick wall." In addition to noting that Standard Oil gasoline is 16¢ a gallon at the general store, the *c.* 1910 image below features the three-bay firehouse that housed the Francis N. Wilson Company No. 5 of firefighting volunteers, which shared its building with the village offices upstairs. Ironically, this building burned down in 1935, taking with it 300 years of irreplaceable village archives. (Courtesy of Robert Carl.)

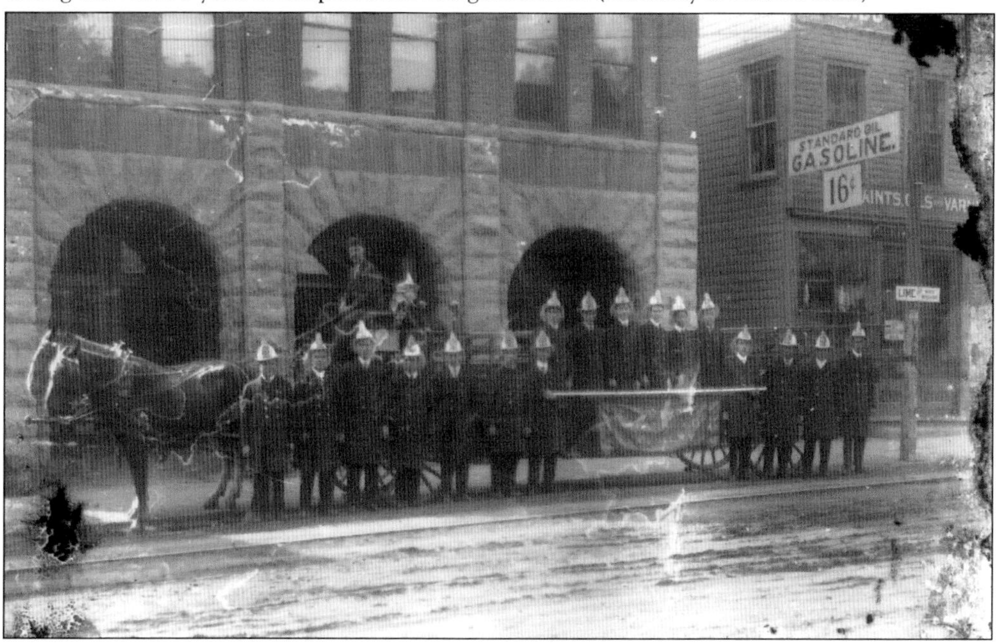

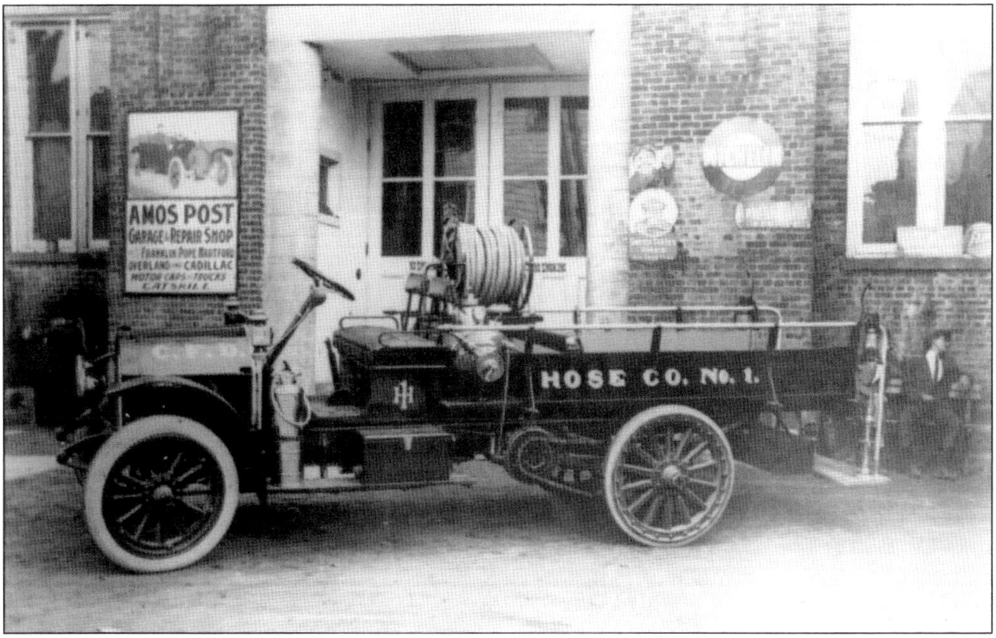


One of the Catskill Fire Department's earliest motorized fire trucks was a chain-driven vehicle used by Hose Company No. 1. It is parked in front of Amos Post's garage where Post not only repaired motor vehicles but also sold Franklin, Overland, and Cadillac automobiles. Post's garage was in the former St. Luke's Episcopal Church that was designed in 1840 by Thomas Cole after a fire ravaged the previous building. Cole's church, having descended into decrepit condition during the 20th century, was finally demolished in 2005 to make room for 10 more spaces in a parking lot serving the new county building. (Courtesy of Robert Carl.)

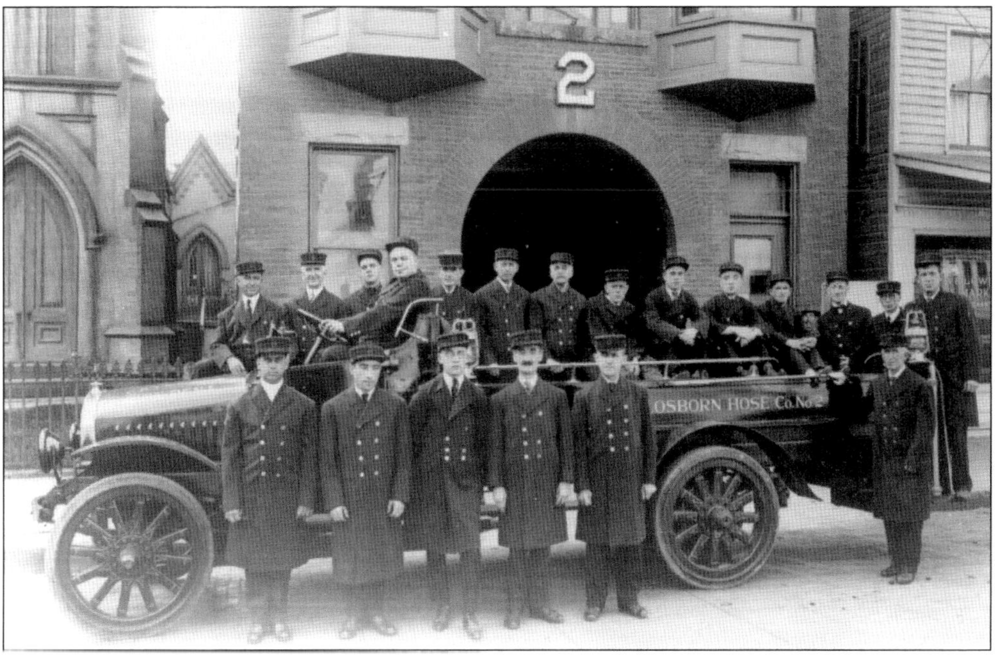

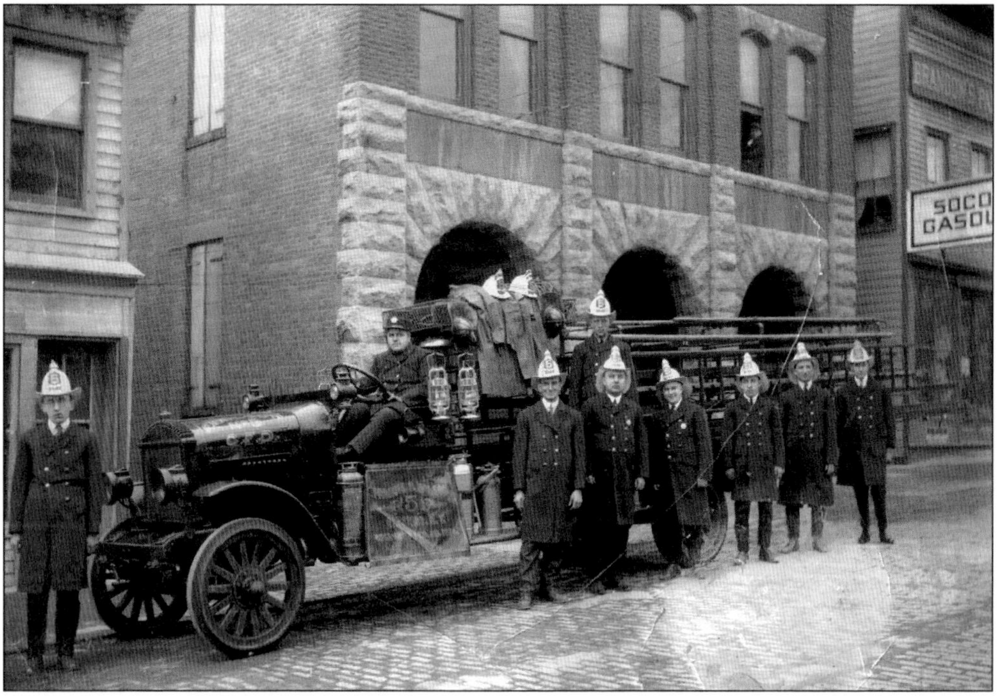


The volunteers of the Francis N. Wilson Company No. 5 (above) that was established in 1854 proudly pose around 1920 with their newest fire truck, this one with rubber wheels, ladders, and kerosene lamps, making it ready for almost anything. They share the three-bay building behind them with the village offices. Below is a picture of this scene after the building was ravaged by fire in 1935. Legend has it that one of the fire trucks parked inside the burning building caved through the floor into the cellar and, rather than go to the trouble of extricating the charred remains from the ruins, the cellar was filled in and the lot paved over for a parking lot—one that has remained to this day. (Above, photograph by Van Dyke, courtesy of Robert Carl; below, courtesy of Robert Carl.)

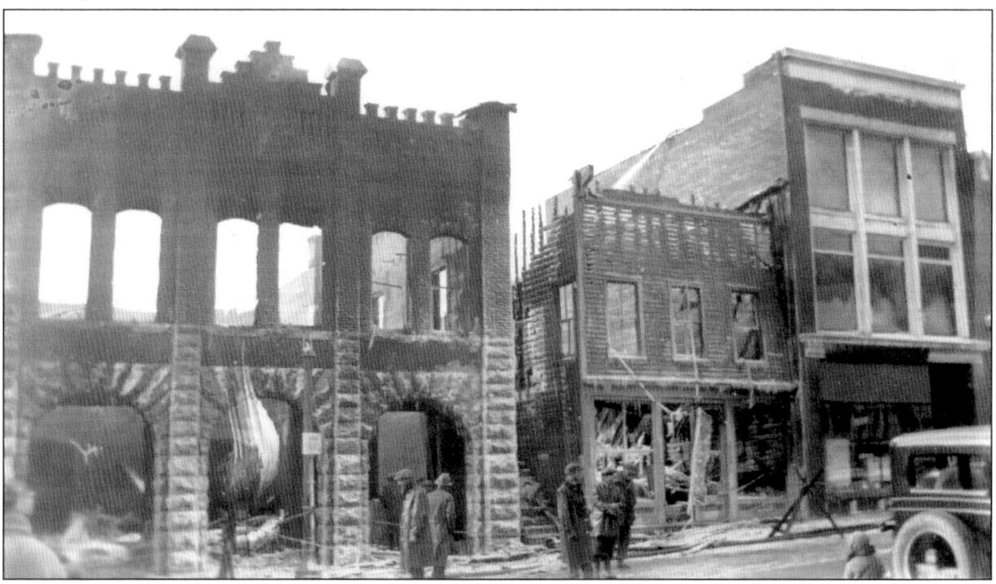

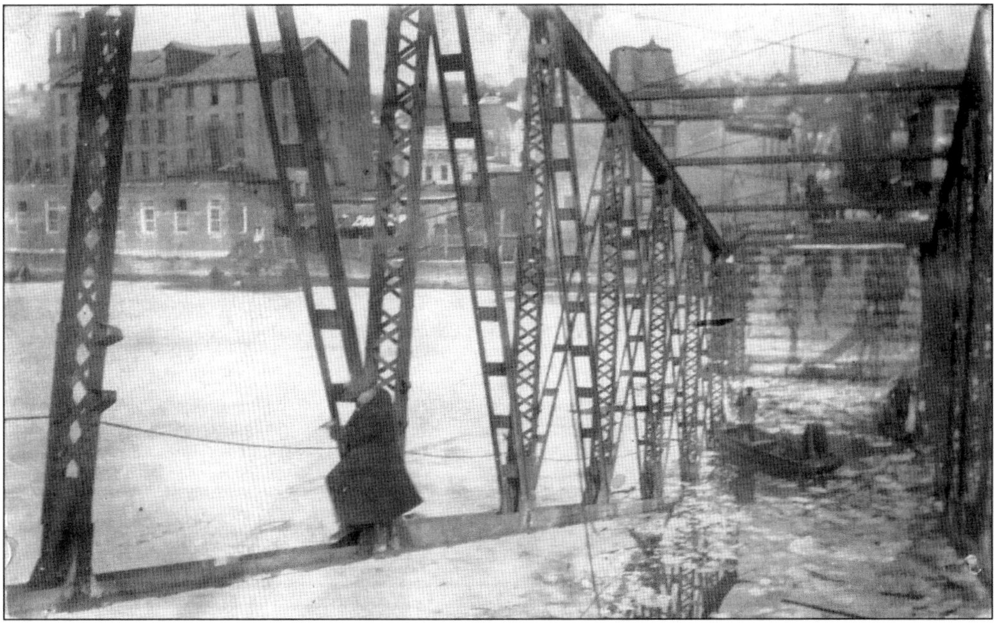

A barge from the Kaaterskill Paving Brick Company broke its mooring farther down the creek in 1901 and, on the rising tide, crashed into the 1871 iron bridge (above), smashing it beyond repair. A man is apparently making his way along an iron girder with the help of a rope handrail. In the distance is the Union Mills. In order to help pedestrians cross the creek farther up from the accident (below), a pontoon bridge was erected connecting West Main Street on the west side of the creek with Water Street on the east side. (Courtesy of Robert Carl.)

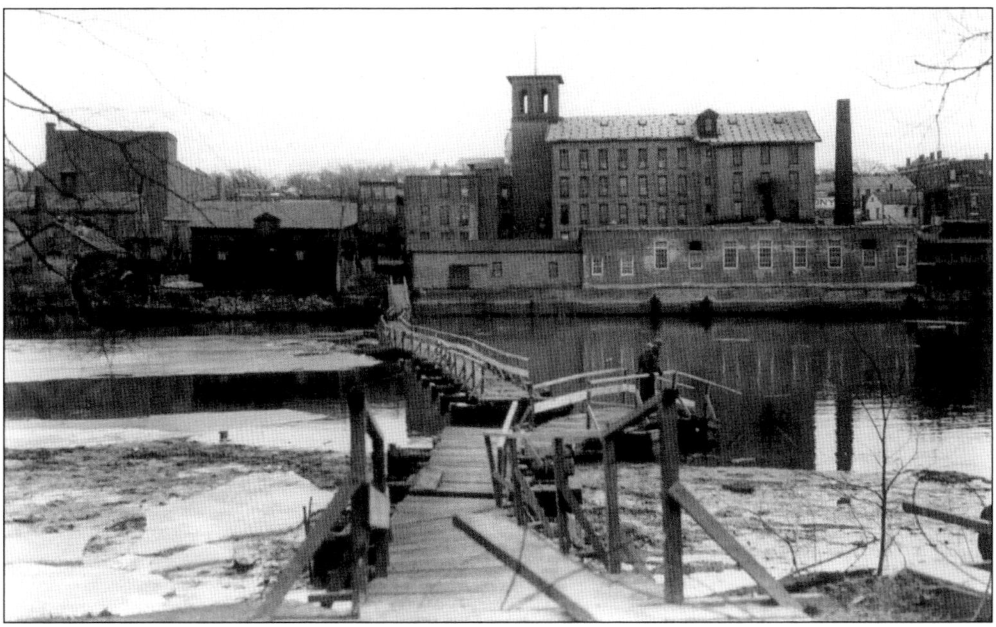

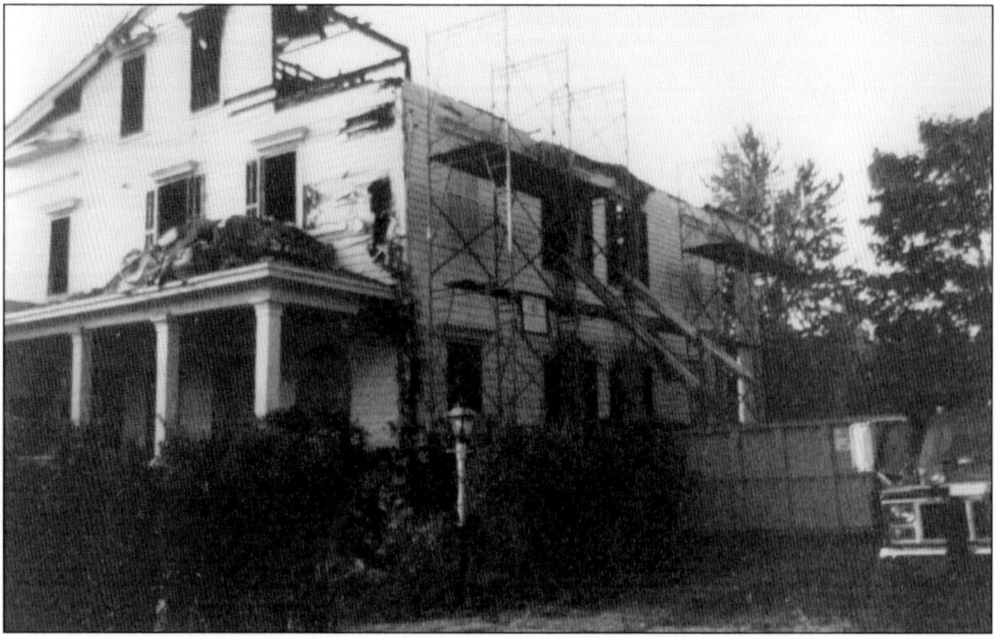

One of the most striking private homes in the village is the Greek Revival mansion Hiram Comfort built in 1838 at the corner of Orange Avenue (now Prospect Avenue) and William Street. It was renovated in the 1980s by Barbara Newcomb (now Weber), who has rescued and restored seven historic homes in Catskill over six decades. During the course of another restoration in 1992, fire ravaged the top floors almost beyond repair (above). The ruin was eventually purchased for $10 and rebuilt (below) by Rich and Kim Rappelyea. Known in the area as the contractor most sensitive to the nuances of restoring historic properties, Rich Rappelyea's success with saving and restoring the Hiram Comfort house is exemplary. (Courtesy of Rich Rappelyea.)

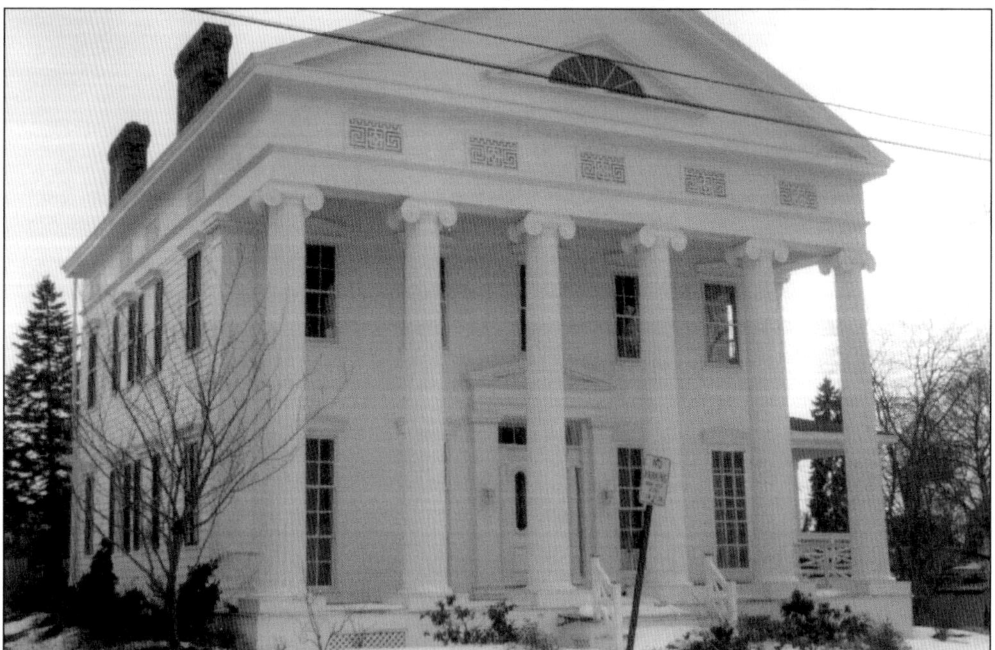

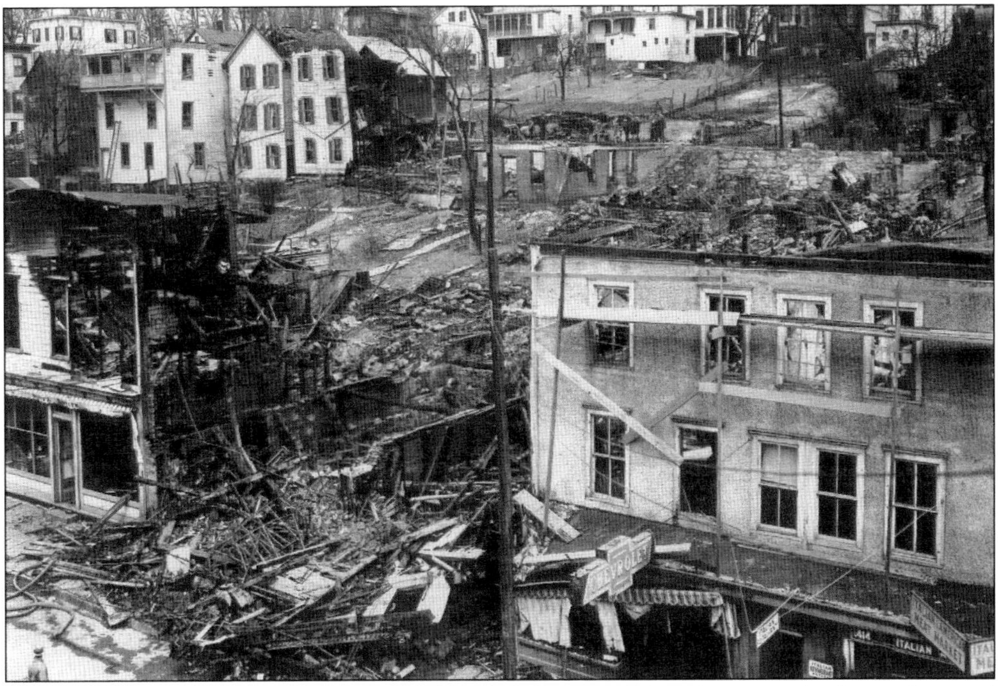


The fire that began on May 1, 1928, in the Kortz barn on Main Street resulted in widespread devastation on upper Main Street (above). After heroic but futile attempts to stop the fire by companies that came from as far away as Poughkeepsie, Albany, and Windham, 16 buildings were consumed, and 15 families and 40 people were left homeless. The entire segment of the village that was consumed was replaced by fireproof buildings of brick and stone. Below, the frozen remains simmer down after the fire that demolished several buildings at Main and Church Streets on February 13, 1934. Another fire destroyed the much-beloved Nelida Theatre on January 1, 1918, when temperatures dropped to 20 degrees below zero. Seven buildings were destroyed in addition to the old vaudeville house. (Courtesy of Robert Carl.)

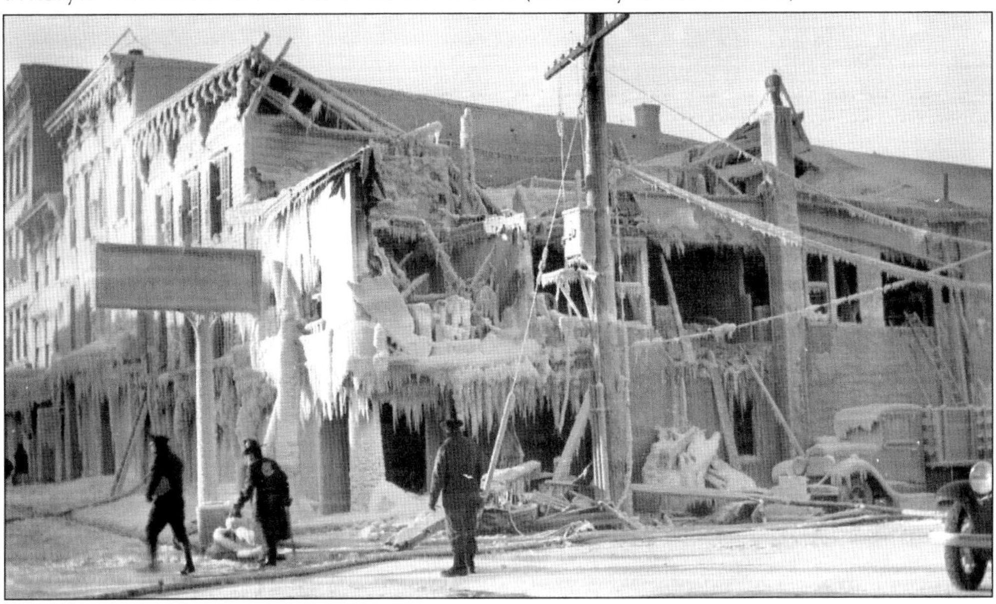

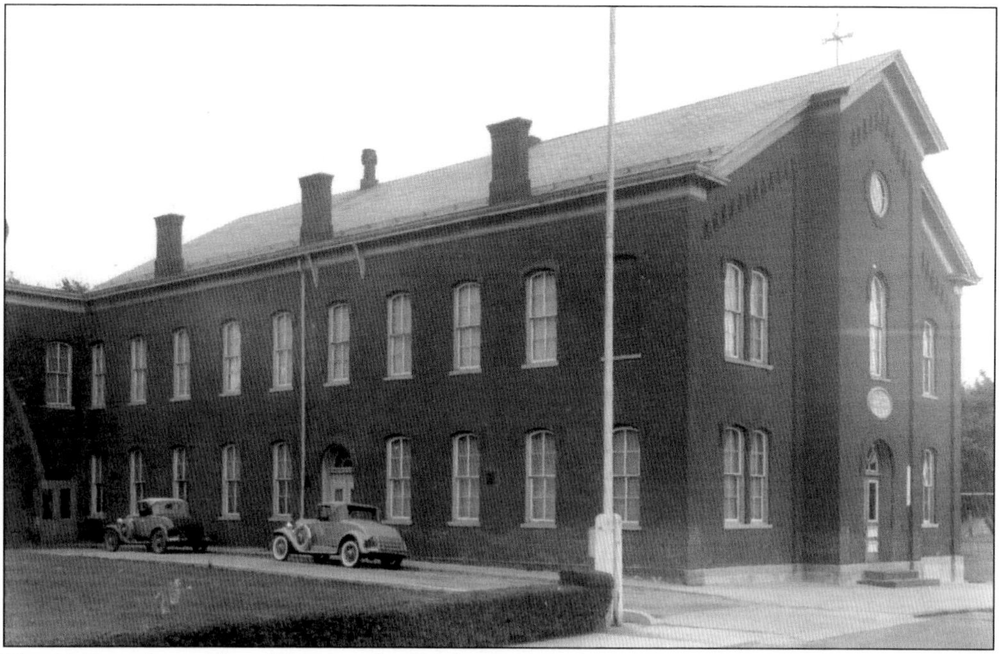

The 1869 academy (above) became the Washington Irving High School and was used for nearly 65 years before it was consumed by a ferocious blaze on March 8, 1935. It is seen below in the aftermath of the fire. Students were transferred to the old Union Mills a short distance away on Water Street where classes were held for the next five years. The new Works Progress Administration high school was completed in 1940 on property on the west side of the creek that was a Dubois farm in the 18th and 19th centuries and a brickyard in the early 20th century. (Courtesy of Robert Carl.)

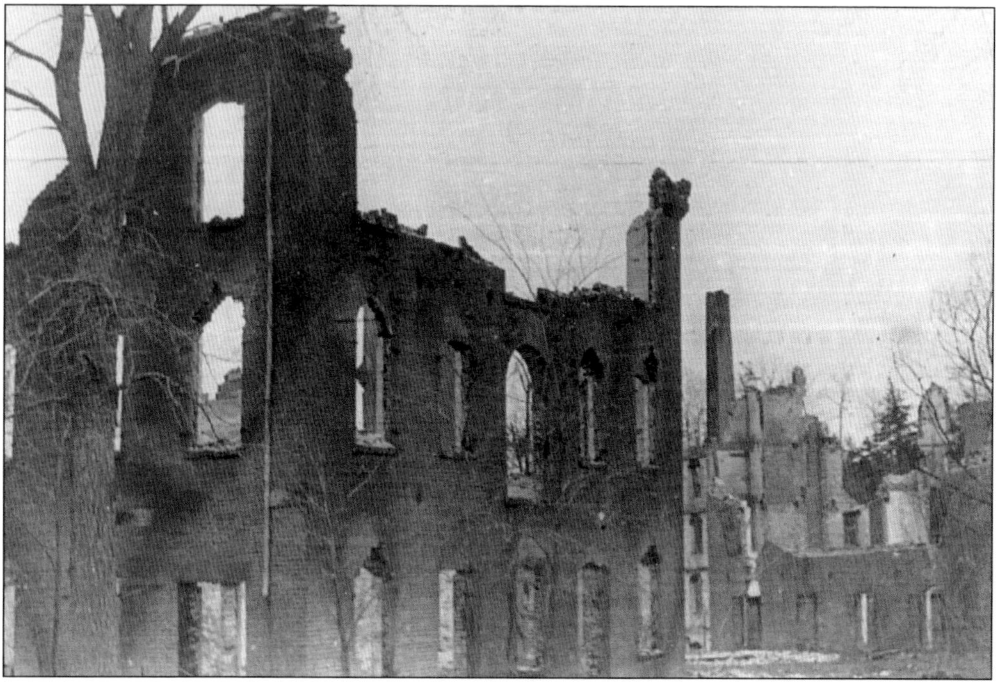

The Catskill Young Men's Christian Association (YMCA) was organized in 1890 with the mission of "the improvement of the spiritual, mental, social, and physical condition of young men." Young women had their own YWCAs elsewhere. The first quarters were located above the Van Valkenburghs' Main Street store, and the present building, pictured at right around 1905, now home to the community center, was built in 1902 on the site of the late-18th-century arcade building. Of the original $40,000 cost, $30,000 was given by F. N. Dubois, one of the YMCA's most fervent supporters. Below, the building burned on April 30, 1957. In the process of restoration, the top two floors were left off. (Right, courtesy of the Arthur Hamm collection; below, courtesy of Robert Meo.)

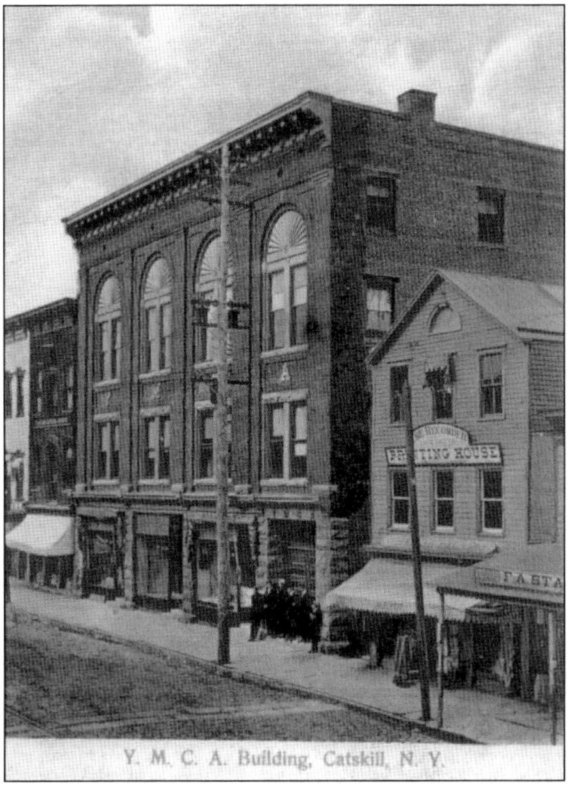


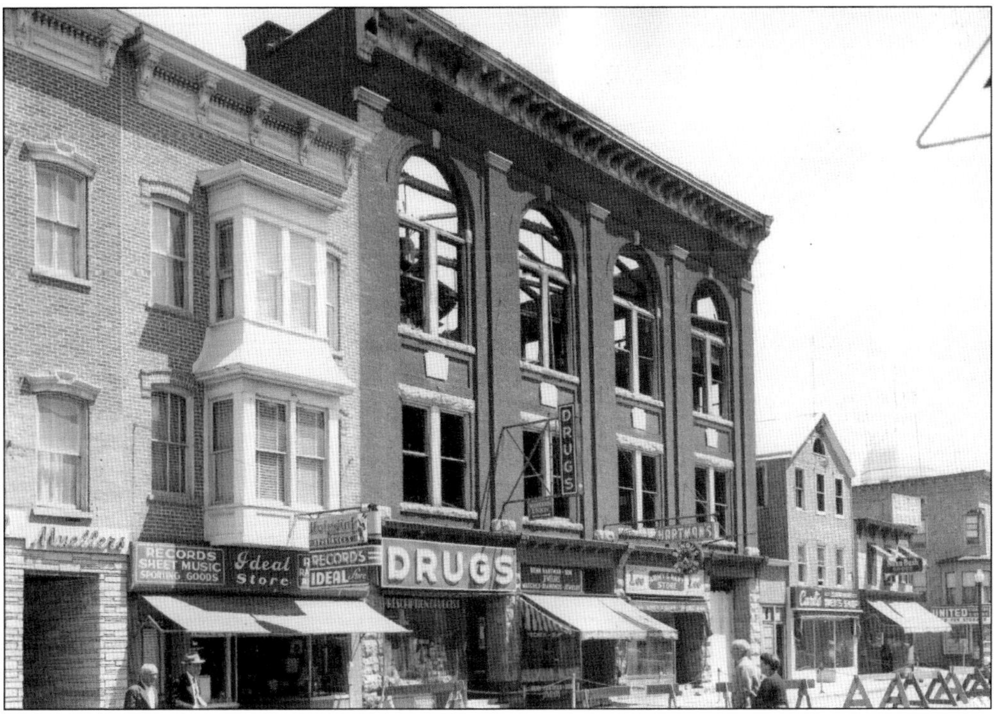

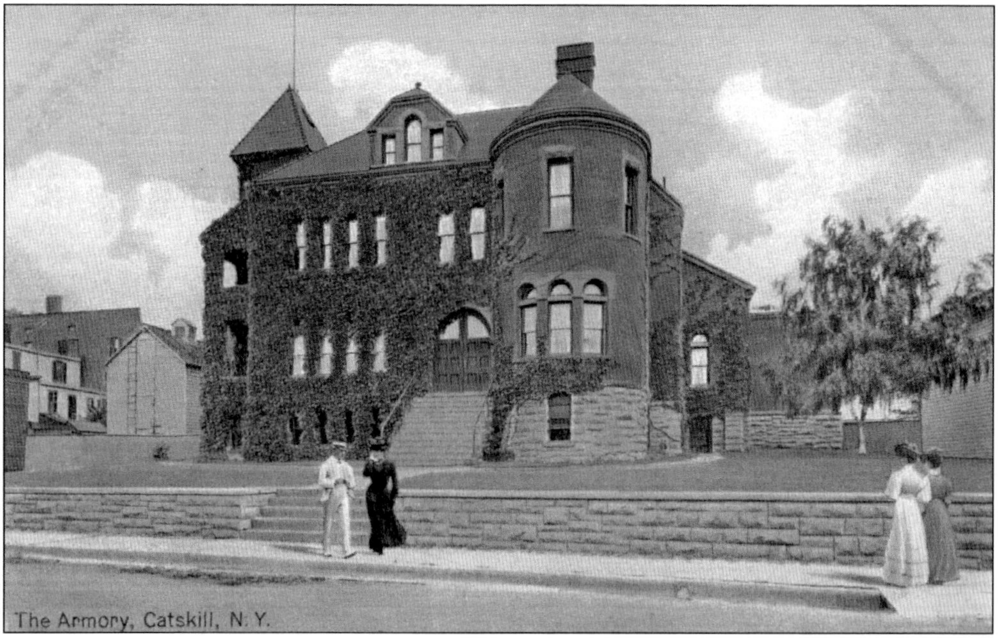


In order to stimulate declining profits on Main Street, an entire business district along Water Street was demolished and turned into a paved-over bald spot to provide hoped-for customers with parking. The demolition of the 1889 Victorian Gothic Romanesque armory (above) might not have happened today in view of more sensitive awareness to the inherent value of old structures. The 1893 Grandview School (below) had withstood the ravages of change until 2006 when it was torn down to make way for a chain pharmacy. Both of these very substantial buildings of native stone and locally made brick were constructed by George W. Holdridge, a Catskill builder who created some of the most enduring civic and domestic structures. (Author's collection.)

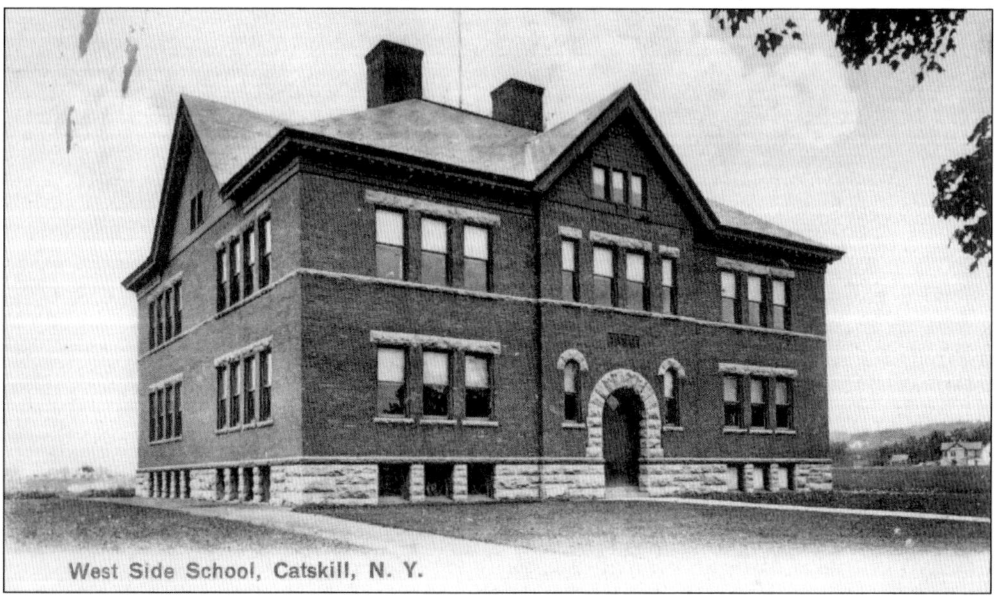

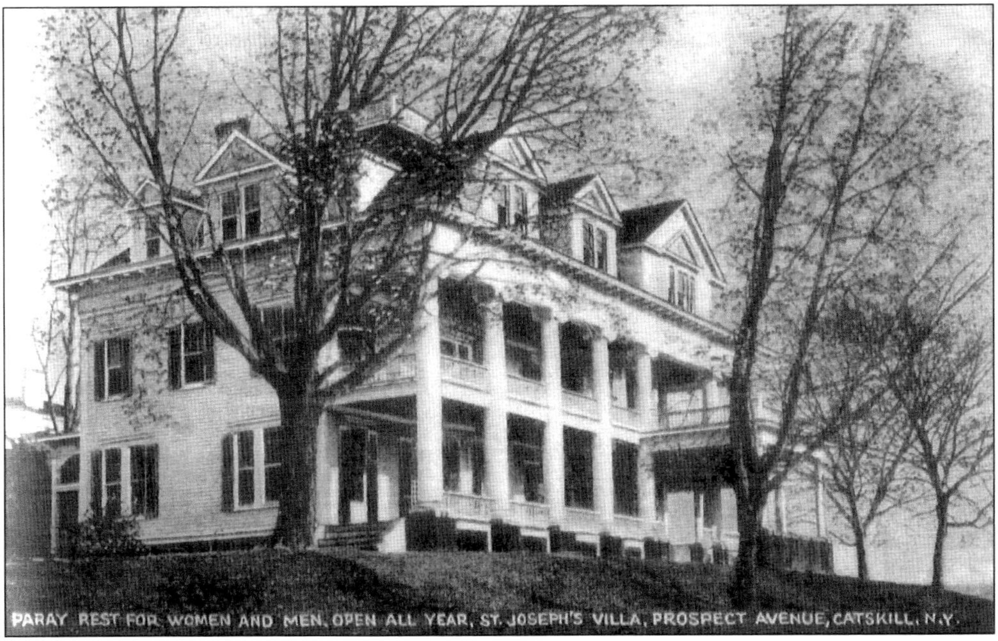


The Paray Rest Home (above) was a private home built in 1866 by the proprietor of the Prospect Park Hotel nearby. In the early 20th century, it was bought by the Roman Catholic Church and used as a nursing home until the mid-1980s when it was torn down rather than having its roof repaired. The Cornelius Dubois Dutch fieldstone house (below) was built in 1762 on West Main Street. In 1803, a substantial addition of 14 rooms was added on the street side of the older stone structure (just visible behind). For reasons still unknown, in 1952, the 1803 addition was torn down by a new owner who started a car dealership on the property. The 1762 house is to the left, and the 1803 addition is to the right in this 1901 snow scene. (Above, author's collection; below, courtesy of Robert Carl.)

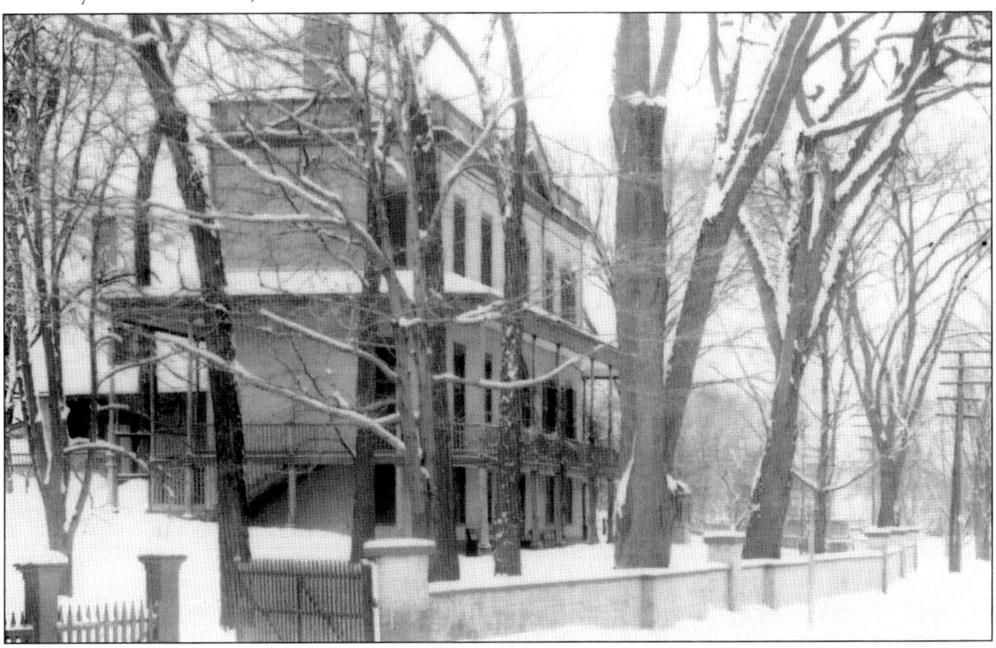

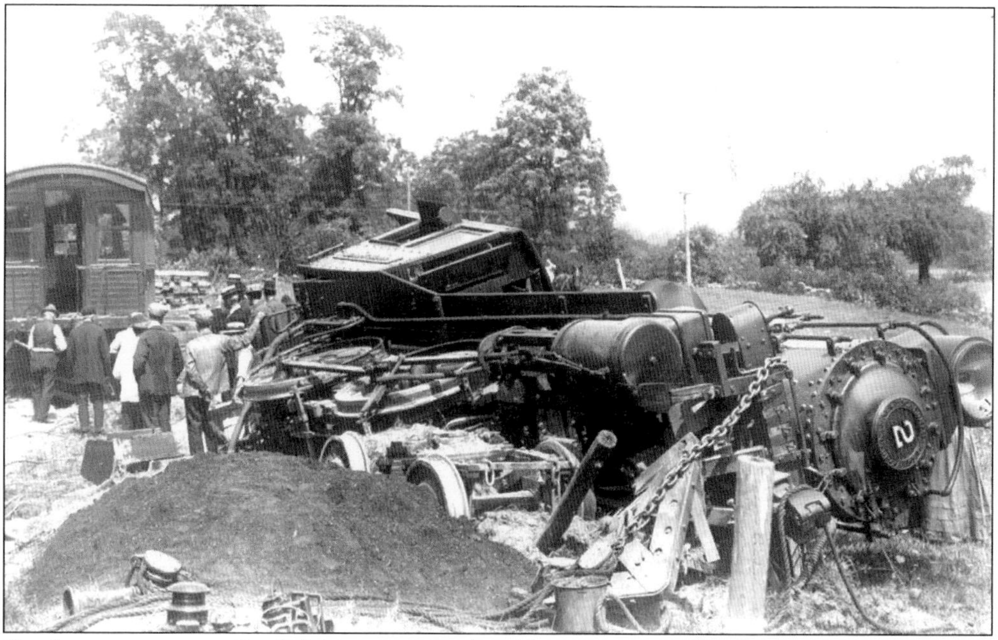

On the narrow-gauge Catskill Mountain Railroad between Catskill's Point and Palenville, "the most frequent accident was derailment, often where schoolboys were likely to congregate." In other words, rocks put intentionally on the tracks caused derailments. While rounding an embankment on April 3, 1910, train No. 2 (above) separated from its baggage car, derailed, and tipped over. Nobody was hurt, and once up-righted back onto the tracks, the little engine was sent for extensive repairs in the village. For well over 125 years, a local landmark at the top of West Bridge Street (below) was a building that housed a chair factory, served as a glass factory, and, for the last 40 years of its life, had been refitted as an apartment house. It was completely destroyed by fire in the winter of 1999. (Above, courtesy of Robert Carl; below, photograph by Ron Welsh.)

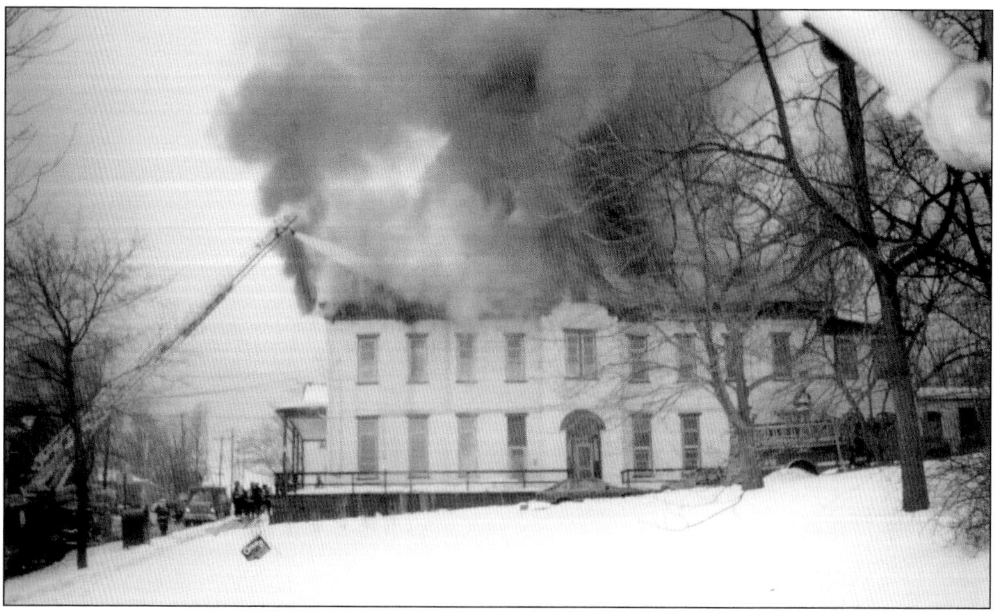

# *Six*

# SERVICE

At the dawn of the 20th century, the village was, to quote a publication from that era, "one of the busiest and most progressive of its size in the whole country," and "it is in the front rank of the lively, up-to-date twentieth century villages of New York State." One of the reasons for its success was its community services, including police, fire, medical, mercantile, churches, library, clubs, banks, courts, jobs, and schools. The Catskill Police Department, for example, occupied new up-to-date headquarters on Main Street equipped with telephones and electric lights. It had new motorcycles, perhaps newly added to the force for enhanced pursuit of criminals. There were five firefighting organizations. Catskill Village was served by three railroads by the late 19th century, and the port on the Point was a major stop on the river for passengers and commerce. Churches played important roles in village life and furnished the services that are provided by community organizations today, such as individual emotional support, family counseling, and education, as well as feeding and housing the poor and destitute and the hungry.

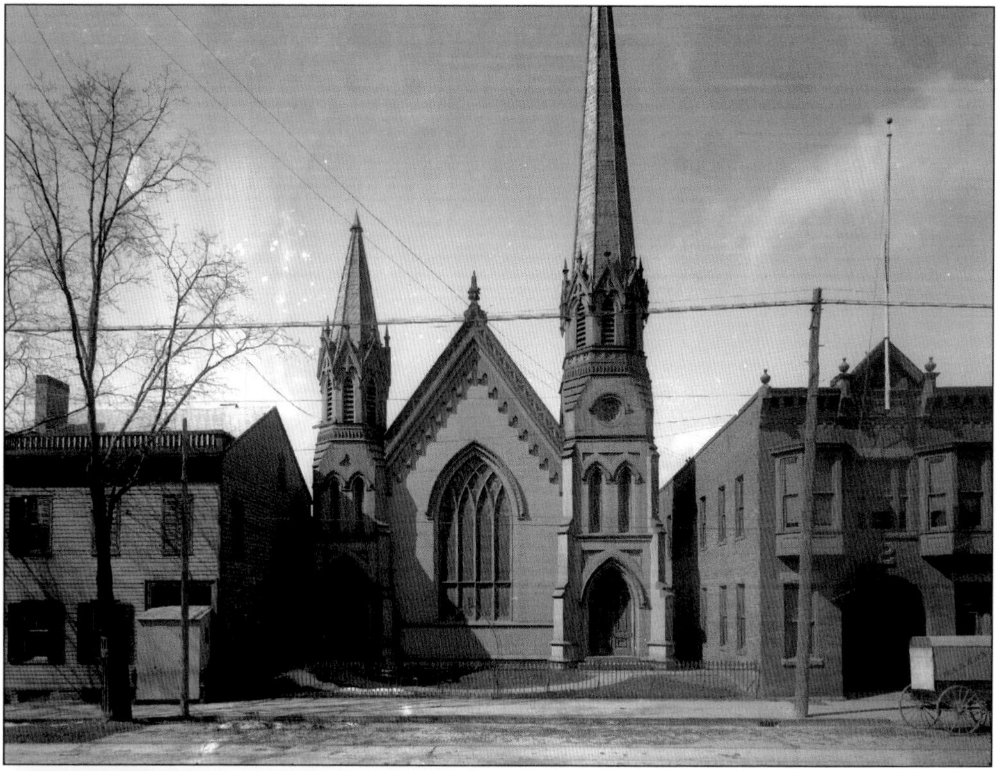

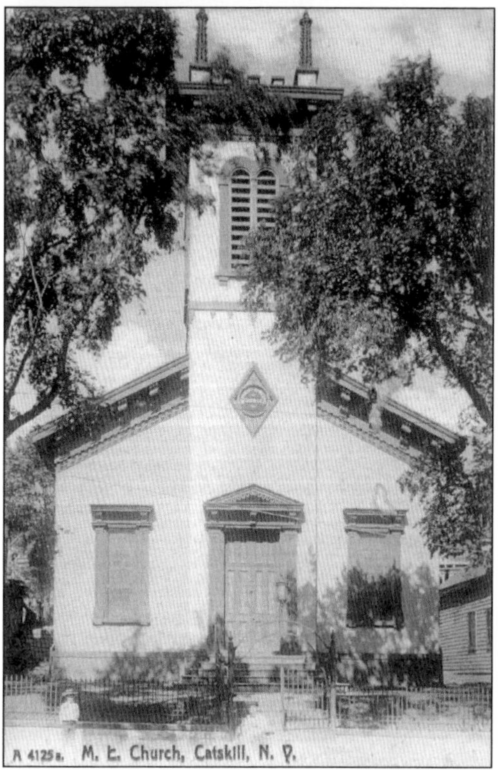


The First Baptist Church (above) was organized in 1803. It was given this Main Street lot, and the first church was erected here in 1840. It burned in the worst fire in village history in 1851, was rebuilt, burned to the ground again in 1871, and this handsome High Victorian neo-Gothic structure was dedicated in 1873. Today this building is a health club. The Methodist Episcopal Church (at left), founded in 1806, moved into this building in 1864. It was the home of Catskill's Methodist Church in the 1960s. In the 1980s, the Second Baptist Church purchased the historic building, which by then had been condemned and was going to be demolished. Primarily through membership volunteer work, the building was rescued from the wrecker's ball. (Above, photograph by Paul Morrison, courtesy of Peggy Ahwesh; left, courtesy of the Arthur Hamm collection.)

Incorporated in 1803, one of the great architectural treasures of the Hudson River valley is Christ's Presbyterian Church (right, around 1880) on Franklin Street in the village. The foundation of the present building dates from 1808. In 1853, one of the wealthiest members of the congregation, Charles L. Beach, of Catskill Mountain House fame, paid for a substantial renovation in the then-popular Greek Revival style, including the addition of six Corinthian columns originally carved in the village for an aborted opera house project in New Orleans. Thirteen more columns from the same lot were put on the front of the Catskill Mountain House. Before Franklin Street was cut through, the Presbyterian church was approached through a pathway (below, around 1890) uniquely called a slide, of which four still exist in the village to this day. (Author's collection.)

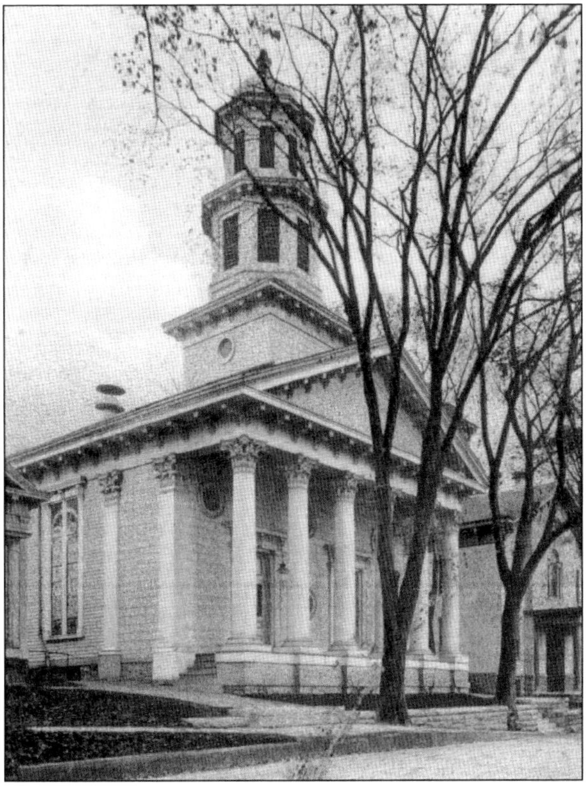

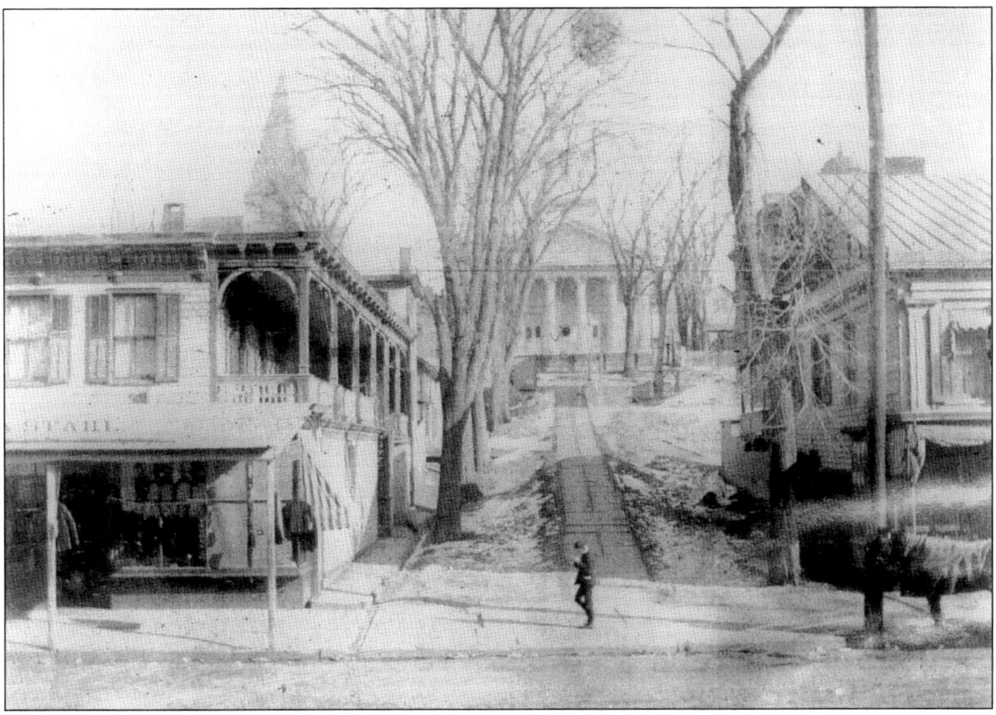

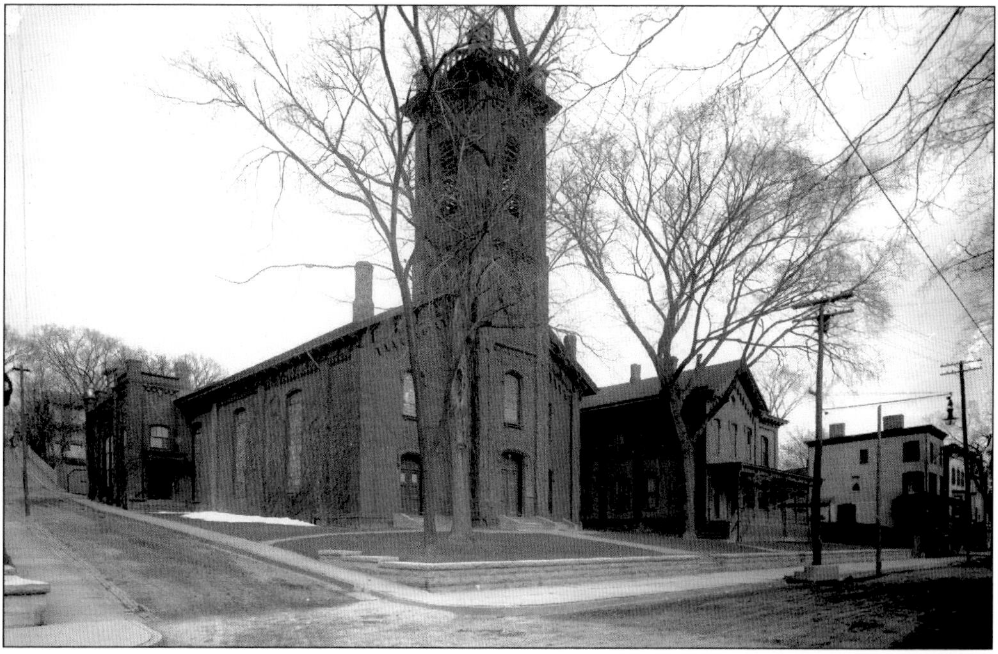

The Dutch Reformed Church (above) was organized in this area in the 1650s and was the earliest and for many years the strongest church denomination in the Hudson River valley. While Dutch was still widely spoken in Catskill Village well into the middle of the 19th century, sermons were requested in English at the Catskill Dutch Reformed Church beginning in 1810. The first sanctuary on this Main Street site was dedicated in 1829 and destroyed in the disastrous fire of 1851. The present church was dedicated in 1852, and the adjoining parsonage dates from 1870. The view of the back of the interior of the church (below) was taken from the front aisle. (Photographs by Paul Morrison, courtesy of Peggy Ahwesh.)

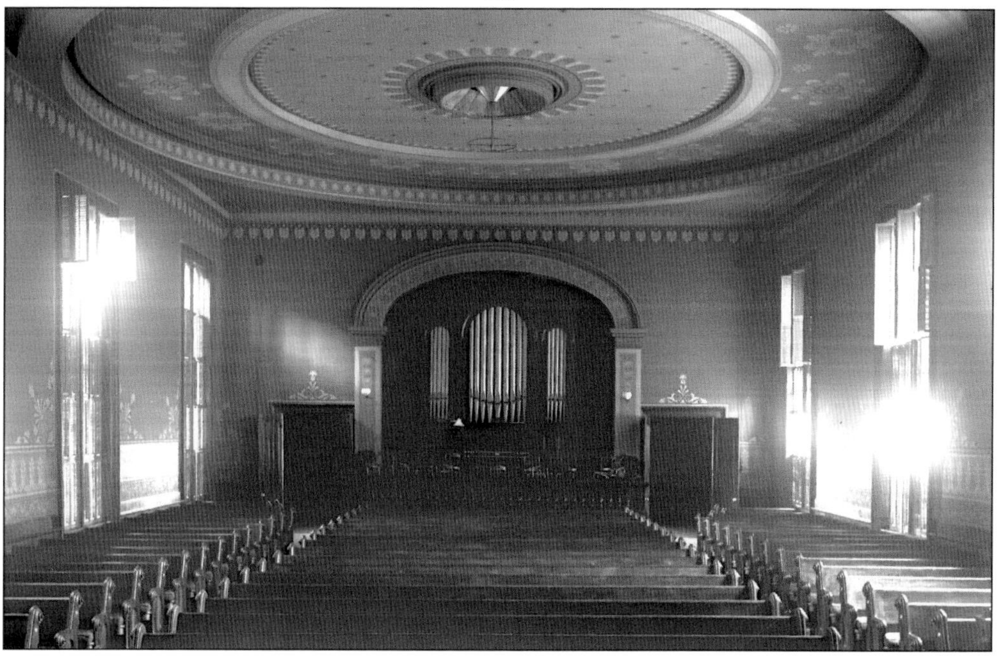

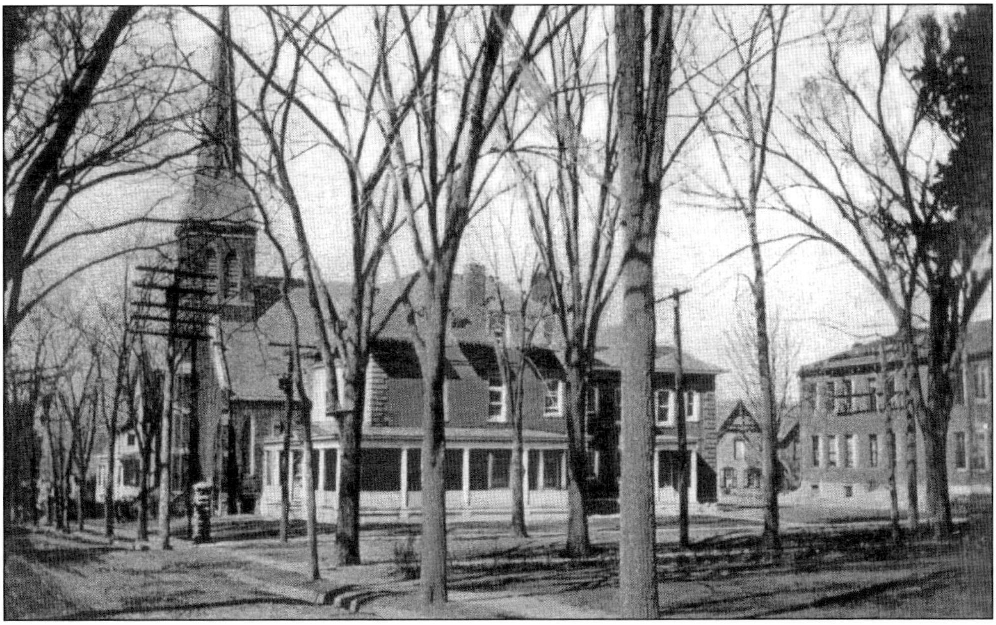

In 1854, the first church of St. Patrick's Roman Catholic parish (above) was built on William Street, and the present church, on the same lot but facing Bridge Street, was dedicated in 1884. St. Patrick's Academy, to the right of the church and facing Spring Street (also above), was opened in 1890, and, having moved in the 1960s to a new building on Woodland Avenue, the academy was in operation until 2006 when it closed for lack of funds and students. In 1905, an Italianate mansion on Prospect Avenue (below) was purchased and turned into a nunnery. Having been abandoned and sold in the early 1990s, this landmark building was rescued at the last minute from the wrecking ball and restored by Barbara (Newcomb) Weber, who received the prestigious National Trust for Historic Preservation award in 1995. (Author's collection.)

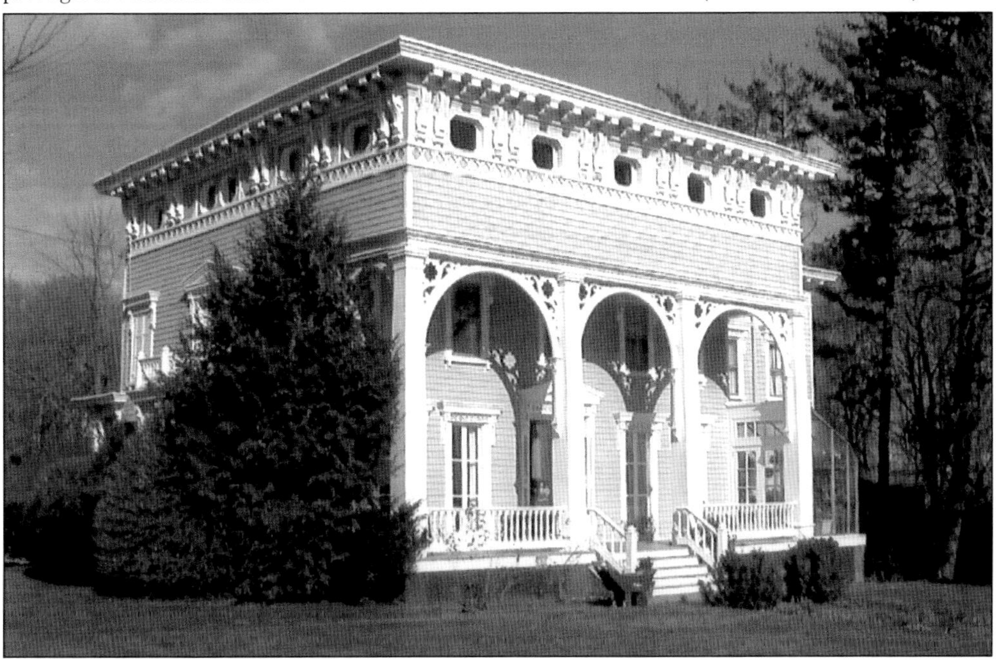

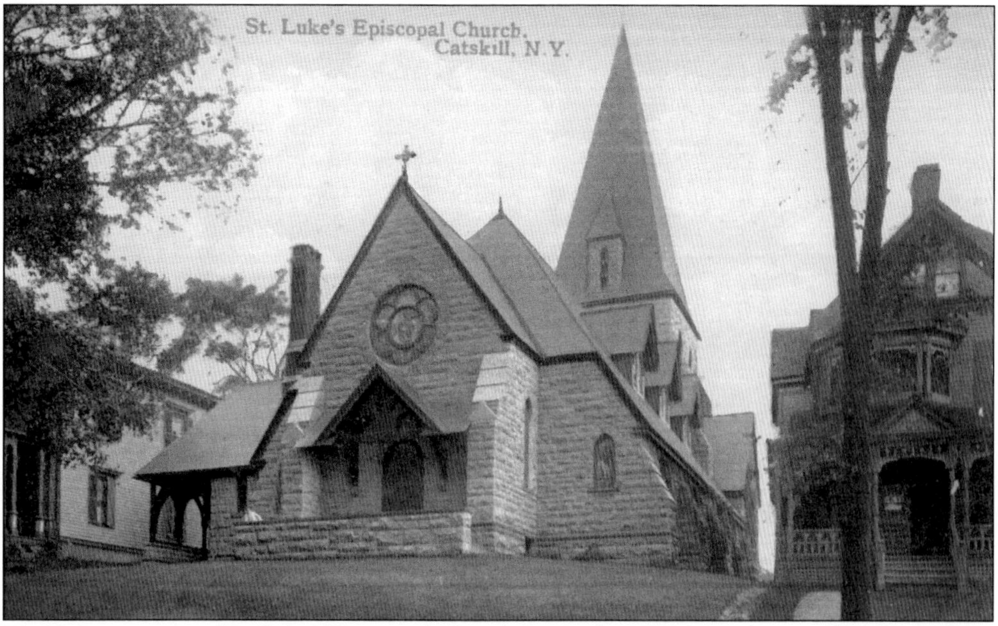


The first sanctuary of St. Luke's Episcopal Church, erected in 1804, was destroyed by fire in 1839. The second sanctuary was designed by landscape painter Thomas Cole. In 1899, the new church on William Street (above), built in the then-fashionable Richardsonian Romanesque style, was dedicated. The Cole church was sold to Amos Post, who turned it into an automobile garage and showroom. It housed the *Daily Mail* after a disastrous fire drove the daily newspaper, founded in the 1790s, from its longtime home on Main Street. The Cole building was demolished in 2002 to provide 10 parking spaces for the new county building. At the corner of Broad Street and Livingston Street (below) in one of the oldest sections of the village is the starkly plain and beautiful arts and crafts sanctuary of the First Church of Christ Scientist that dates to the 1920s. (Above, courtesy of Robert Meo; below, courtesy of the Arthur Hamm collection.)

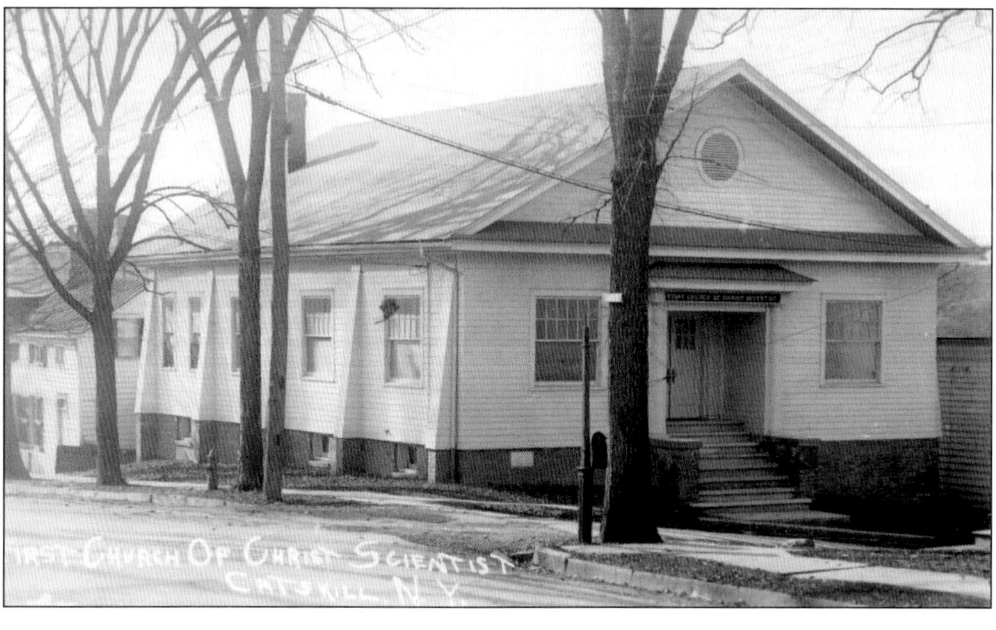

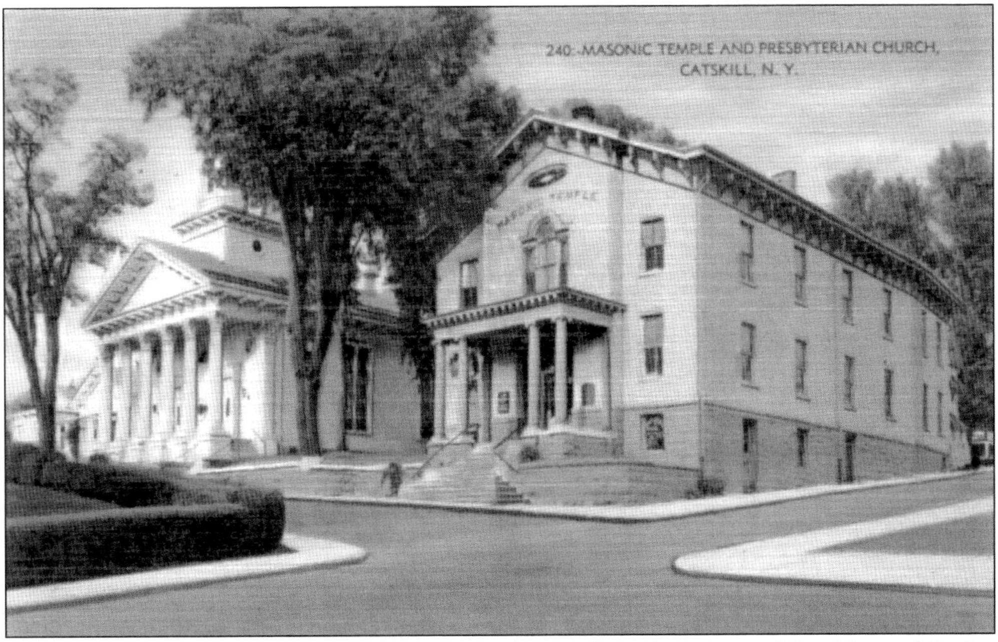


The Federal-style courthouse (above) was erected in 1813 on the corner of Franklin and Bridge Streets. Authorized by an act of the legislature, a courthouse was first built on a site nearby, burned down, and was then built again on this site in 1813. It served Greene County as courthouse and jail for almost 90 years until the new courthouse opened in 1910. The 1813 courthouse is being used today as a law office. Across from the 1813 courthouse on Franklin Street is the 1902 Catskill Public Library (below), funded with a $20,000 gift from the industrialist and philanthropist Andrew Carnegie, who built libraries throughout the United States from 1885 to 1919. It is a fine example of the neoclassical style that characterizes so many of the Carnegie libraries. (Courtesy of Joan Jacobs.)

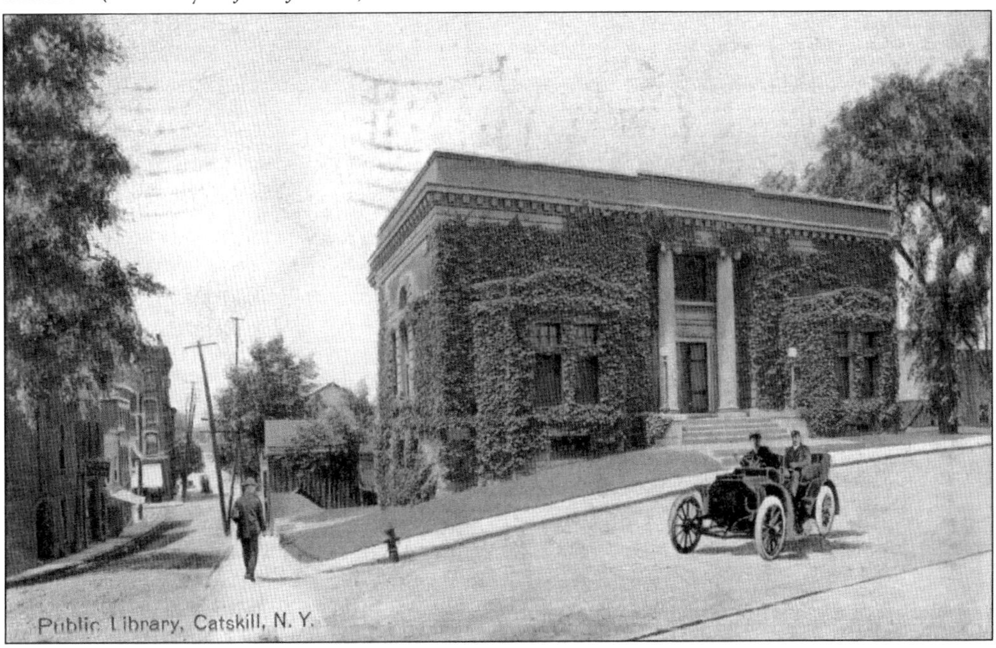

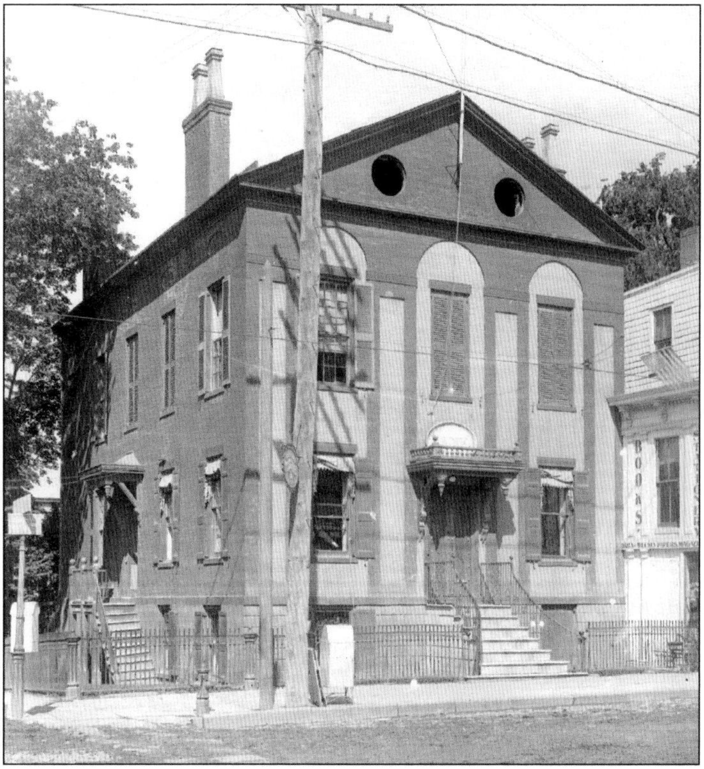

Catskill's "Little Wall Street" has been regarded fondly for many years as the sturdy repository and reservoir of the wealth of the village. The photograph at left shows the Catskill National Bank in the late 19th century before its remodeling and renovation. It was located at the corner of Bridge and Main Streets. The second bank in the row was the Catskill Savings Bank (below, left) with its neoclassical facade. The third in the row, the Tanner's National Bank (below, right), was the oldest. (Left, courtesy of Robert Carl; below, courtesy of the Arthur Hamm collection.)

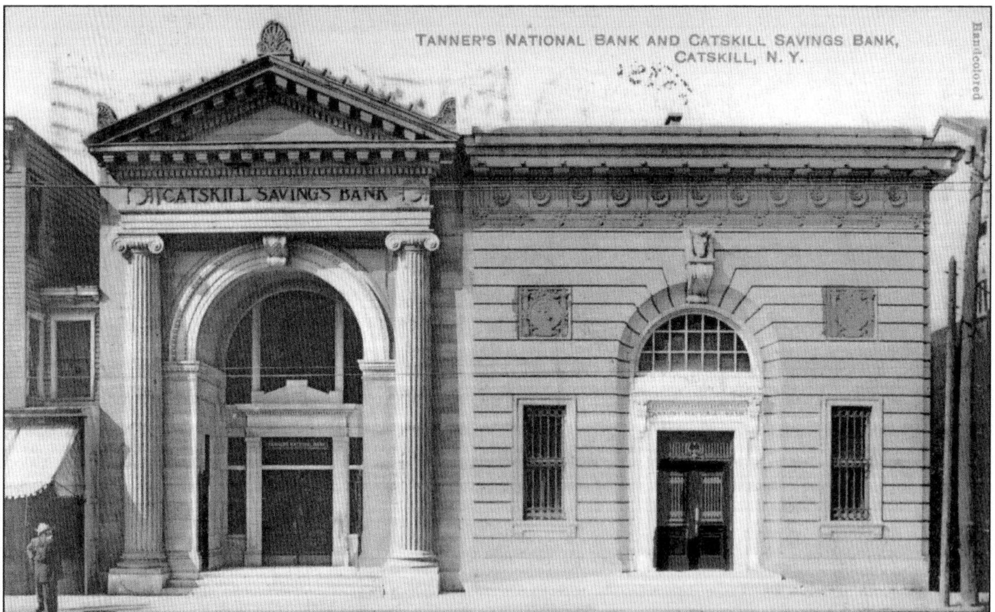

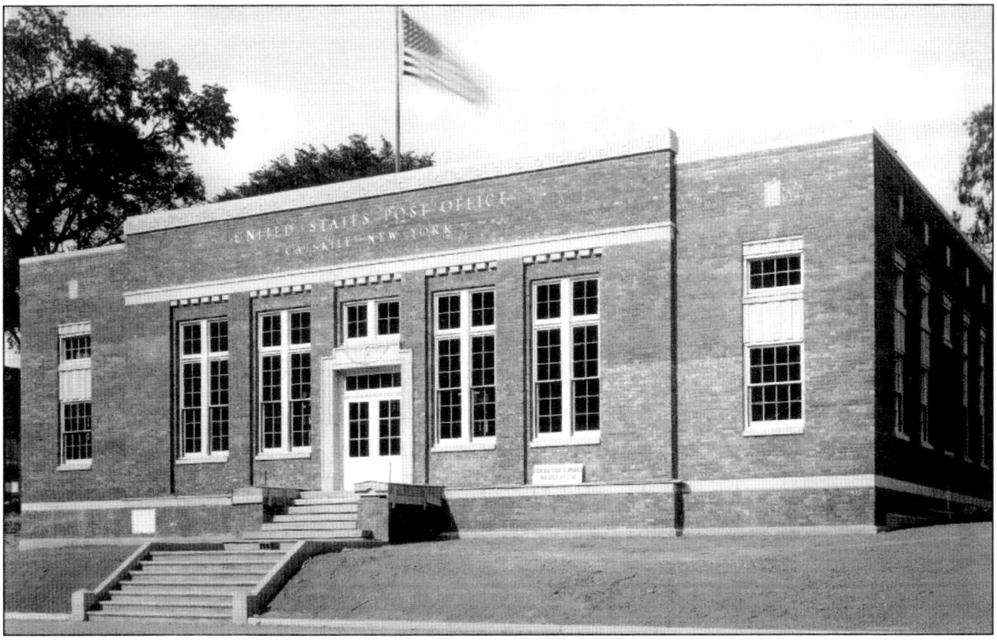


Over the years, the general post office was located in various places within the village since the first postmaster was appointed by George Washington. The location just before the post office was moved back to Main Street was the old mattress factory on Water Street. The present post office (above) with up-to-date sorting equipment must have been a welcome change when it was completed in 1936. The facade was considerably altered by the addition in the 1980s of a wheelchair ramp, which gave easier access for people with disabilities. Although the bus service today is probably more comfortable, the Catskill–Stamford line (below) was well served by this elegant conveyance from around 1920, which appears to have eight rows of seats that could seat as many as 24 passengers. (Above, courtesy of the Catskill Post Office; below, courtesy of Robert Meo.)

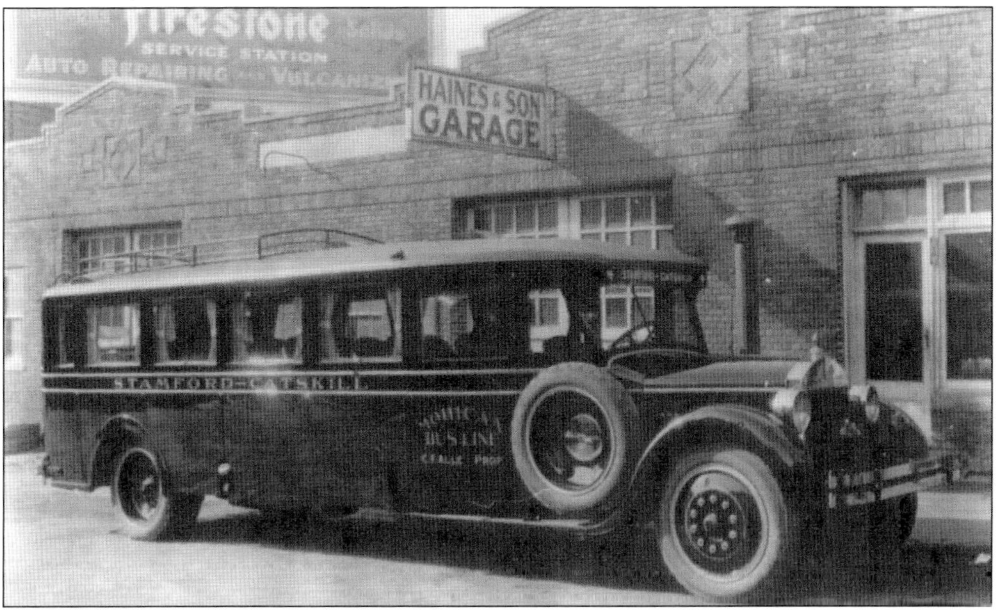

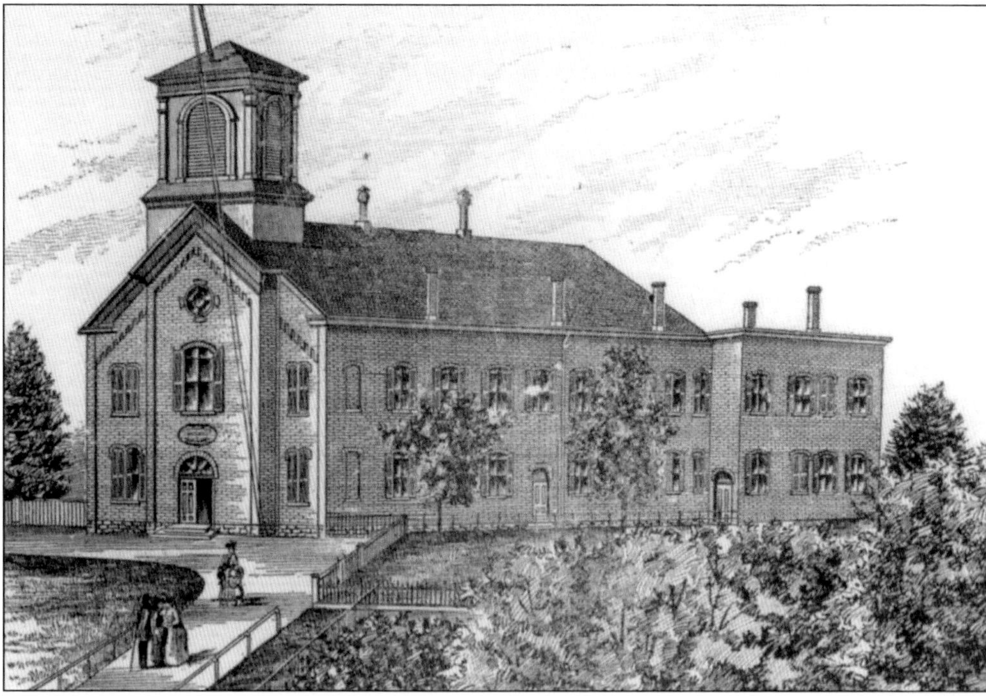

In 1803, there were three schools in the village, and education was held in high esteem. The Catskill Free Academy and Grammar School (above) was built on a hillside above the village off Thompson Street in 1869 and added to in 1882, consolidating several smaller schools around the county. The Washington Irving School (below, left) and the Academy High School were reported to be excellent schools in their day, offering languages and relatively advanced high school courses in mathematics, physics, and chemistry. An unusually high number of students for those days went on to college and made distinguished careers in law, medicine, and education. The academy succumbed to flames in 1935; today the site is occupied by the senior center. The Irving School has been converted into condominiums. (Courtesy of the Arthur Hamm collection.)

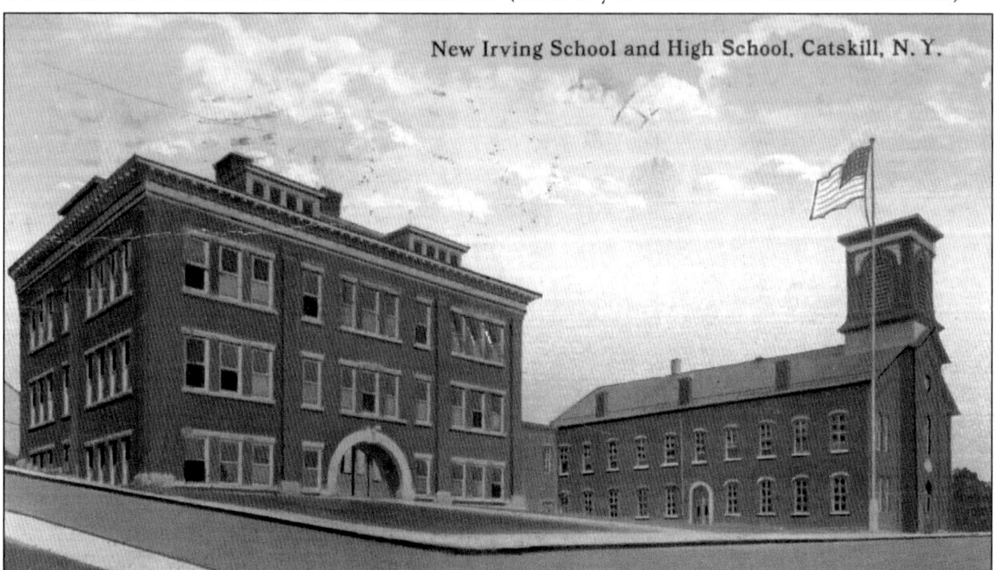

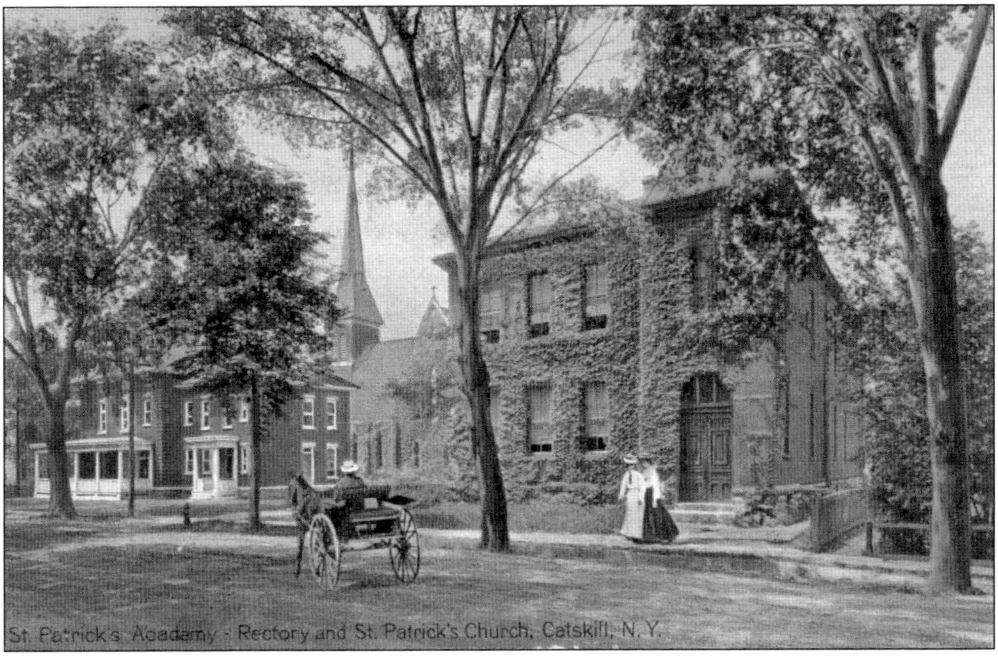


St. Patrick's Roman Catholic Church (the steeple is seen in the background of the photograph above) opened a parochial school in 1890 for children of the parish, and through the efforts of a zealous pastor, it was put on a level with the best schools in the state, according to the official parish history. Sisters of Charity were brought in to take charge of the school's classrooms and administration. After a fire demolished the old Academy High School on the east side, a new high school (below) in the popular Colonial Revival style was completed in 1940 and still serves the community as the middle school. The site of the new school is of historical significance, having been a brickyard and before that a field connected with Cornelius Dubois's 1762 fieldstone house and 600-acre farm. (Author's collection.)

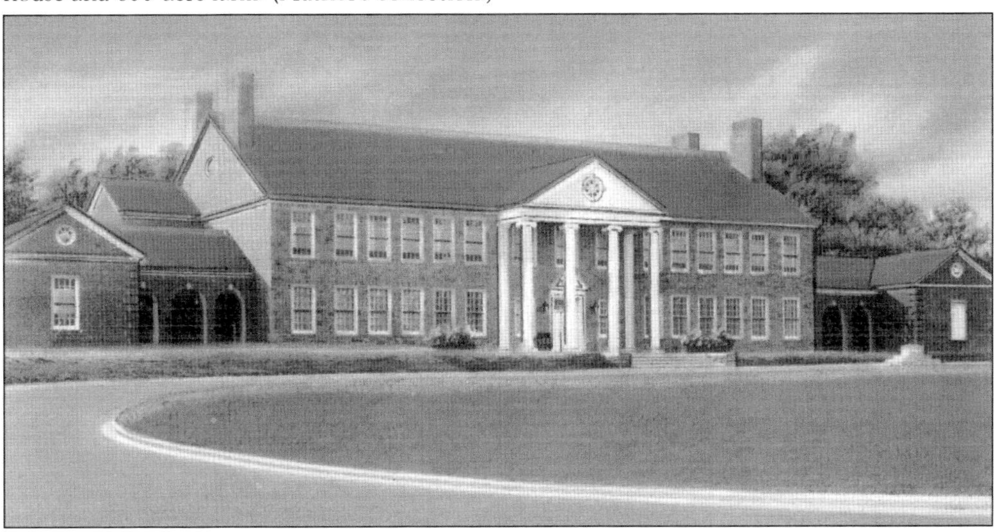

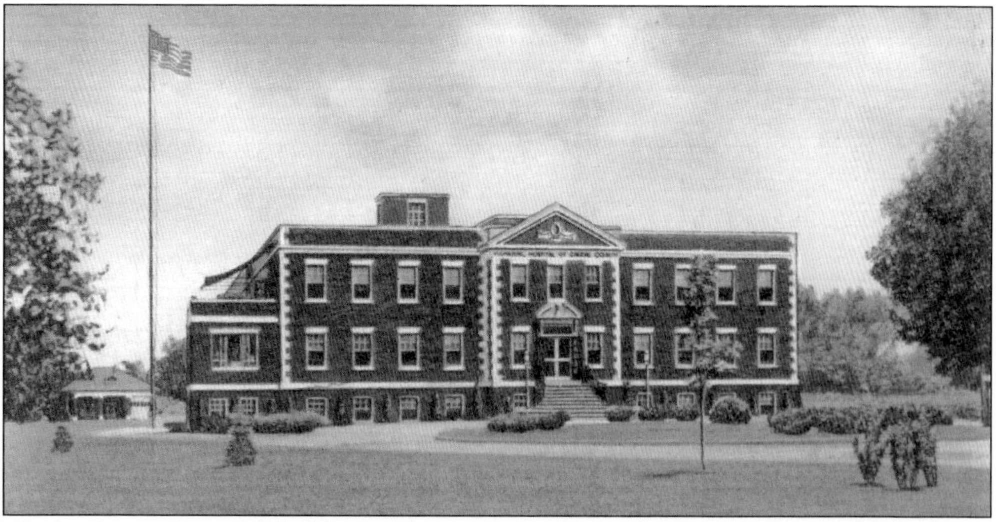

The first hospital was a 13-bed facility that opened on Broome Street in 1915. Under Dr. Lyle B. Honeyford and his brother-in-law, Dr. Wardell Jennings, the Greene County Memorial Hospital (above) opened in 1933. Built on the site of the Grant House Hotel, which had burned in 1923, the new hospital originally had 25 beds. A 10-day stay, including surgery, bed and board, operating room fees, and laboratory work in 1933 cost $54. A nurse on a daily 12-hour shift earned $80 a month. Catskill Village was served by two railroads, one on the east shore of the river stopping at Greendale opposite Catskill's Point and the other was the West Shore Railroad that carried people between New York City and Albany until 1955. Below is the first Catskill station before it burned down. (Author's collection.)

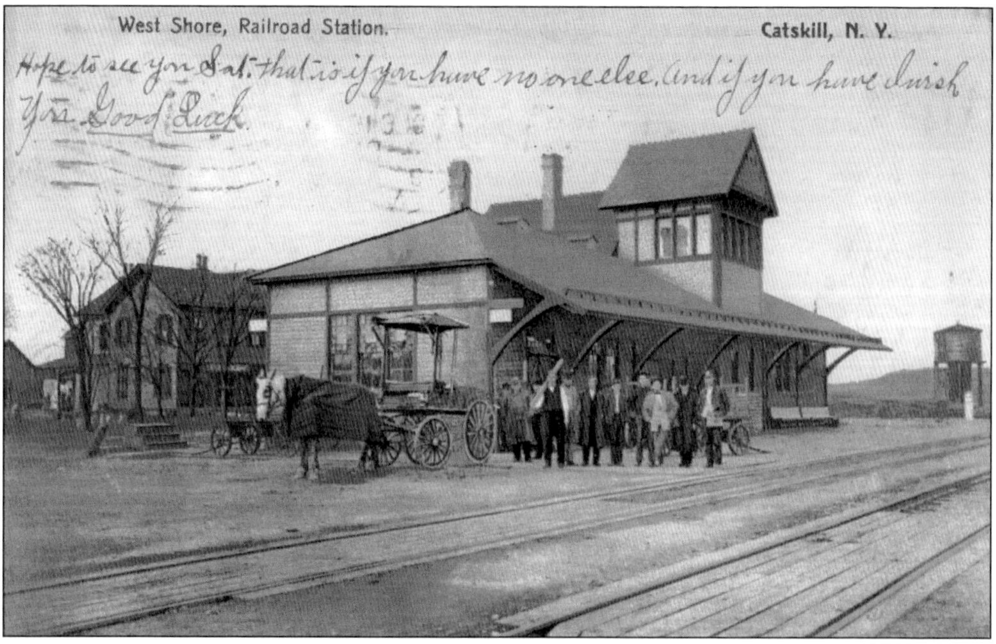

# *Seven*

# VILLAGERS

Despite the gradual shift by 1900 away from farms and into industrialized centers, living in rural America was thought to be healthier than living in crowded, polluted cities. A great many myths about crime, disease, crowds, noise, and pollution existed in rural America about the dangers of living in cities, all of which had some basis in facts but were probably not as bad as believed. Infant mortality was about 15 percent, high by today's standards even for underdeveloped countries, and the life expectancy for the average American male in 1900 was 46.3 years, and for women, it was 48.3 years. Photography filled an important role in American life; it served as a reminder of loved ones who had left the nest. In a culture where death was a constant presence, photography provided the desirable memento mori of those who had passed on. Many of the photographs taken at local studios—there were as many as five professional photographers working in Catskill Village by 1900—have survived, but they are often unidentified, undated, and therefore unknown. Who might have thought that there would be an interested audience for those camera images a century later? Paul Morrison was arguably the best of the professional photographers working in the village in the early 20th century, and from his photographs is learned as much as one may ever know about the forgotten faces, unless years ago some thoughtful person scribbled a name on the reverse sides. Some of Catskill's more prominent families have been here since the 17th century, while others came here later as immigrants from Europe and the American South to take advantage of available opportunities in one of the busiest and most prosperous ports on the Hudson River.

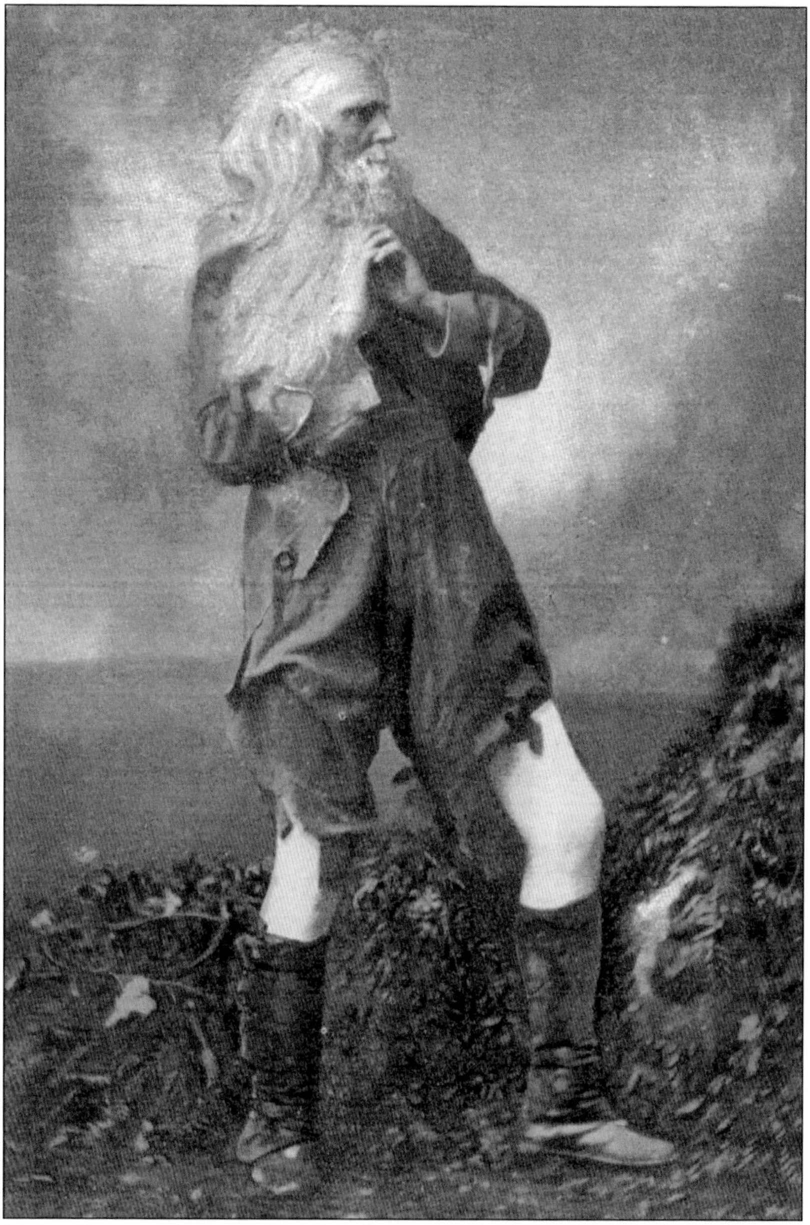

Perhaps the best-known character associated with Catskill Village is not a real person at all but Washington Irving's fictional composite of the idle rural Dutchman of his day, Rip Van Winkle. When Irving wrote the story, first published in 1819, he had never been to Catskill Village and had never visited the famous bald spot on South Mountain where Henry Hudson's ghostly crew was bowling and drinking a mysterious draft that puts poor Rip to sleep for 20 years. Irving saw the Catskill Mountains at a distance from a boat on the river and was deeply impressed, and he was familiar with local and European legends that he drew on for his plots. But in his story, Irving never names Rip's home village, leaving that to the reader's imagination (nearby Palenville is a good guess). The most impressive 20th-century monument to the tipsy Dutchman is the Rip Van Winkle Bridge that opened in 1935. The oil painting of Rip's awakening is by Thompkins Harrison Matthews about 1860. (Author's collection.)

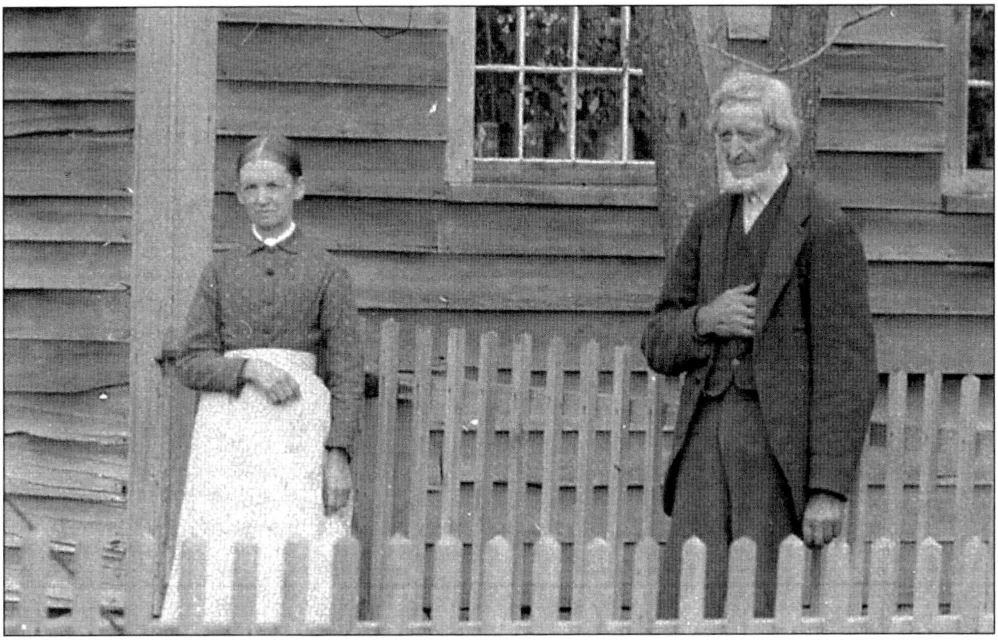

Photographer Paul Morrison's sensitivity to simple country folk and their environment is evident in this moving portrait of a couple, probably long married, who may have had hard lives and not much in the way of material possessions. The photograph probably dates to about 1910. Below is a characteristic Morrison photograph of what appears at first to be a family out for a drive. One may wonder about the mysterious-looking veil (possibly to keep down on dust from the roads), the fancy car, and the rigid (posed?) passengers. (Photographs by Paul Morrison, courtesy of Peggy Ahwesh.)

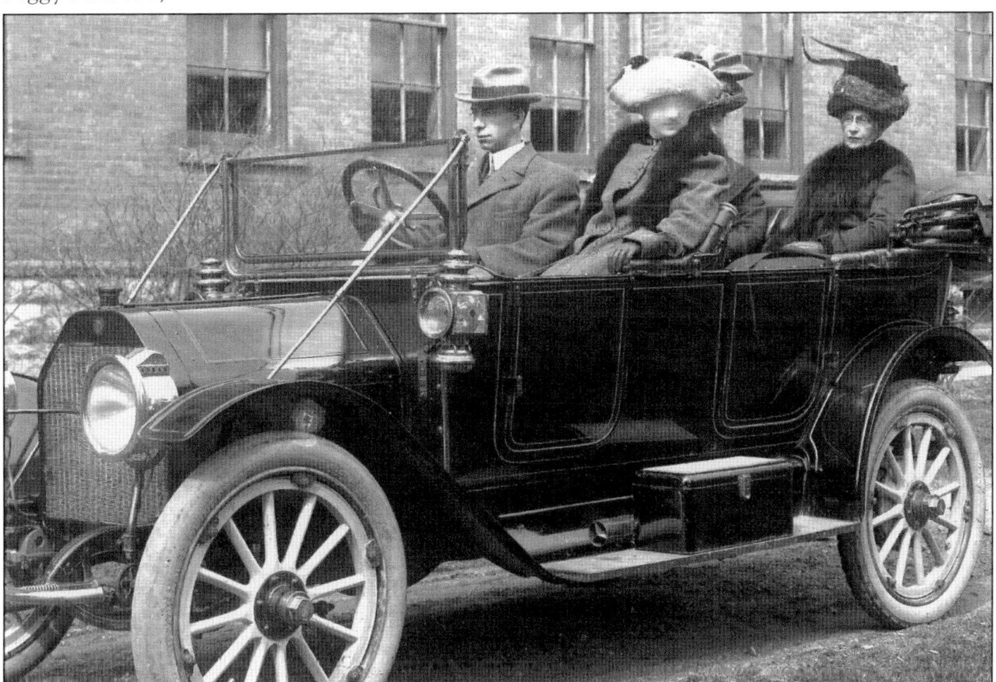

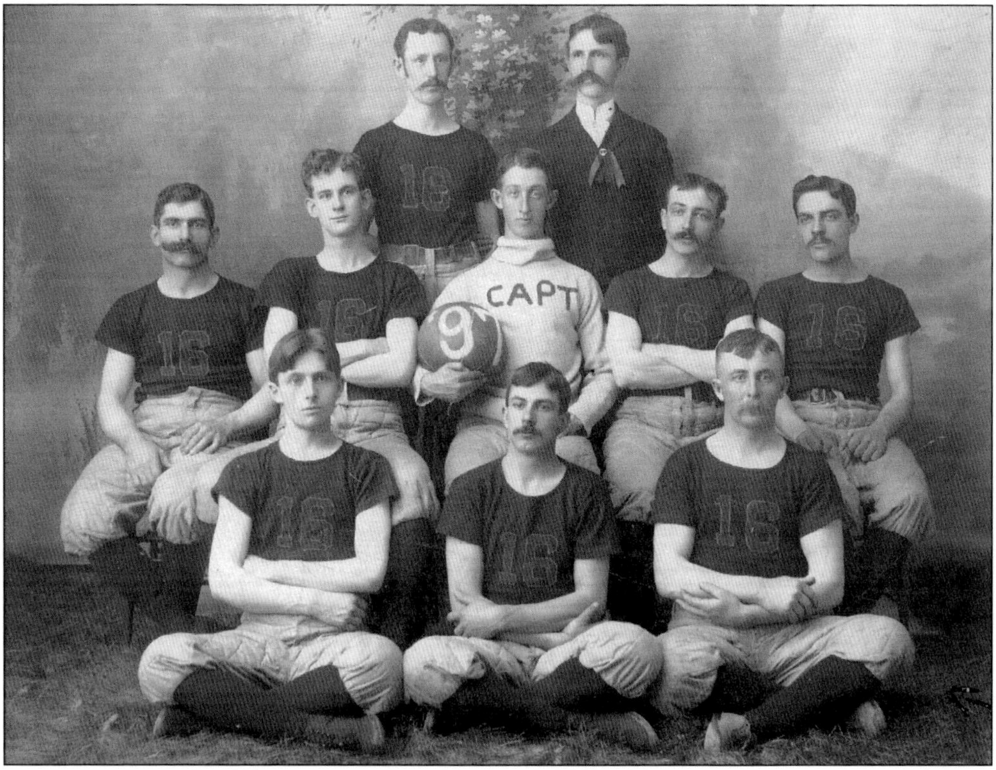


Basketball was, judging from reports of the day, probably the most popular sport in Catskill Village around 1900. The armory on Water Street (demolished in the 1960s for a parking lot) had an excellent gymnasium that had many uses, including basketball. The captain of this 1897 team proudly holds a basketball. A penciled note on the photograph says that this was the first professional team. Catskill's baseball team did very well by making it into the minor leagues. The photograph below is dated 1919 and shows clearly that Catskill's team was integrated far ahead of the days when Major League Baseball began to accept African American players on its teams. (Above, courtesy of Bill Oravsky; below, courtesy of Charles Swain.)

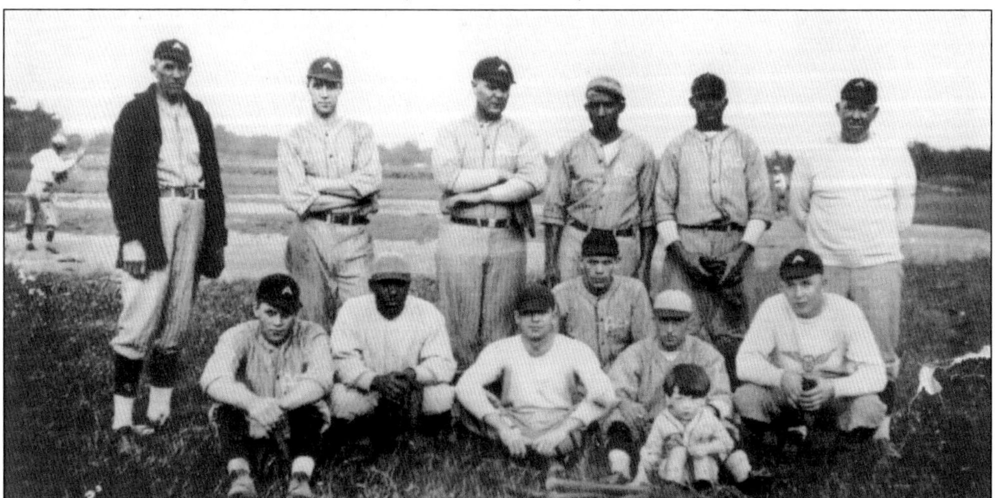

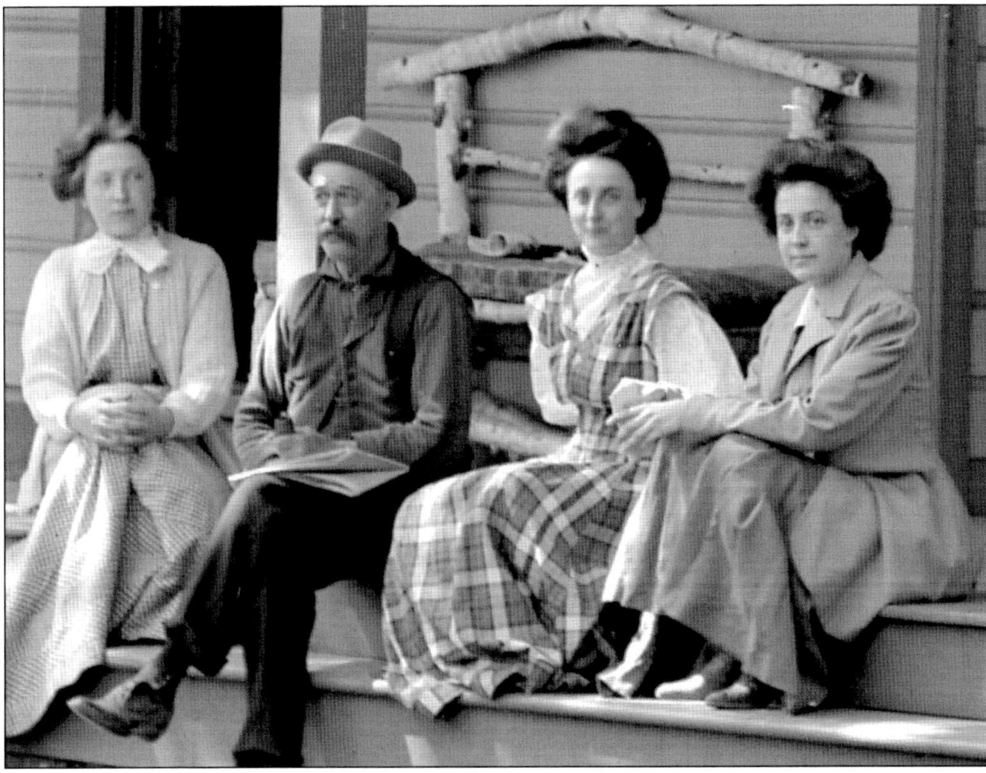

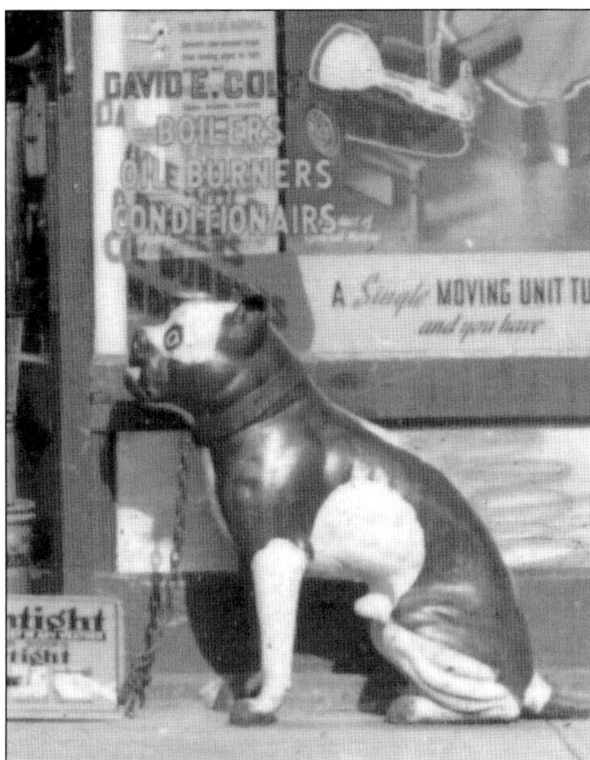


Photographer Paul Morrison's work with village people catches moods of the moment. Above, three fashionably dressed young women around 1915 seem to have been interrupted by the photographer's request to pose for a picture, while the gentleman in his porkpie cap just might be eager to escape to read the newspaper he holds in his lap. The Adirondack-style birch wood bench suggests this may have been taken at somebody's summer cottage. The iron dog (at right) is the informal mascot to Catskill Village, having been one of a pair headed for the scrap yard in New York City in 1849 when John Brested rescued it and sent the 200-pound bull terrier to Catskill where it stood guard at a Main Street paint store for more than 100 years. (Above, photograph by Paul Morrison, courtesy of Peggy Ahwesh; below, courtesy of the Floyd Du Mond collection.)

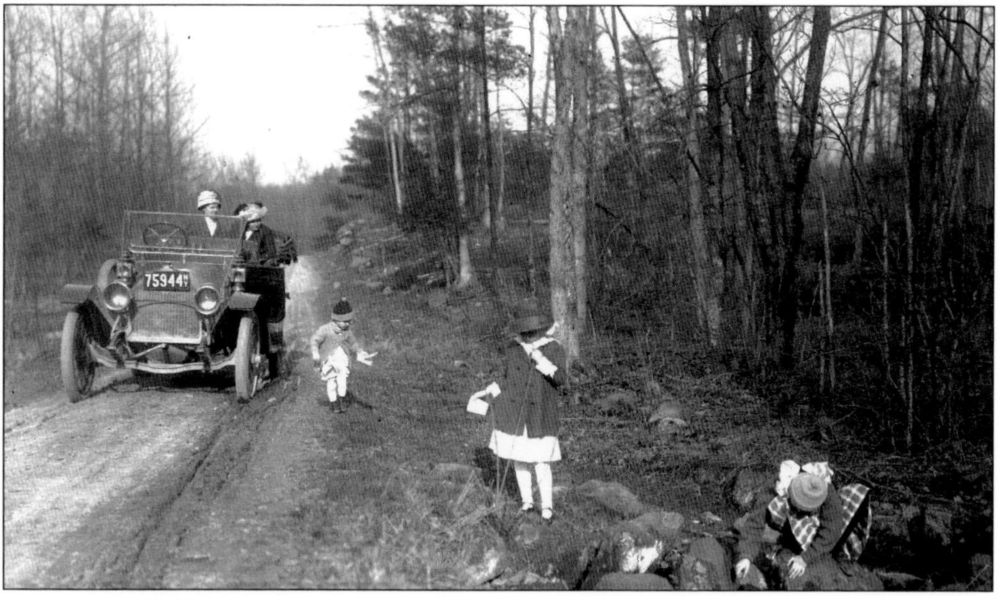

Another of photographer Paul Morrison's beautiful compositions (above) probably dates to about 1914. The Alsen Cement Company machine shop crew (below), seen on June 15, 1920, was composed of many first-generation immigrants looking and hoping for a better life in Catskill Village. Alsen provided villagers with work for a long time, although in recent years, the plant was closed, unable to comply with new pollution standards and competition in the Midwest. (Photographs by Paul Morrison, courtesy of Peggy Ahwesh.)

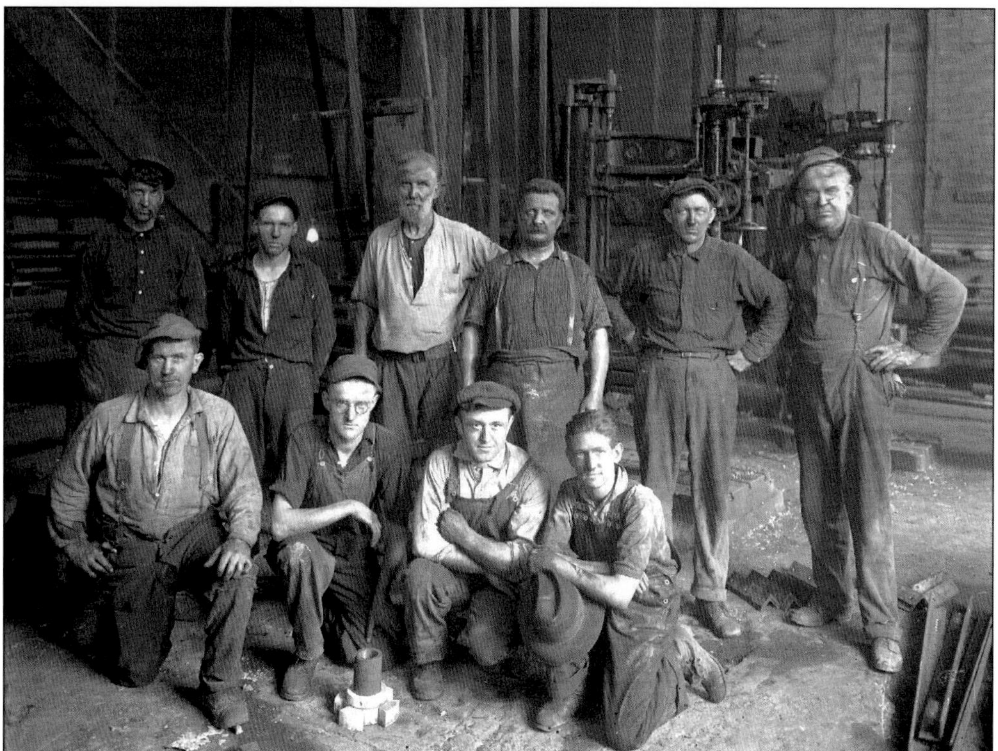

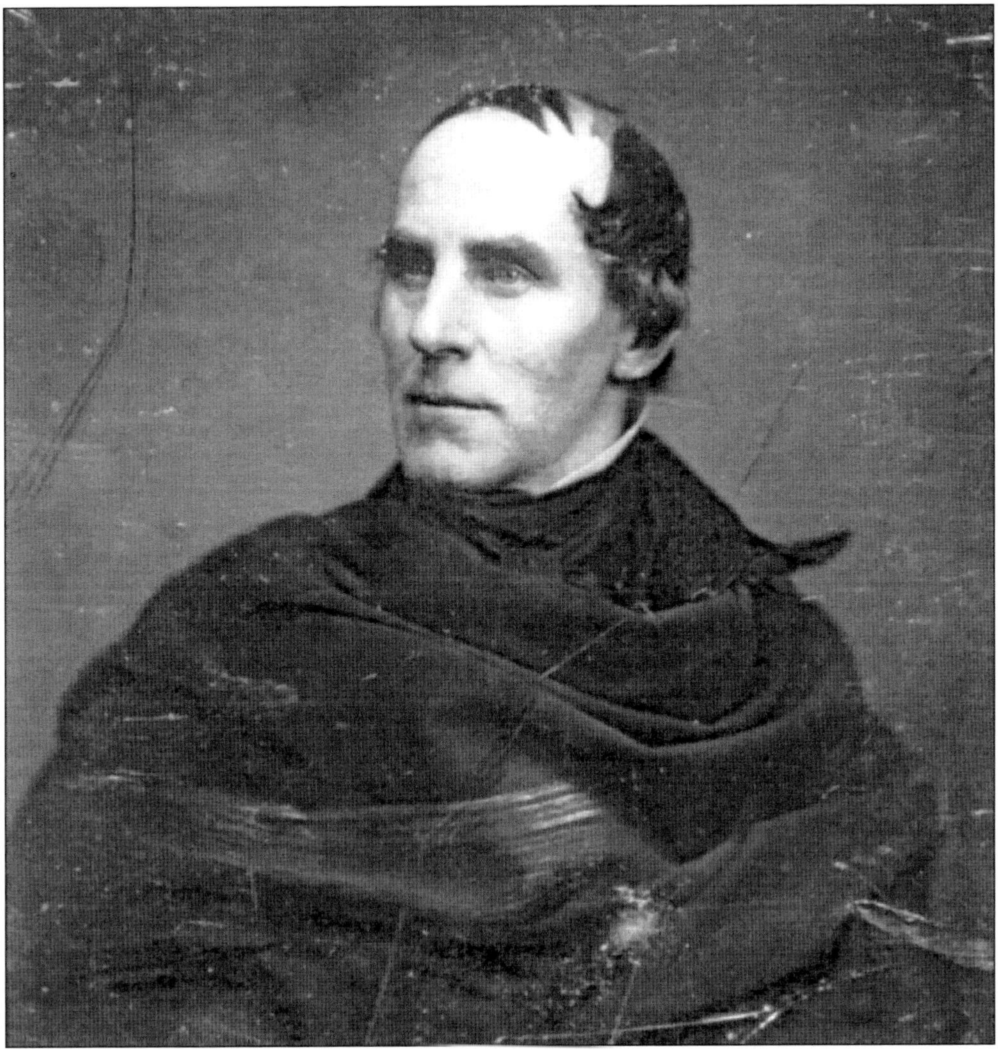

Thomas Cole posed for this 1846 Matthew Brady attributed daguerreotype, about two years before his untimely death at the age of 47. Cole first came to Catskill Village in 1825, rented space at Cedar Grove that he used for a studio during the summers, and took up permanent residence in 1836 when he married one of Cedar Grove's owner's four nieces, Maria. He is considered the founder of the Hudson River school of landscape painting and had only three students. The most successful of his students was Frederic Church, who built a Moorish-Victorian "castle" directly across the river from Cedar Grove. By the time of Cole's death, the style of painting he had made so popular—landscape painting with, as he said, "moral content"—was beginning to decline in fashion and marketability. Apparently like so many men his age, Cole tried in vain to cover up his bald pate by combing wisps of long black hair forward over his scalp. The black cloak was probably a prop he used on one of his models. (Courtesy of Edith Cole Silberstein.)

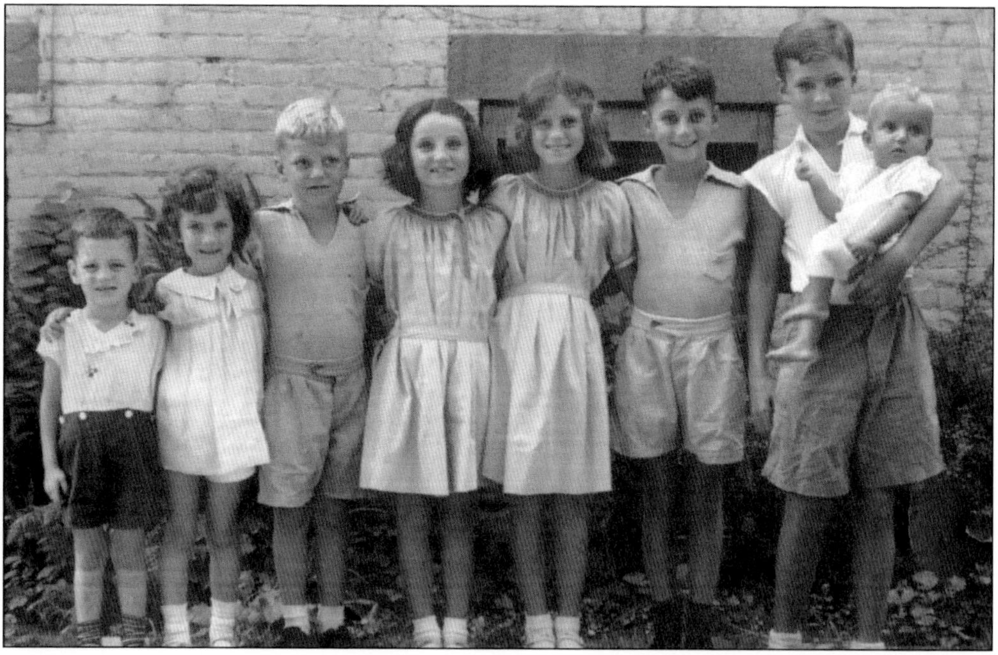

Large families have been a kind of insurance against disaster from time immemorial, but by the 20th century, as populations moved from rural communities to cities, and health care improved making "backup" children unnecessary, the smaller nuclear family became the norm. A family with nine children became noteworthy, as did the Englerts, with eight of the nine children (above) lined up here in their dentist father's garden on Main Street in 1934. Young Paul Englert, third from the left, grew up to take over his father's dental practice on Main Street and have nine kids of his own. Below, the Catskill High School class of 1925 is formally posed in front of the Romanesque arch of the Irving School, and it seems to be taking this rite of passage very seriously. (Above, courtesy of Mark Cooper; below, courtesy of Nancy Ursprung.)

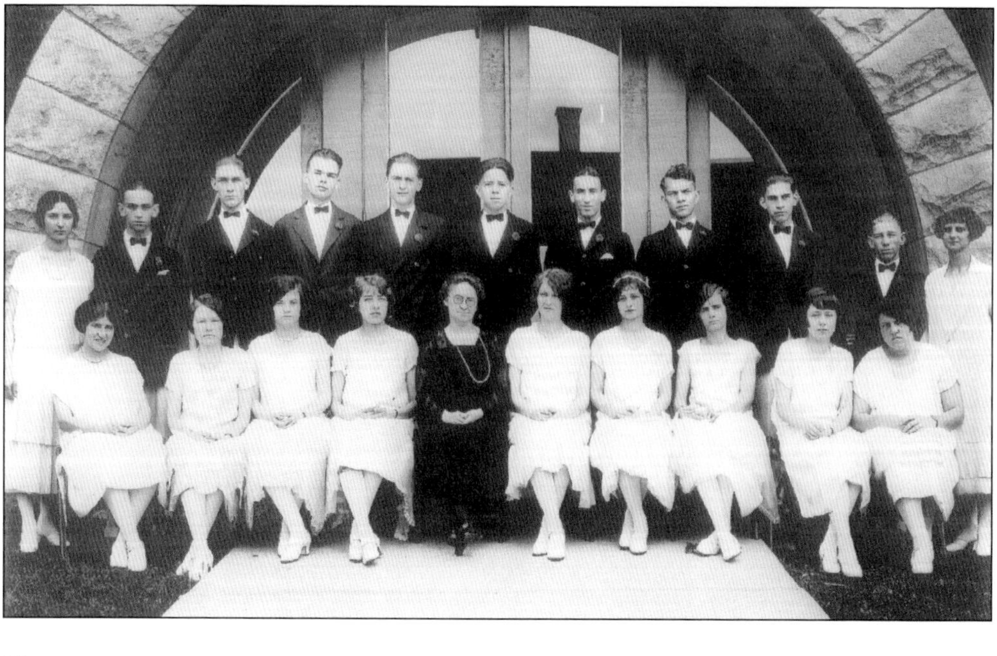

Chauncey and Aravesta Smith of West Main Street in the village pose in 1890 with their eight children. (Courtesy of Nancy Ursprung.)

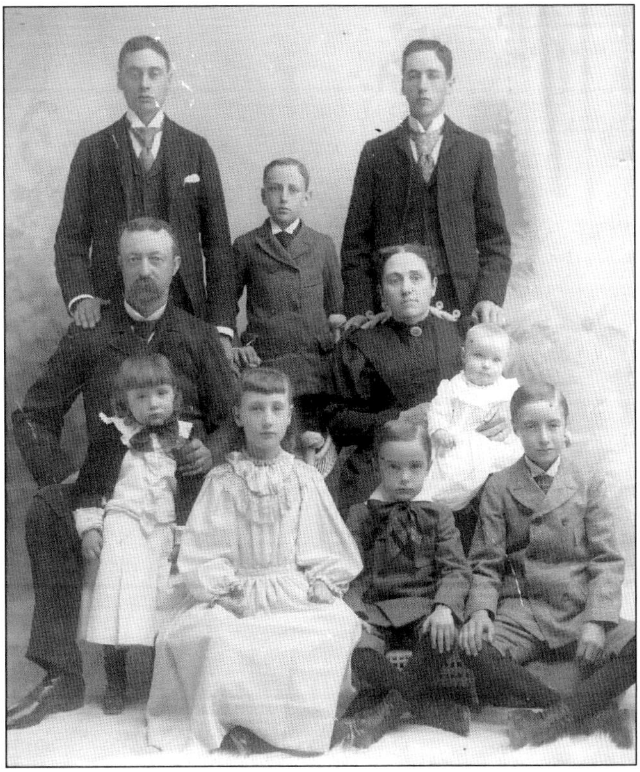

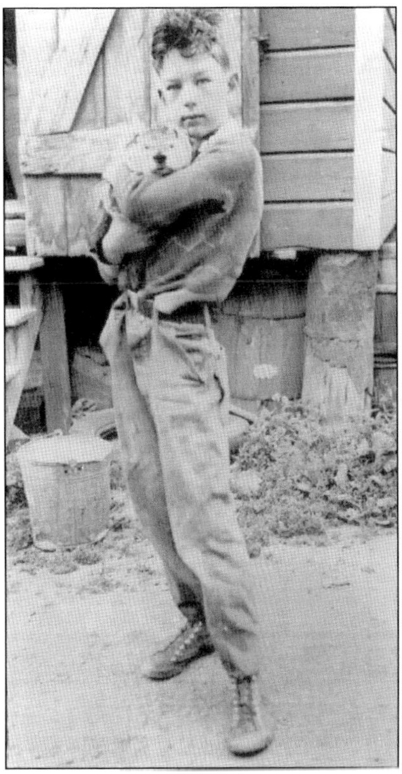

William Van Vechten Jr., a descendant of one of the oldest families in the county, was in ninth grade in 1942 when he found a baby woodchuck in a field, named him Lucky, tamed him, and for several weeks took him every day to school where the animal usually stayed pretty much under his desk. But when his teacher told young Van Vechten to leave Lucky at home, he chose instead to leave school altogether with his woodchuck, ending his formal education. Lucky and Van Vechten were inseparable for a number of years. (Courtesy of Kevin Van Vechten.)

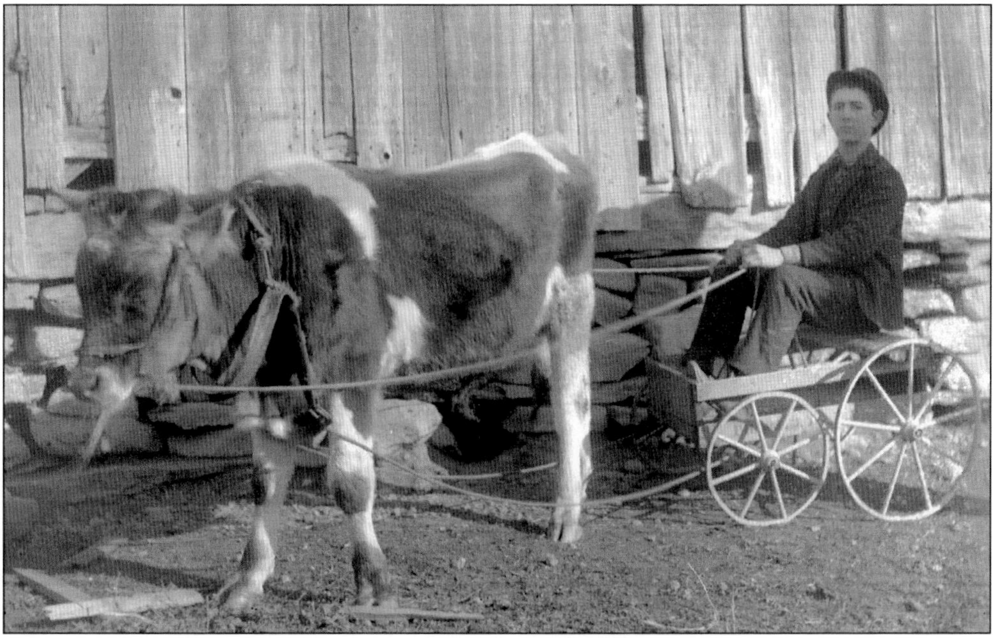

The glass-plate photograph (above) appears to be a setup because neither the calf nor the boy will be going anywhere very fast with that child's wagon. Photographer Paul Morrison did not keep a record of who the boy was or where the photograph was taken, but it is probably Catskill Village sometime around 1900 when glass plates were still being used. While the unidentified photographer (below) has recorded a momentary pickle caused by the broken left front wagon wheel lying sideways on the road, four ladies in black hover in the background, looking bemused, while the gentleman with the cap scratches his lower lip in perplexity. (Above, photograph by Paul Morrison, courtesy of Peggy Ahwesh; below, courtesy of Robert Carl.)

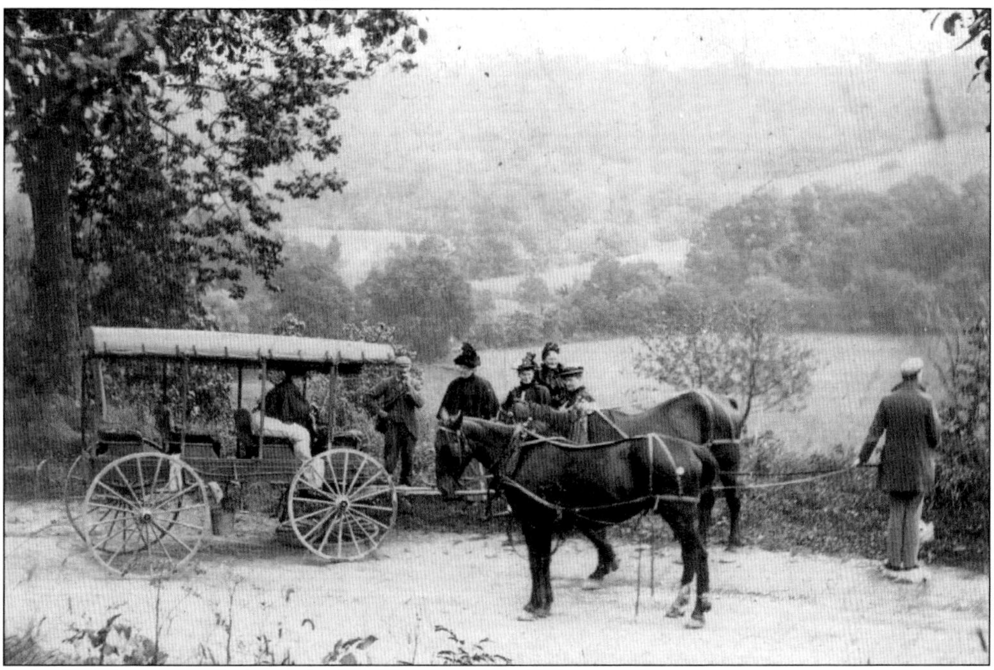

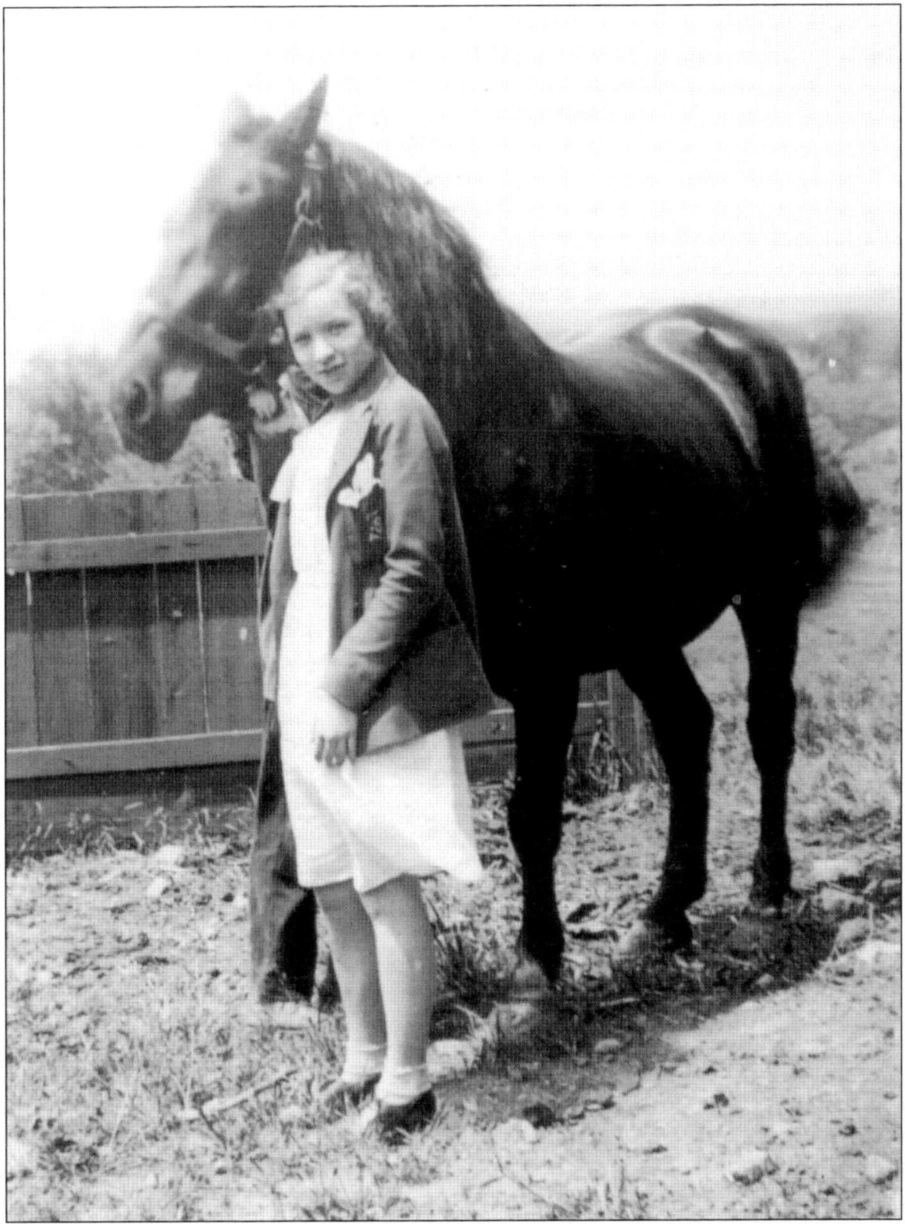

Edith Mary Cole, great-granddaughter of painter Thomas Cole, lived in New York City while she was growing up in order to go to school, but when she was not in school, she was at her family's home, Cedar Grove, which was run for many years with a velvet-gloved iron fist by her aunt Florence Cole Vincent. Edith has written at length about her delightfully batty family in Catskill Village in *Our Lovable Eccentrics*. When her aunt died in 1961, Edith inherited Cedar Grove, and her children were the sixth and the last generation to live there. Seen here in the early 1930s, 14-year-old Edith holds her horse for the camera in back of the large 18th-century unpainted Cole barn that stood for years on what is now the corner of Spring Street and Route 23 (where the gas station is today). She always rode bareback, she remembers, because her aunt was too careful with money to buy a saddle, regardless of the real danger of her niece being thrown and breaking her neck. (Courtesy of Edith Cole Silberstein.)

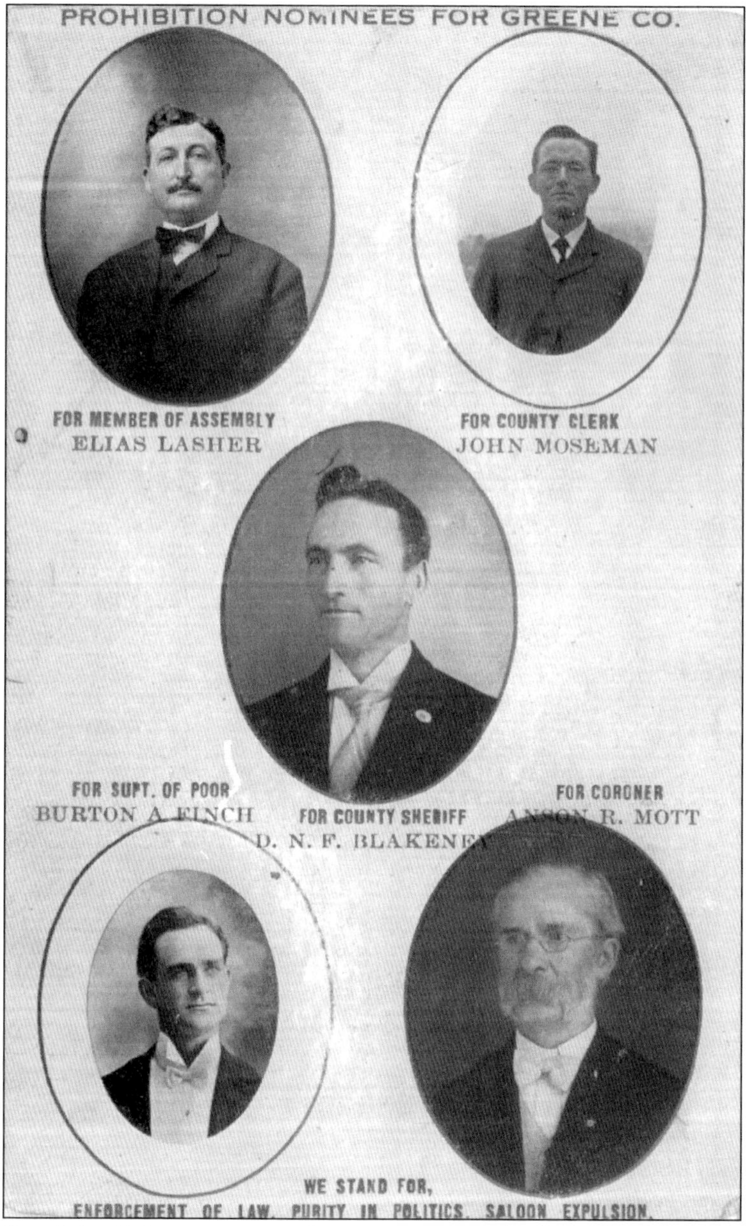


By the middle of the 19th century, antiliquor movements had sprung up in the village, but the profits to be made from the sale of grog, not to mention the pleasures of drinking it, made temperance an unpopular uphill battle. By the early 20th century, the Women's Christian Temperance Union had small chapters in towns or villages of any size in Greene County, and by 1912, Catskill Village had voted out saloons, although that did not require retail stores that sold liquor to close. Prohibition was made law in 1919 and lasted until 1933, when it was generally agreed that Prohibition had not stopped the sale of illegal alcohol. It had attracted organized crime, and the use of alcohol had continued behind closed doors, in clubs, and in homes. Greene County had an active Prohibition Party by 1910 when this political postcard was sent, and the party's stated goals were the "enforcement of law, purity in politics, [and] saloon expulsion." Its success was limited. (Courtesy of the Arthur Hamm collection.)

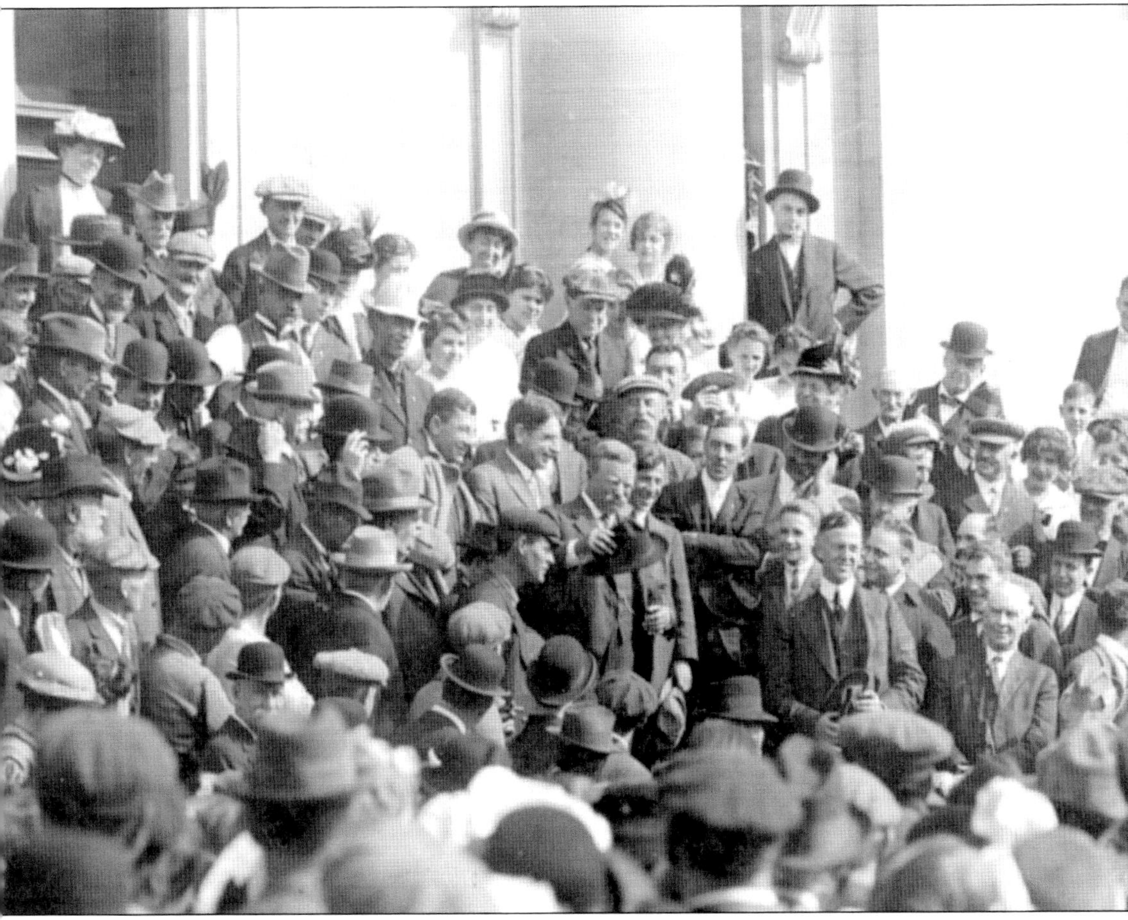

Theodore Roosevelt visited Catskill Village on a campaign trip around 1912, making a pitch for a third term as president. His record was well known, having served in New York State government and two terms in Washington as president from 1901 to 1909. He was a reformer, an environmentalist, and a prolific author whose four-volume *Winning the West* was in every public library across the nation. He established parks, preserved millions of acres, promoted wildlife refuges and national monuments, and even put a stop to women using the plumage of wild birds on their hats. In 1912, he founded the Progressive Party, which was nicknamed the Bull Moose Party after its progressive leader. That is when the famous Catskill visit took place, and he seems to have found supporters for his progressive causes. Roosevelt (holding his hat) can be seen in the middle of a crowd on the steps of the new courthouse on Main Street. He lost the presidential race to Woodrow Wilson. (Courtesy of Robert Carl.)

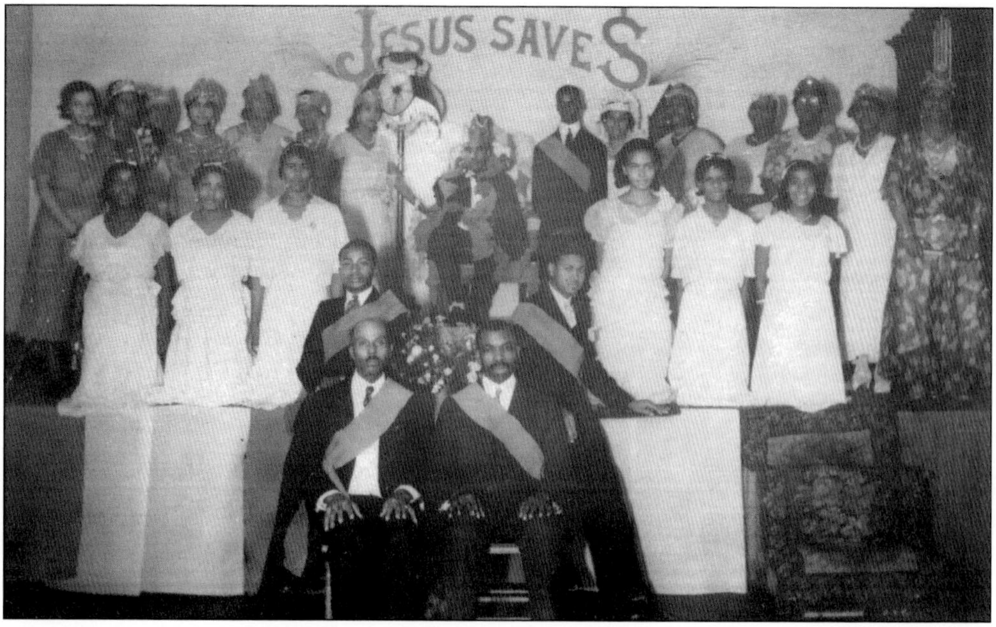


The role of African Americans in Greene County has historically been underplayed. For example, abolitionists in the county played important but mostly unrecorded roles in the Underground Railroad movement before and during the Civil War. There was a large exodus of African Americans from the South in the 20th century to Greene County to fill the demand for low-wage workers in the brickyards and cement factories. Through all this, religion has played an important part in African American communities. The choir, pastorate, and members of Catskill's Second Baptist Church (above) were the center of social and spiritual life for many African American citizens of Catskill Village in 1920. The pastors and trustees (below) of Mount Tabor African Methodist Episcopal Zion Church on Water Street gather in front of their altar on a Sunday in 1998. (Author's collection.)

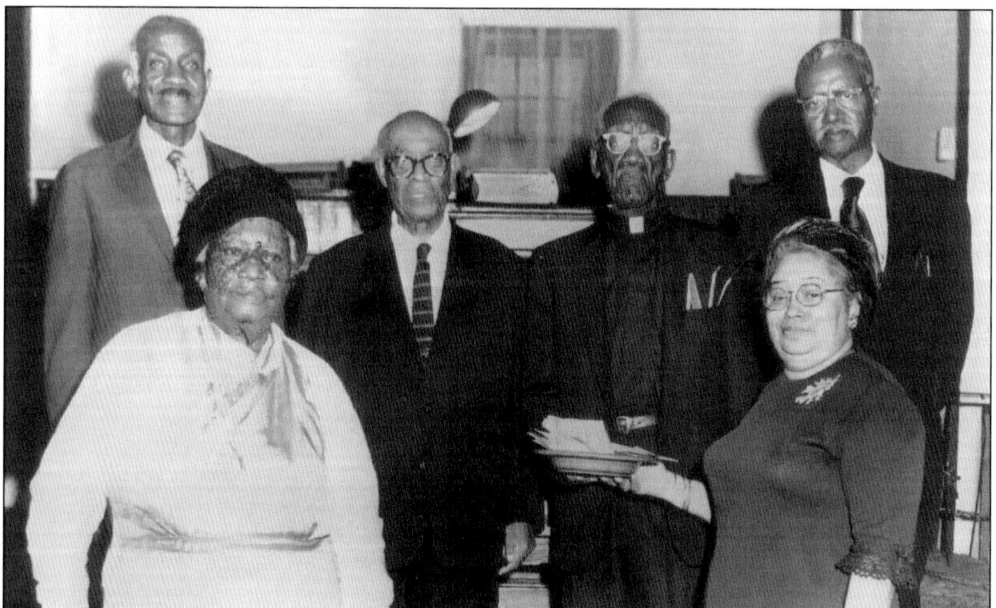

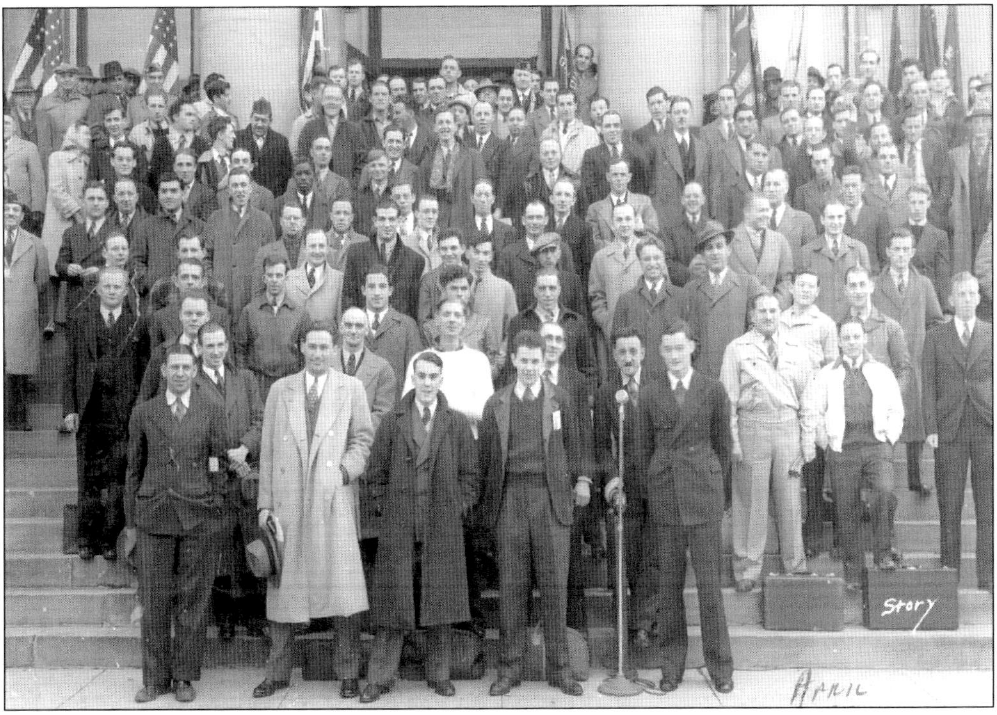


From the beginning of time, young men have been sent off to fight wars. Catskill's uniformed future (above) poses on the steps of the old armory on Water Street in 1917 before being shipped off to France. History repeats itself 25 years later in April 1942, as Greene County draftees (below) pose on the steps of the courthouse before being bused to Albany, sent by train to Long Island, and from there shipped to the European or Pacific fronts. (Above, photograph by Story; below, photograph by Fred Clarke.)

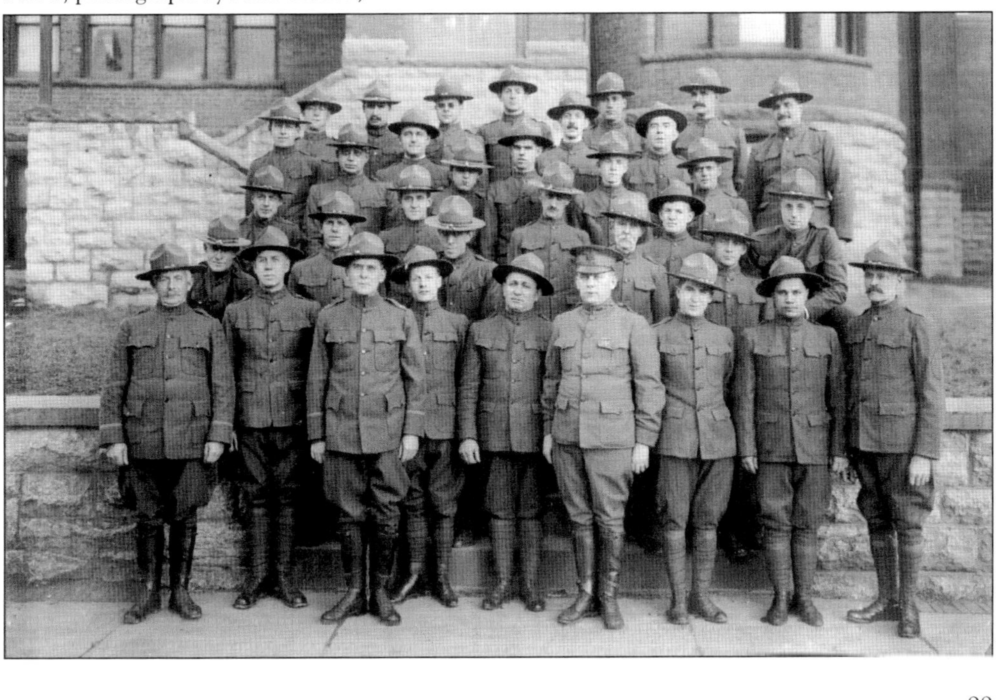

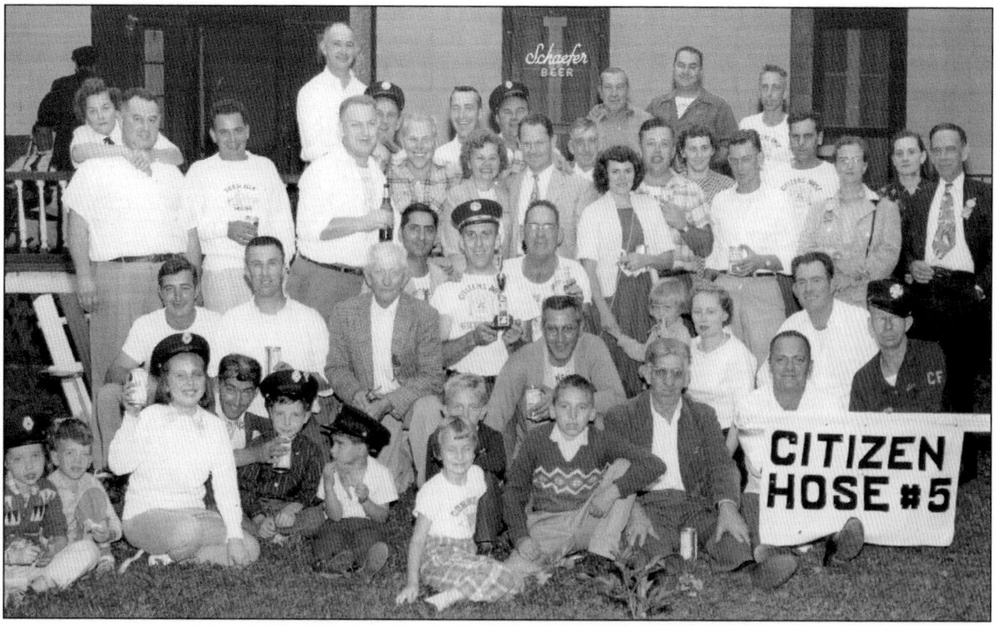


In the village fire companies, there is a strong sense of fellowship among the men and their families, as is evident in this photograph taken at a picnic for Citizen Hose Company No. 5 in the early 1980s. Another village fraternal organization, the Rip Van Winkle Club (below) was founded in 1886 and over the years thrived with as many as 145 members. A brief history that appeared in 1908 claims that the club was "a fixed institution that enjoys the esteem and respect of the entire community through its policy . . . of no gambling, no Sunday games and temperance." A more contemporary charter from about 1965 states that "there [is] to be a maximum of enjoyment and freedom, with a minimum of rules and regulations." The photograph below of the membership was taken in the late 1970s; the club today is quiescent. (Above, courtesy of Robert Carl; below, courtesy of Damon Pouyat.)

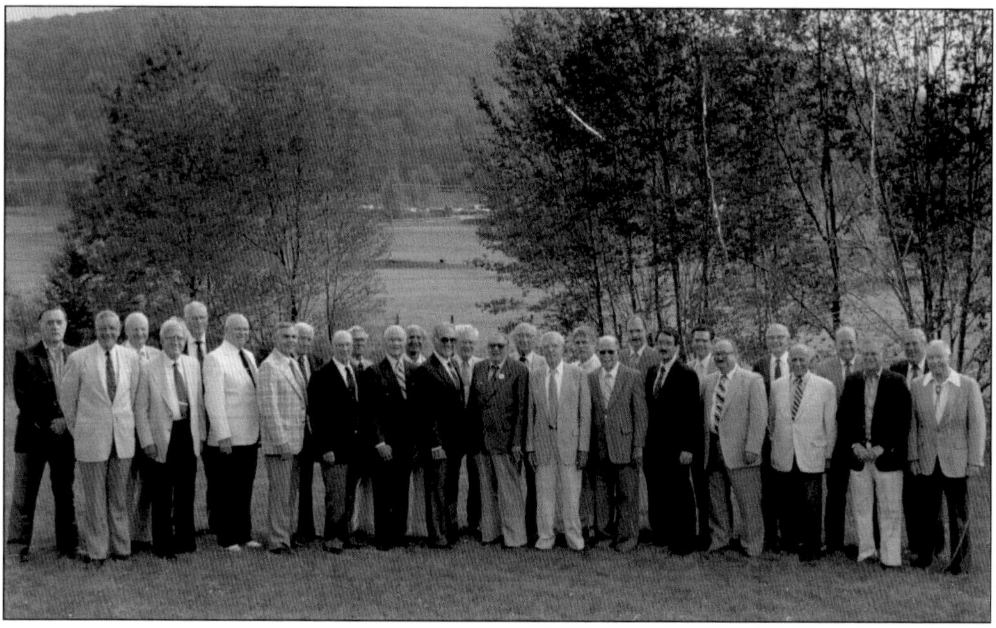

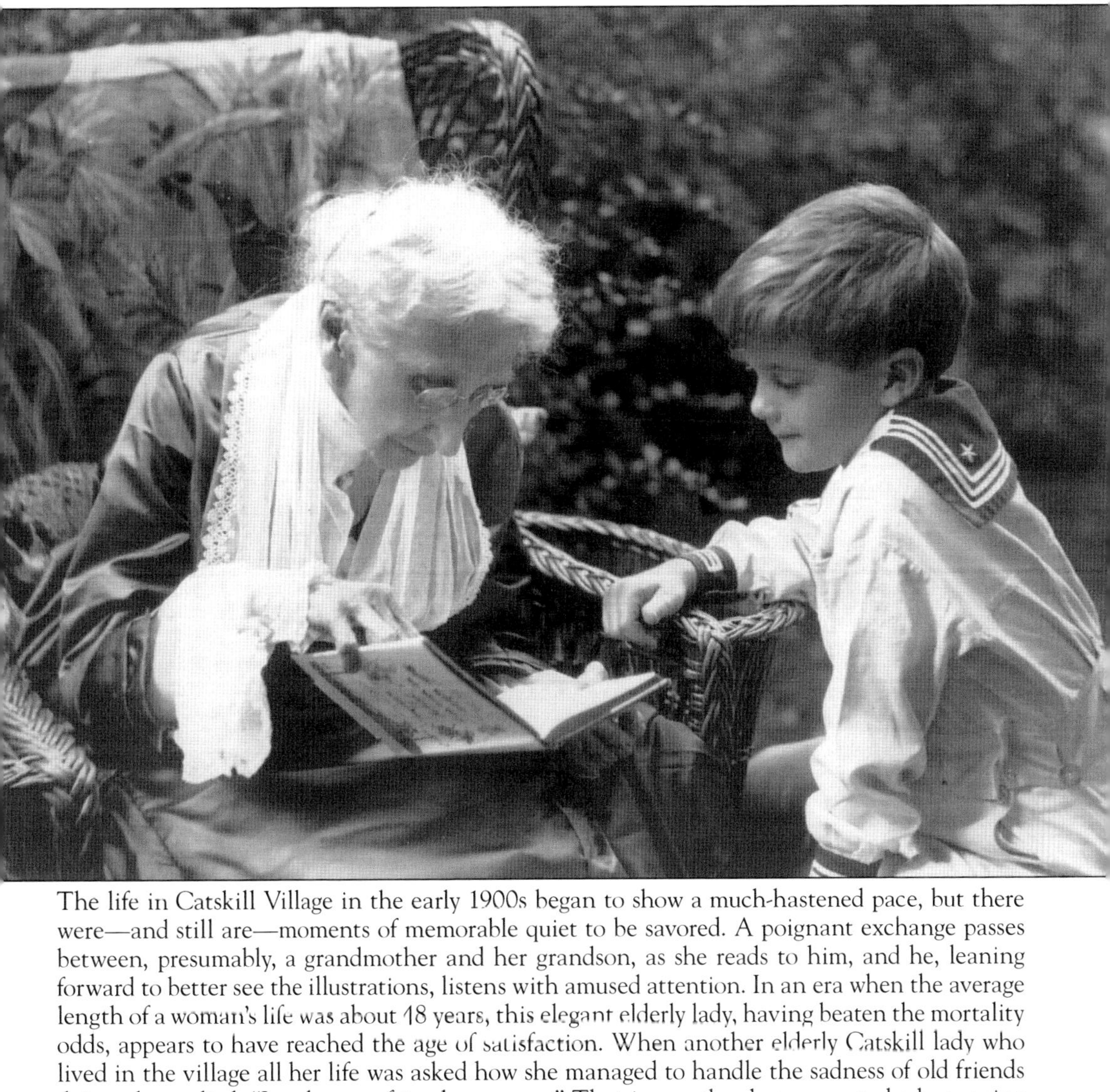

The life in Catskill Village in the early 1900s began to show a much-hastened pace, but there were—and still are—moments of memorable quiet to be savored. A poignant exchange passes between, presumably, a grandmother and her grandson, as she reads to him, and he, leaning forward to better see the illustrations, listens with amused attention. In an era when the average length of a woman's life was about 48 years, this elegant elderly lady, having beaten the mortality odds, appears to have reached the age of satisfaction. When another elderly Catskill lady who lived in the village all her life was asked how she managed to handle the sadness of old friends dying, she replied, "I make new friends, younger." That is exactly what seems to be happening here. This photograph by an unknown photographer of unidentified subjects was purchased in an antique shop on Main Street. (Author's collection.)

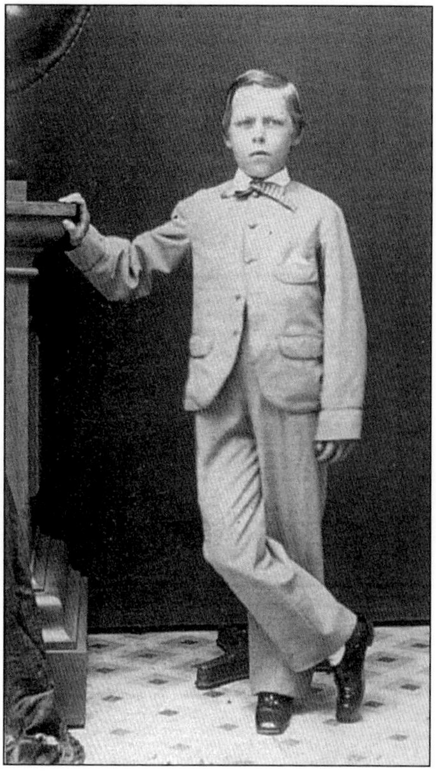

An unidentified young man poses for this daguerreotype around 1855. The legs of the iron stand behind him that keep him from fidgeting while his still image is burned on the plate are visible. That, no doubt, is one of the sources of his apparent displeasure. (Courtesy of Edith Cole Silberstein.)

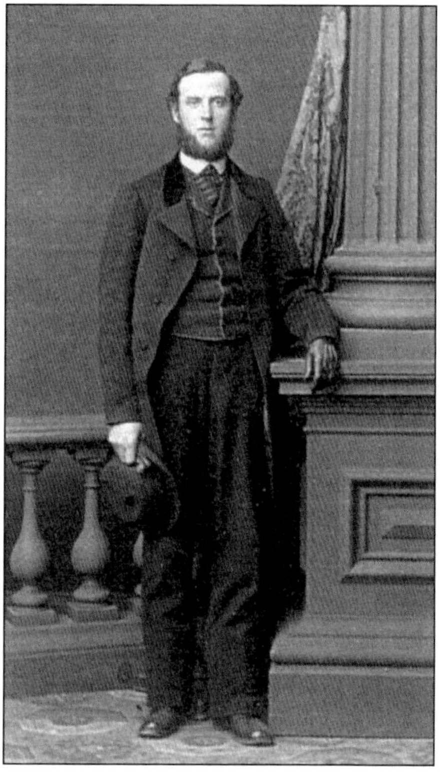

Theodore Alexander Cole (right, about 1862) was Thomas Cole's elder son, who, to make money, worked directly across the river from Cedar Grove at the estate of one of his father's most successful pupils, Frederic Church. (Courtesy of Edith Cole Silberstein.)

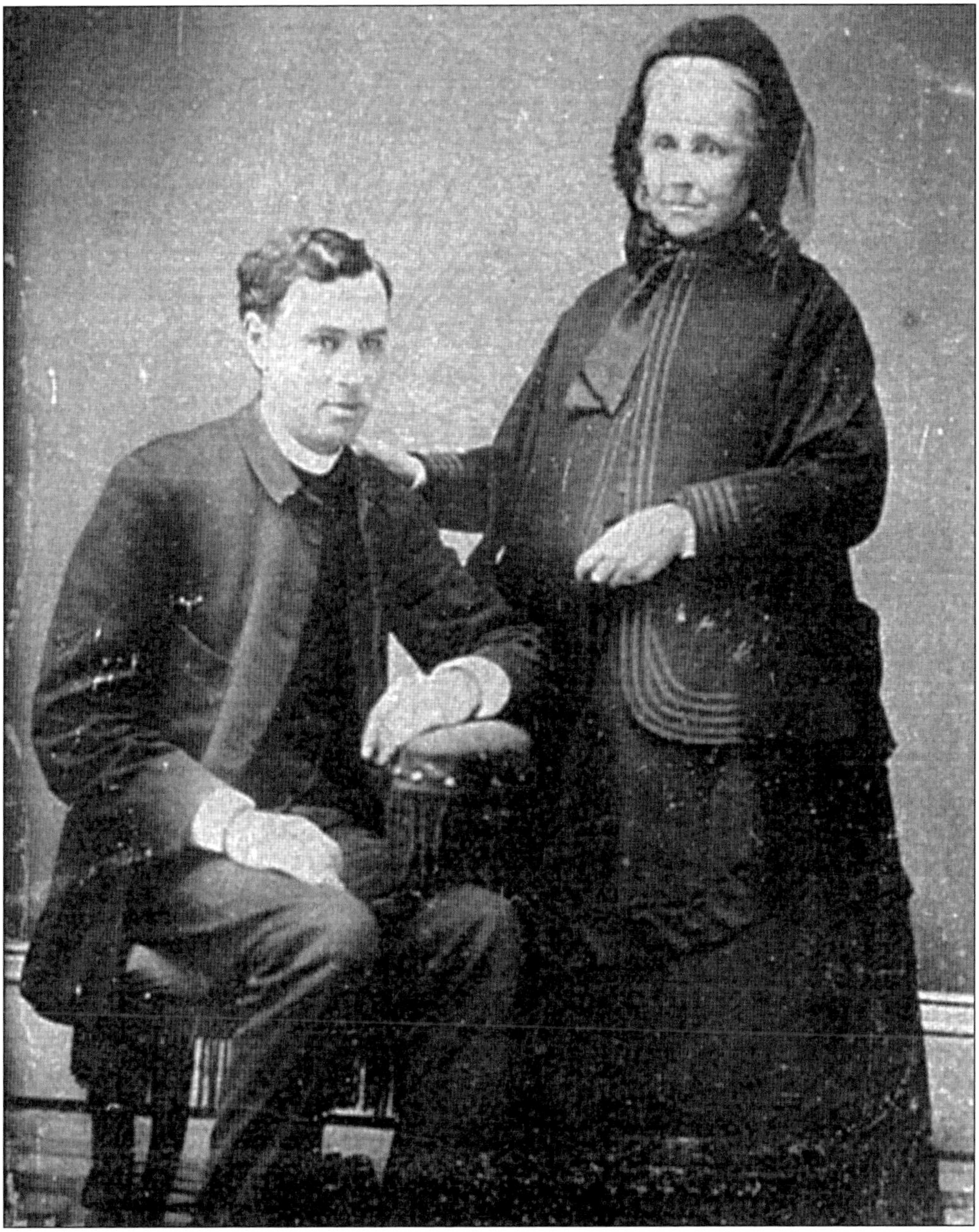

This never-before-published tintype from about 1864 shows Thomas Cole's widow, Maria Bartow Cole, still in her widow's weeds at least 16 years after her husband's death in 1848, with her younger son, Thomas Cole II, born in 1848. Maria and her three sisters inherited Cedar Grove in 1846 upon the death of their uncle John Alexander "Uncle Sandy" Thomson and lived there until their deaths. Maria kept the house and grounds very much the way they were during her husband's lifetime, seldom selling any of his paintings, as they had already gone out of fashion. She only rented his studio to accomplished artists. Strapped with debt going back to the years when Thomson ran the farm, she eventually was able to turn its management over to her older son, Theodore. She died at Cedar Grove in 1884, and the house and much of its Cole memorabilia stayed in the family until 1979. (Courtesy of Edith Cole Silberstein, author's collection.)

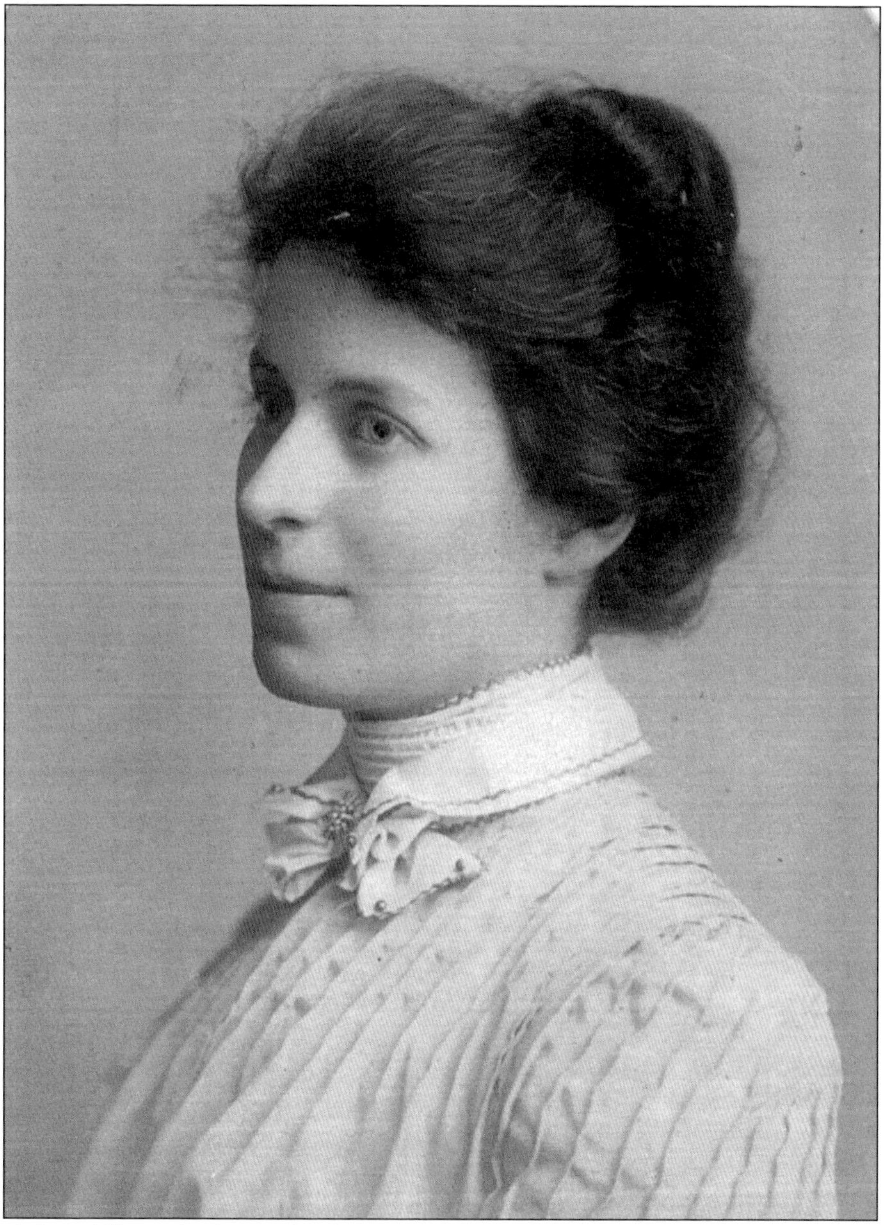

If Catskill could be said to have a first family, a case could be made for Thomas and Maria Bartow Cole and their descendants. Maria came to Cedar Grove in the 1820s with her three orphaned sisters. The English-born Thomas first visited Catskill in 1825 and rented space at Cedar Grove until he married Maria in 1836 and took up permanent residence in the main house. They had five children, including Theodore (born in 1838), Mary Bartow (born in 1839), Emily (born in 1843), Elizabeth (born in 1847), and Thomas II (born in 1848). Theodore's daughter Florence Cole Vincent (born in 1876) lived at Cedar Grove all her life and was considered a stunning beauty (above). When she died childless in 1961, she left the estate to her niece Edith Cole Silberstein, the daughter of Thomas Cole III. For years, stories abounded in the village about this independently minded, strong-willed, handsome woman called Aunt Florence, as she is still fondly remembered to this day. (Courtesy of Edith Cole Silberstein, author's collection.)

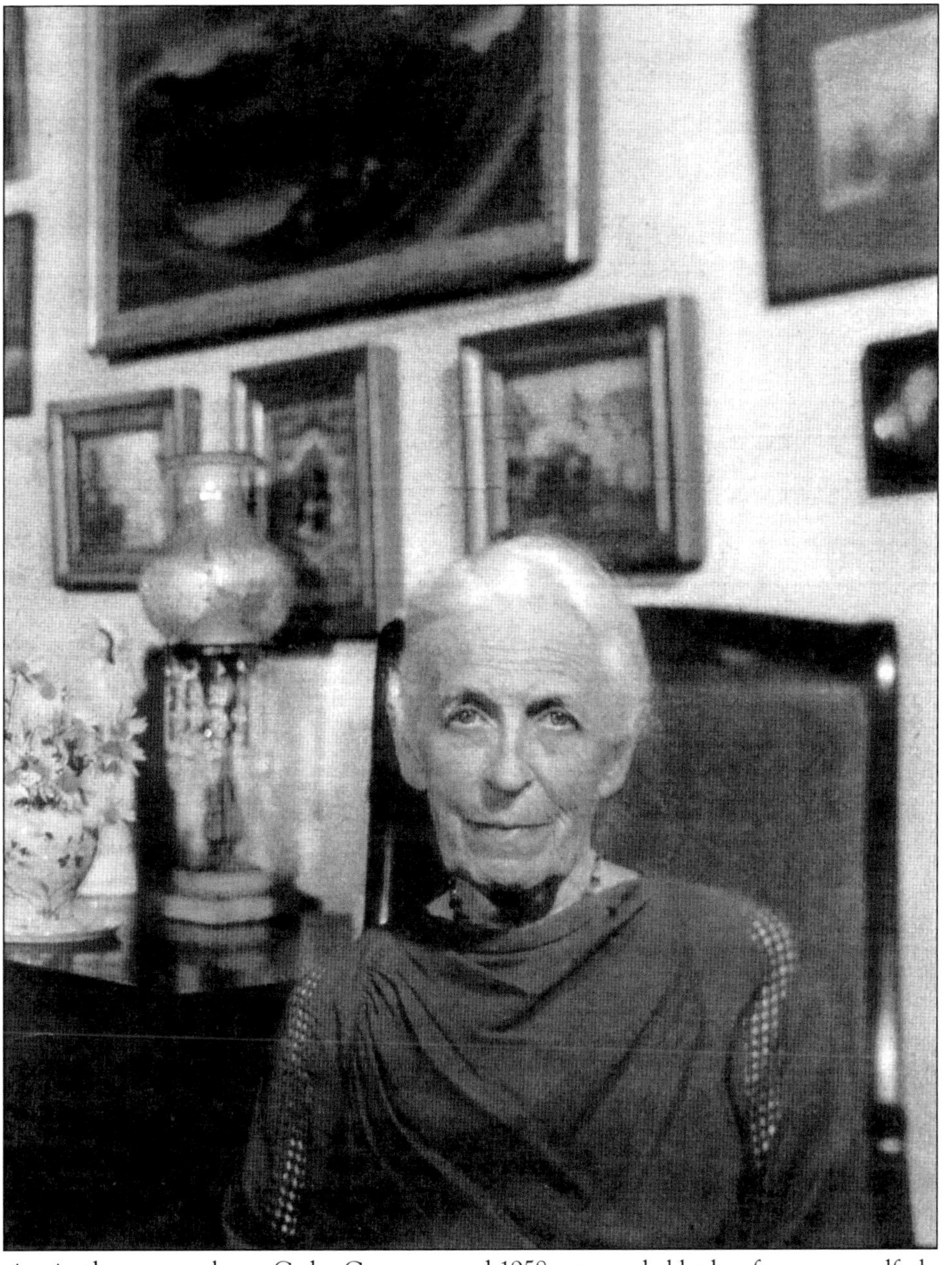

Sitting in the west parlor at Cedar Grove around 1958 surrounded by her famous grandfather's paintings, Aunt Florence emanates the determination and focus that kept her family estate intact for many years. Her tenacity saved the house in 1933 when New York State wanted to condemn the land in order to build the Rip Van Winkle Bridge approach over her house. It did not happen. She oversaw the distribution of her grandfather's paintings and papers to museums and libraries in a day and age when just about anything having to do with the Hudson River school had fallen out of favor and was undervalued. It is almost impossible to talk about Cedar Grove today, where six generations of the Thomson-Bartow-Cole families have lived, without mentioning this fascinating character whose entire life was lived at Cedar Grove. (Courtesy of Edith Cole Silberstein, author's collection.)

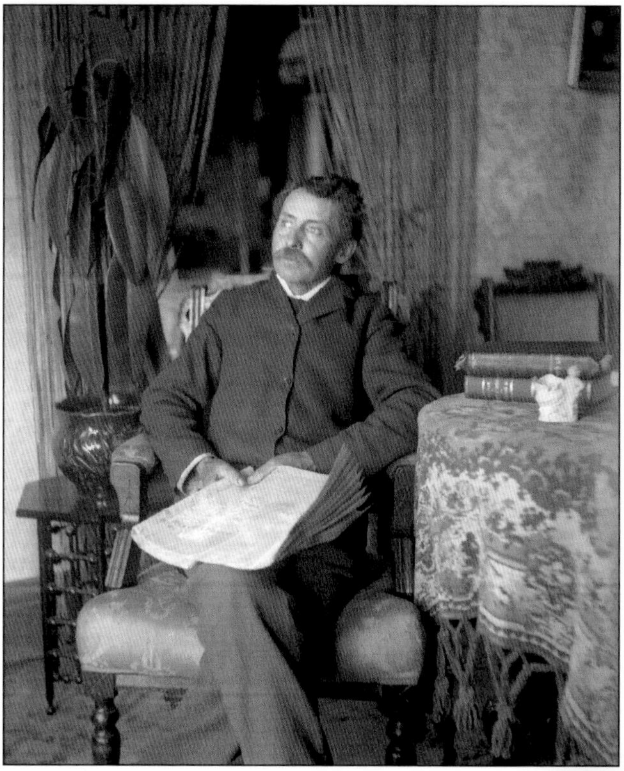

The four glass-plate portraits on these pages from the Catskill Village studio of photographer Paul Morrison probably date to between 1900 and 1910. This gentleman appears to have been caught by surprise by the blinding flash used in those days in indoor photography. (Photograph by Paul Morrison, courtesy of Peggy Ahwesh.)

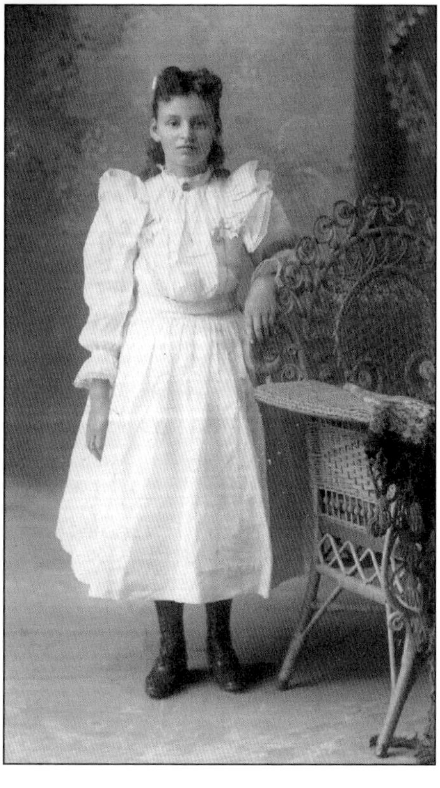

This washed, starched, and primped young lady looks as if she is going to graduate from the academy or perhaps take her first communion at St. Patrick's Roman Catholic Church. (Photograph by Paul Morrison, courtesy of Peggy Ahwesh.)

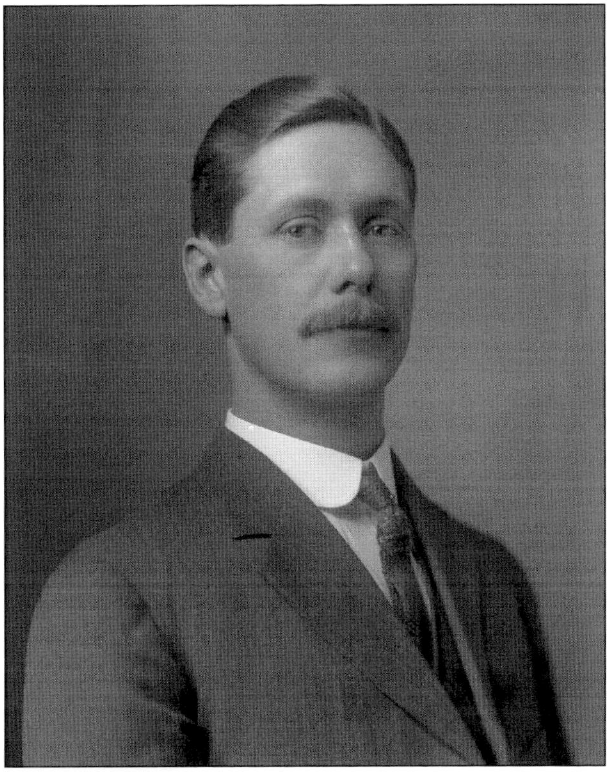

Village men at different stages of life are the subjects of these portraits by Morrison. One is young and proud (at right) and appears to be on top of his world. The other (below) must be a man of means who is probably nowhere near as old as he looks in this portrait and who must have found that walrus mustache in his way when eating. (Photographs by Paul Morrison, courtesy of Peggy Ahwesh.)

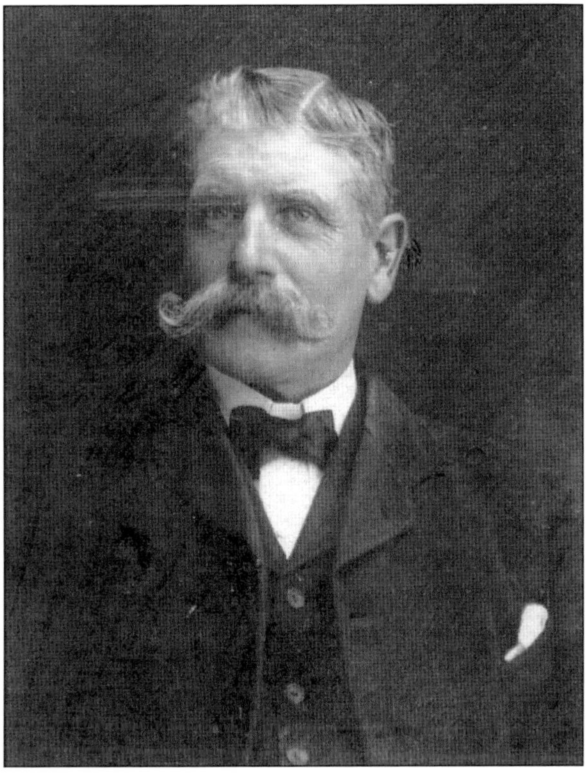

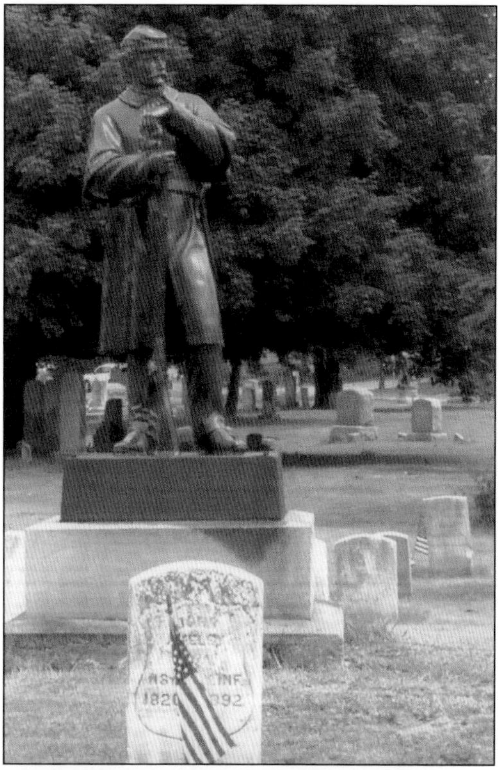

Permanent residents of the village can be visited in the Thompson Street Cemetery, which was founded about 1810. In Greene County, there are 63 family cemeteries dating back to the 17th century, and the Thompson Street Cemetery was used into the 1940s. Today people generally use the newer cemetery in Jefferson Heights. The records detailing who is buried where in the Thompson Street Cemetery were destroyed in the disastrous town hall fire in 1938, and since not all the graves were marked with headstones, identifying unoccupied space for new burials is a risky and potentially embarrassing business. The recently restored Civil War monument (at left) still faces south, and the graves visited most often these days (below) are those of Thomas Cole, his wife, Maria, and their children and extended family. (Author's collection.)

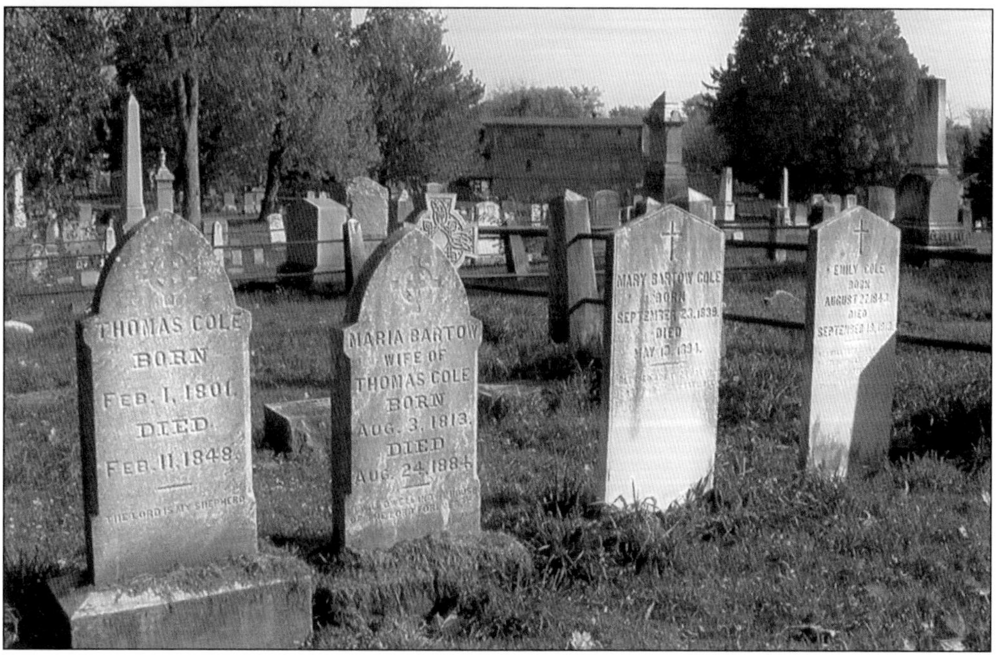

# *Eight*

# WORKING

In 1910, the national census showed that about 13 million people out of a total population of 50 million still worked in agriculture. Just a few years before that, the national average wage for a factory worker putting in a 60-hour week was $500 annually. Factory workers were doing better than most farmers. Figuring that in those days steak cost 10¢ a pound, bacon was 9¢, and a whole frying chicken was 15¢, it gives an idea of how tight the economy of the average household must have been just to survive. People in the workforce still had very little leverage for negotiating with their employers, with unions not having established a foothold in the American workplace yet. The great number of immigrants from Europe, Asia, and the American South were willing to work for subsistence wages with the prospect of someday earning enough for a better life than they had had back home.

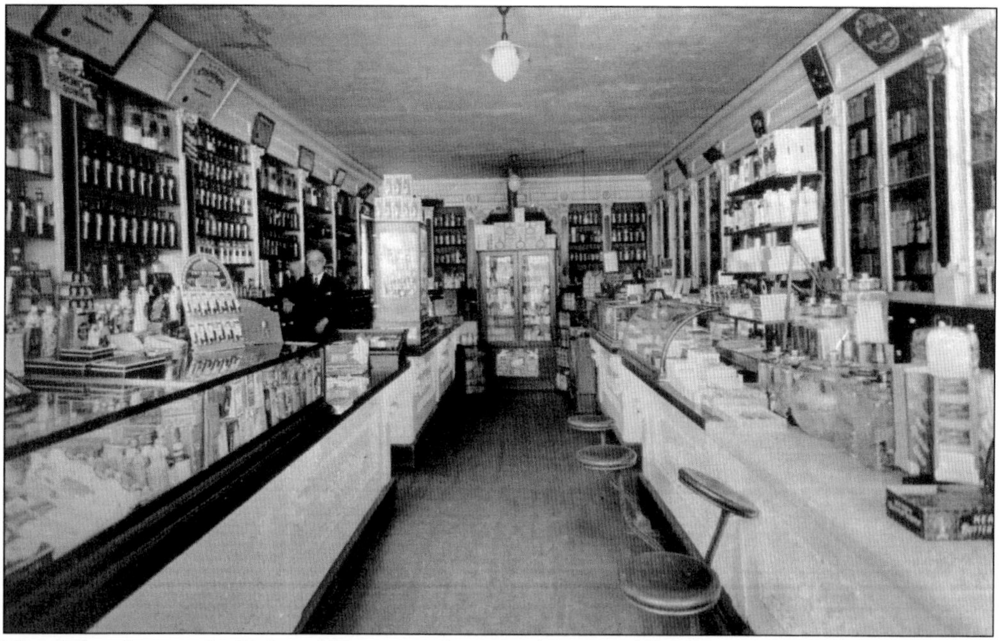

The folks who ran the Dubois Pharmacy always took great pride in its village origins in the late 18th century, although it had long since passed out of the family. On the left side of the 1910 photograph above is the area in which one could buy everything from hairbrushes and nail polish to patent medicines and prescription drugs (which in those days might contain addicting cocaine or marijuana). The soda fountain on the right has newfangled fold-up chairs that made washing the floors easier and a white marble counter offering an array of confections. Below, the freight master's office at the Point is where one could buy tickets for the passenger steamships. The calendar on the wall reads July 1914. (Courtesy of Robert Carl.)

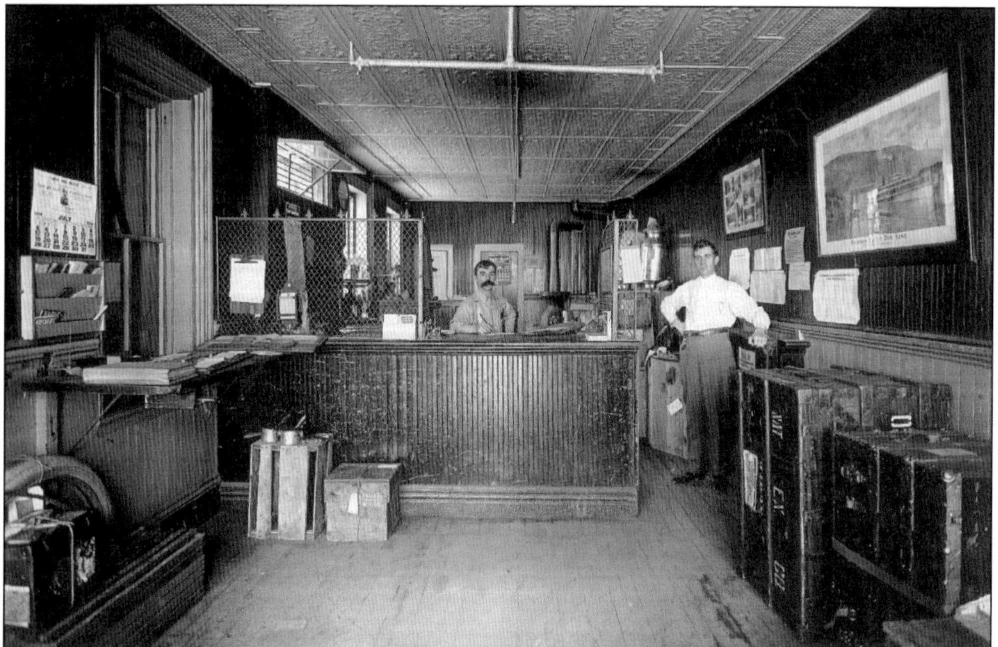

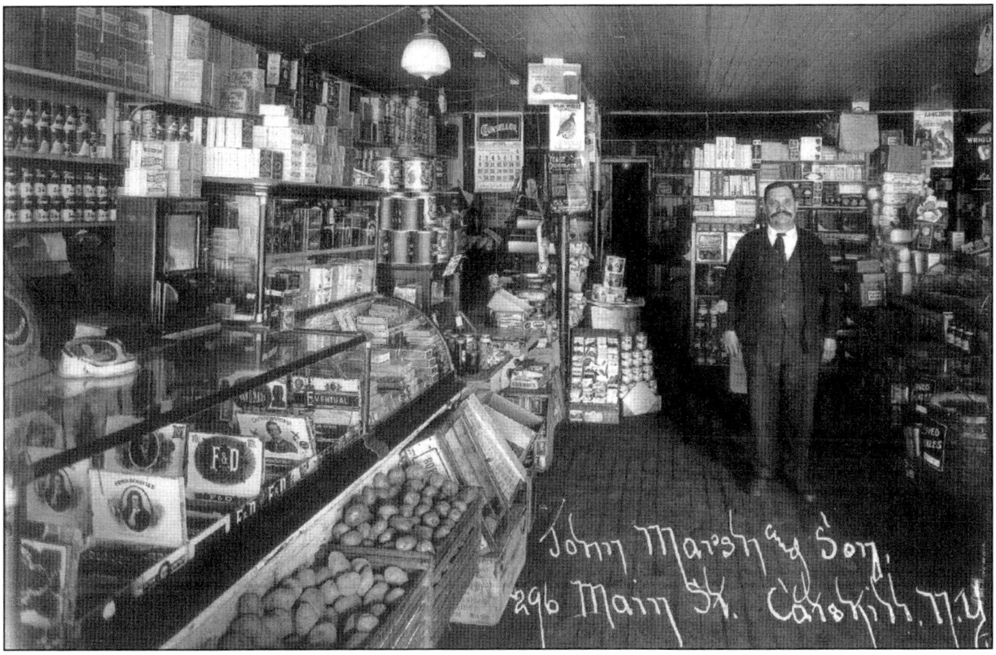


Village people relied on getting their news as much from the general store as they did from newspapers or the telephone. John Marsh and Son was a Main Street general store that was an institution for 63 years. Its closing in 1980 marked the end in the village of the "special service grocery," which would select groceries from customers' lists and then deliver them to their homes. At the intersection of Bridge and Main Streets (below) across from the new courthouse was the Davis market with a display of vegetables on the sidewalk, a staff that is seen here clowning around for the camera with officer O'Reilly, and a sign over the door that reads "Drink Davis' Coffee and Live Forever." (Author's collection.)

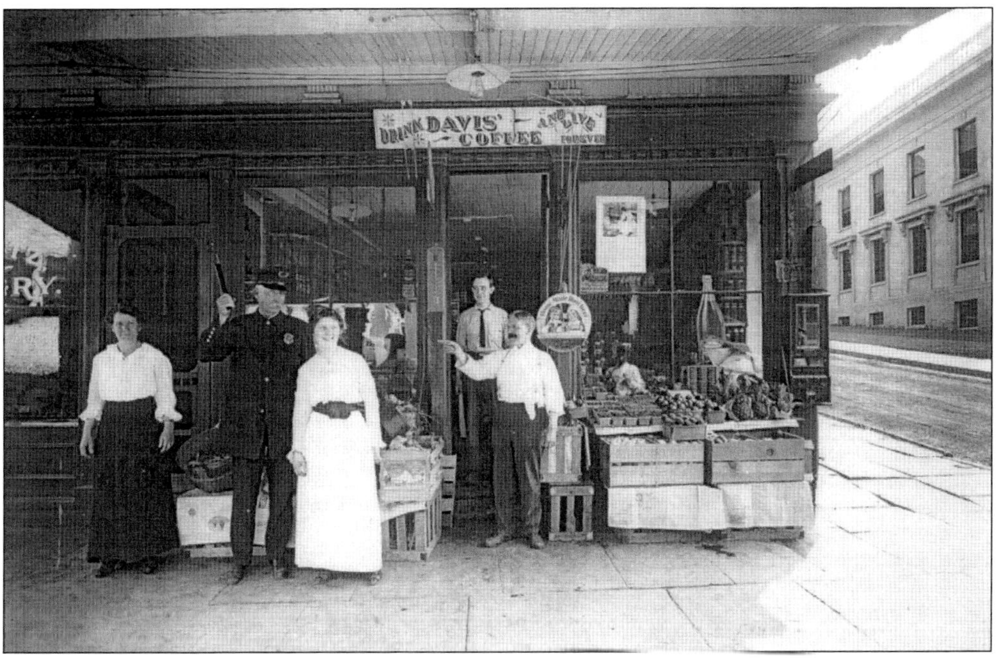

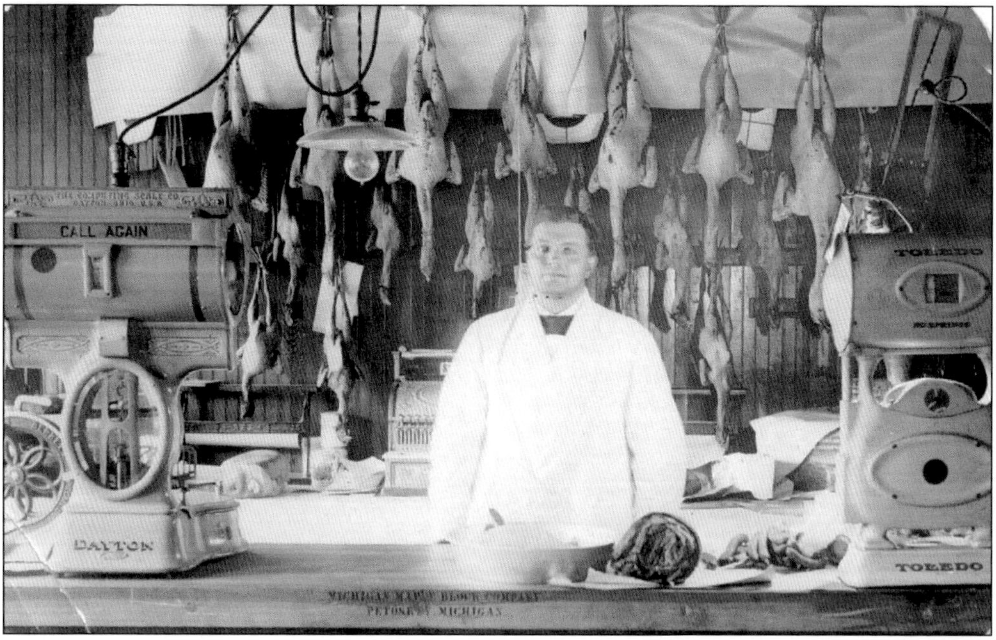


What is interesting about the scene above of an unidentified butcher somewhere along Main Street is the origin of the equipment he is using. The commuting scale is from Dayton, the butcher-block counter is from Michigan, and the no-spring scale on the right is from Toledo. The strangled chickens are undoubtedly fresh and from farms nearby. Day and Holt hardware (below) has been a fixture on Main Street for almost 200 years, having opened under Apollos Cooke's name in 1817 and taking the name Day and Holt by 1883. After serving the community's hardware needs so well for so long in the same building, the owner shifted merchandise a bit to better compete in the Main Street renaissance taking place, and it is now an antique store called the Swamp Angel. (Courtesy of Pat Walsh.)

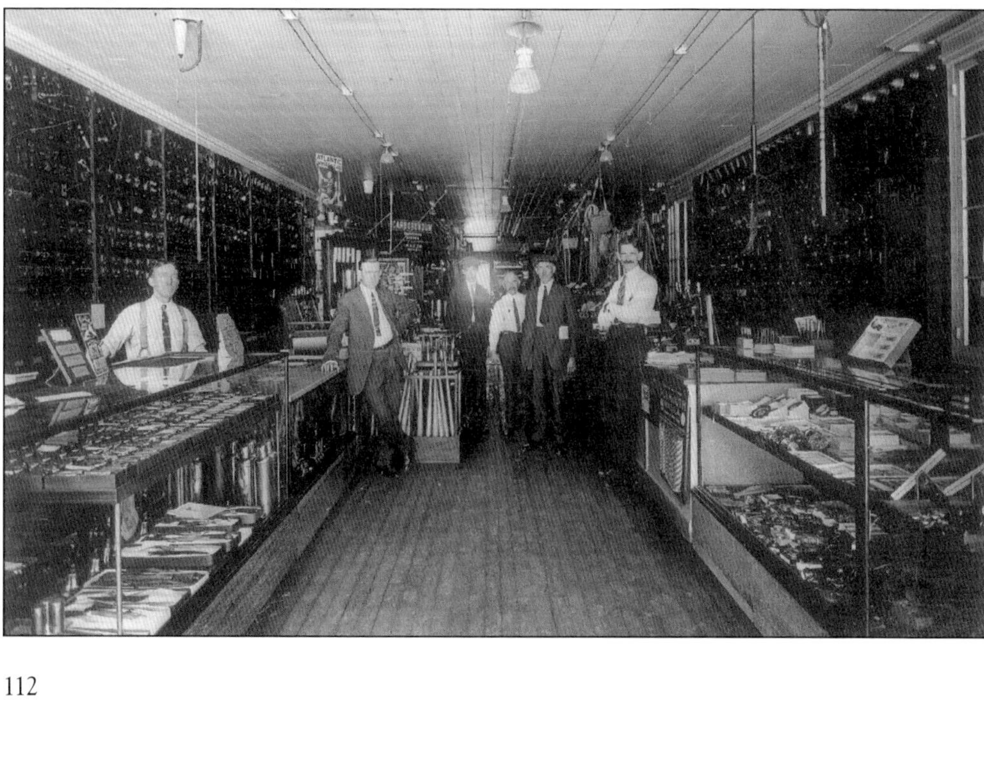

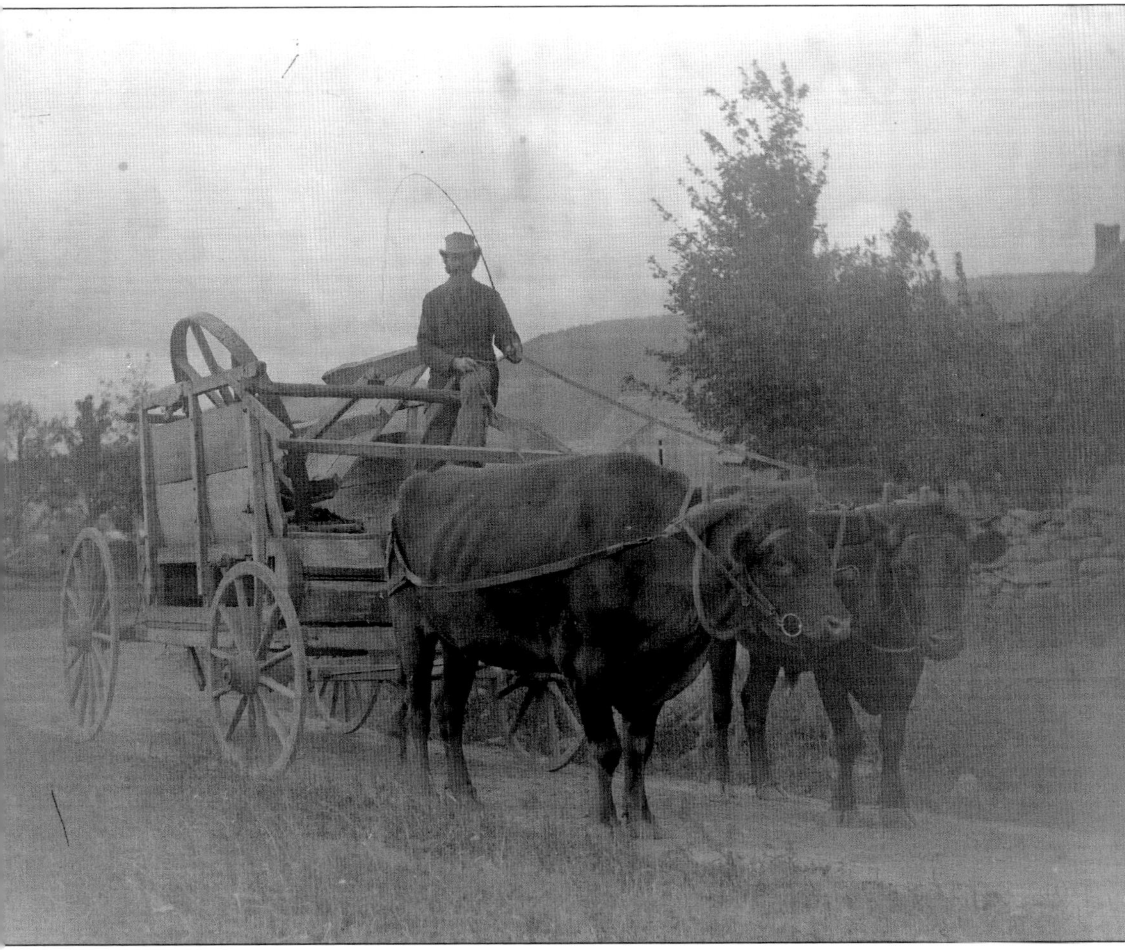

Roads were often rough and poorly maintained. Even Main Street in the village was tamped-down earth until the dawn of the 20th century when cobbles were laid at the intersection of Main and Bridge Streets. The rest remained rutted muddy tracks until bricks and finally macadam were laid down, helping to control the choking dust that must have penetrated every building on the street. In more rural areas when a heavy load had to be hauled, as this wagon might have been able to manage, extraordinarily powerful beasts of burden were needed to negotiate the rutted washboard roads. These patient oxen were perfect for the job. (Photograph by Paul Morrison, courtesy of Peggy Ahwesh.)

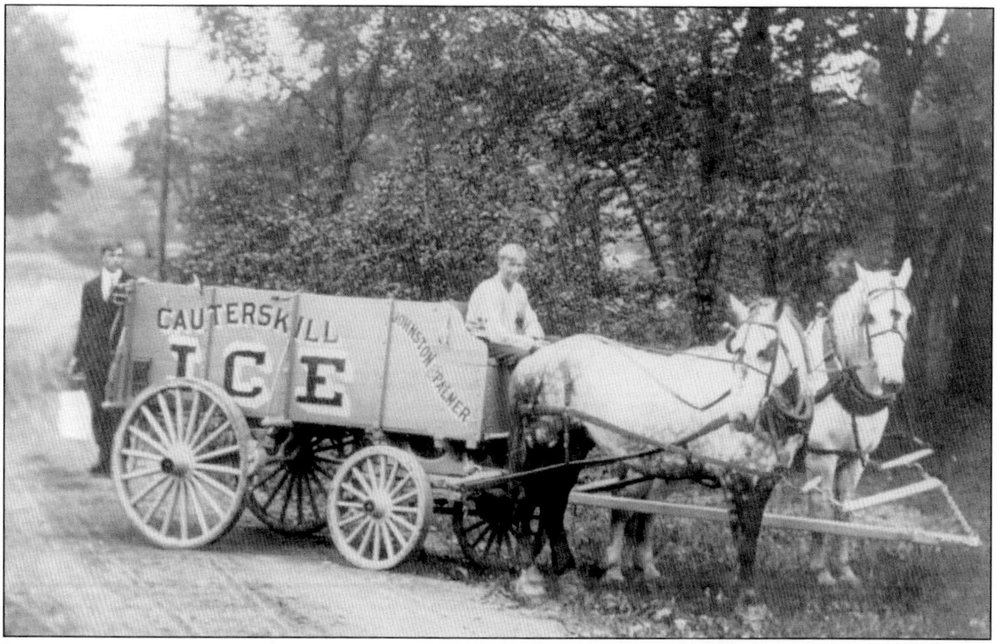


Ice was an important industry in upriver towns such as Catskill Village, and in the winter, it provided men otherwise out of work with six weeks of good money. Local deliveries in the village were made twice a week, and it cost a nickel for a block that could last three days. The ice was stored in large, often oak, insulated containers that were appropriately called iceboxes, a name that stuck even after artificial refrigeration was introduced in the 20th century. Above are two men making local ice deliveries for Johnston and Palmer's Cauterskill Ice Company. F. M. Slauson (below) was a Main Street butcher for many years in the village, and, dressed in his white butcher's apron, he poses on his delivery wagon around 1910. (Above, courtesy of Robert Carl; below, courtesy of Nancy Ursprung.)

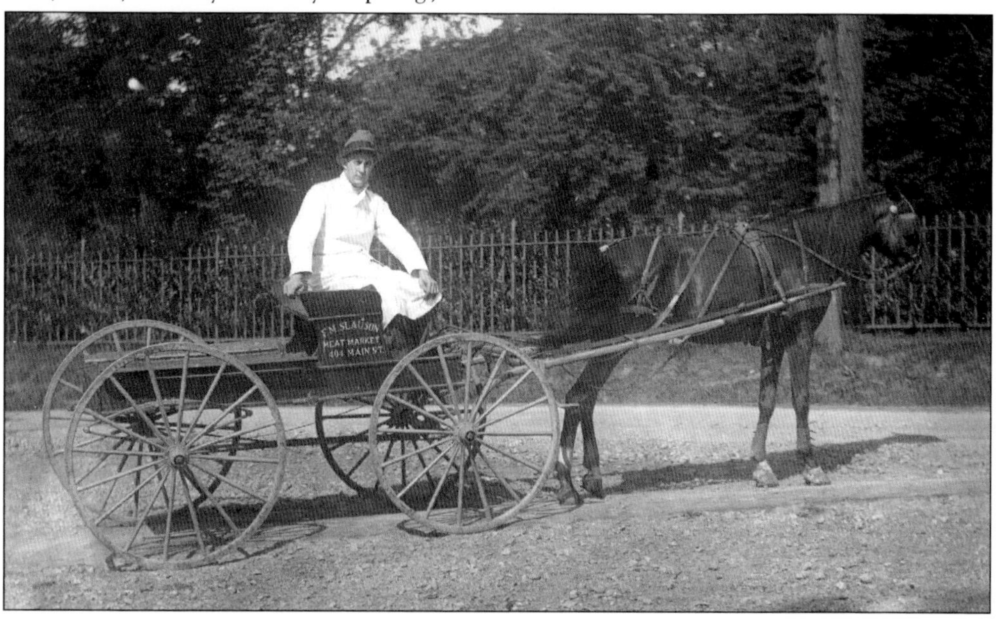

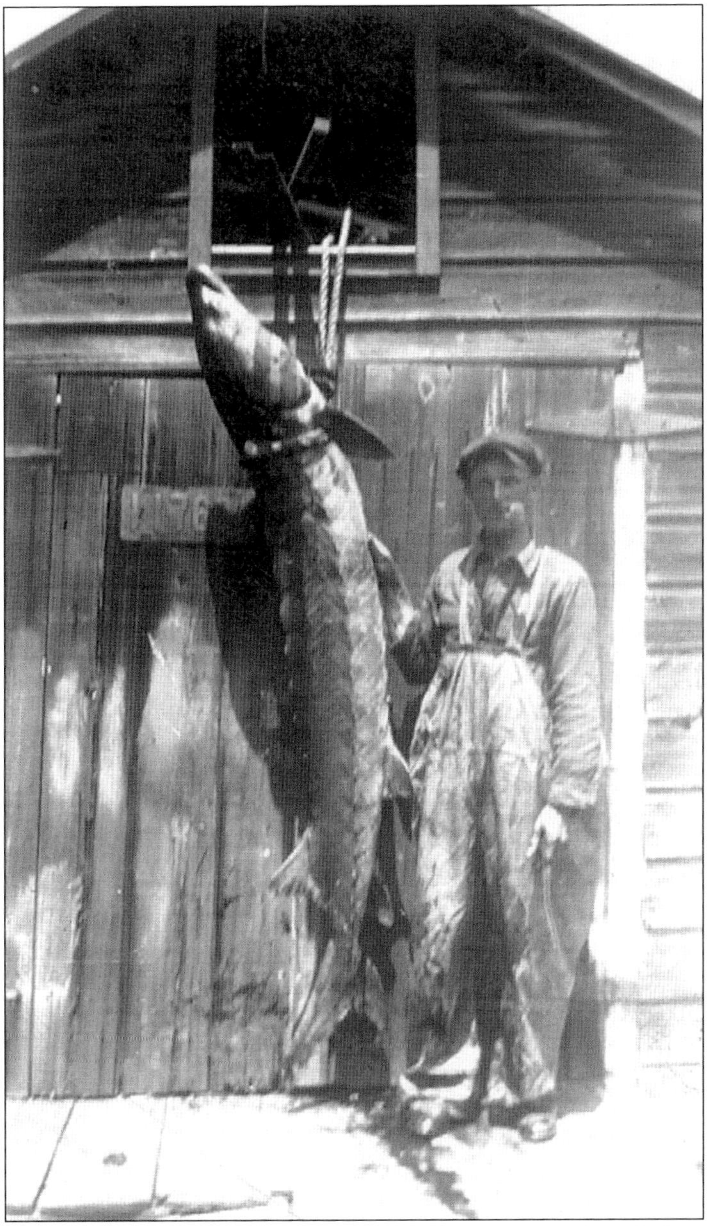

Pollution in the Hudson River from the chemical companies up north and along the Mohawk River as well as the raw sewage from every city, town, and village at water's edge had a disastrous effect over the years on the river's marine life. As awareness of the damage done to the river evolved so did the green movement to undo it, and heartening results are beginning to be seen. For example, large flocks of wild turkeys are once again encountered in the woods and fields, the almost extinct bald eagle has begun to breed again, and the sturgeon (above), belonging to a group of fish that are 300 million years old, have returned after being overexploited and poisoned almost into extinction by waterborne waste. The fishing industry is returning. This proud fisherman, pictured about 1890, stands beside a 12-foot sturgeon, a good-size catch for an ancient species that has been known in the past to reach 20 feet and 1,600 pounds. (Courtesy of Mark Krstovich.)

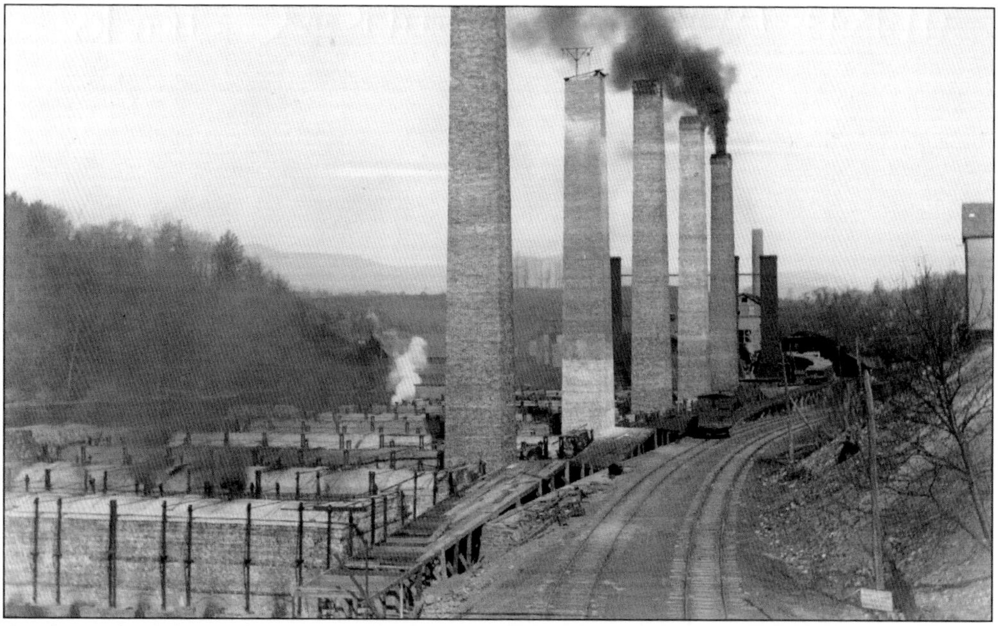

At the end of the 19th century, the Kaaterskill Paving Brick Company in Catskill Village became the recipient of a new invention called "the improved continuous kiln," which meant, basically, that it ran all the time. But the smoke and dirt from the new kiln (above) drove people from their homes along lower Main and Broad Streets. Answering the public outcry, Kaaterskill ineffectively raised the height of its kiln chimneys. The brick industry in the village collapsed soon afterward. And the cement business (below) at Smith's Landing, renamed Cementon, and now named Smith's Landing again, closed down in the 1990s due to federal enforcement of pollution control standards after providing employment to several generations of workingmen and workingwomen in the area. (Above, author's collection; below, courtesy of the Arthur Hamm collection.)

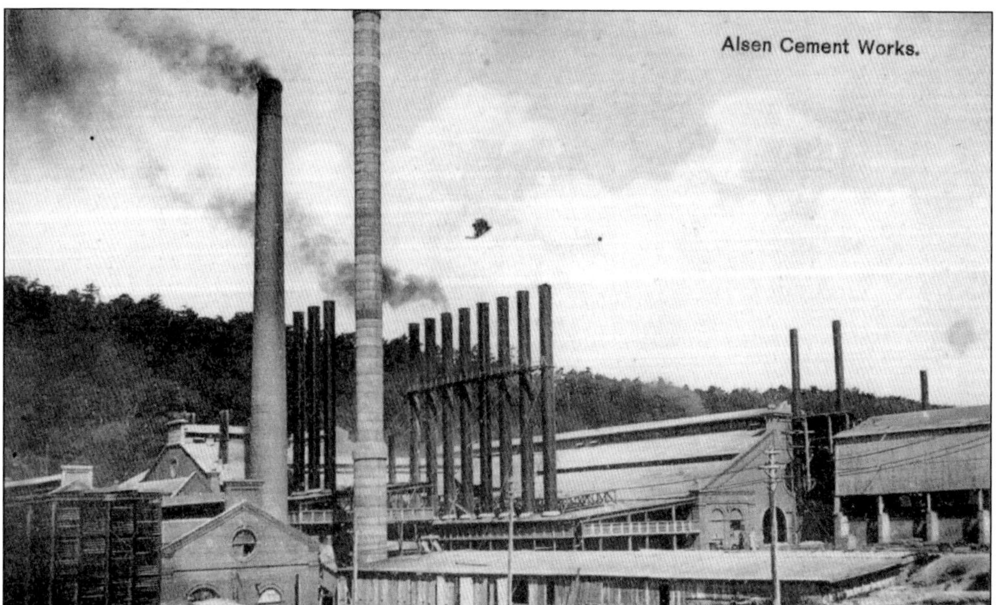

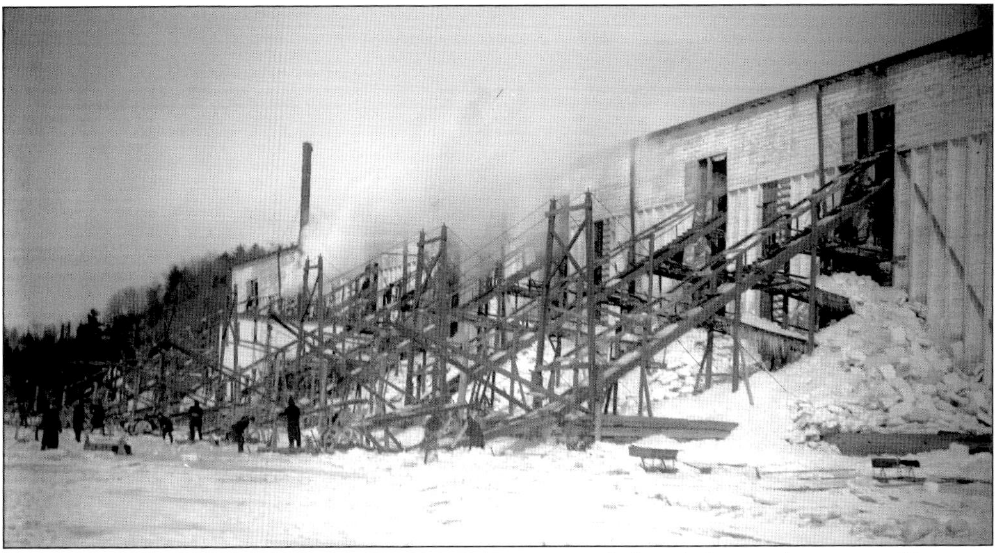

For almost a century, the profitable local ice industry provided work during the winter off-season. Large blocks of ice were cut from the frozen Hudson River with special saws with large teeth and then pushed down channels to the conveyor belts that hoisted the blocks into the barnlike icehouses (above) where they were kept and later sold. By 1900, however, pollution in the river from sewage and chemical waste originating upriver was recognized as a danger to the ice industry. The ice companies tried to improve their product by relocating to local freshwater lakes and upstream on the Catskill and Kaaterskill Creeks. Mechanical refrigeration eventually toppled the ice business. Below, Catskill's finest pose in front of their new quarters around 1920. (Above, photograph by Paul Morrison, courtesy of Peggy Ahwesh; below, courtesy of Robert Carl.)

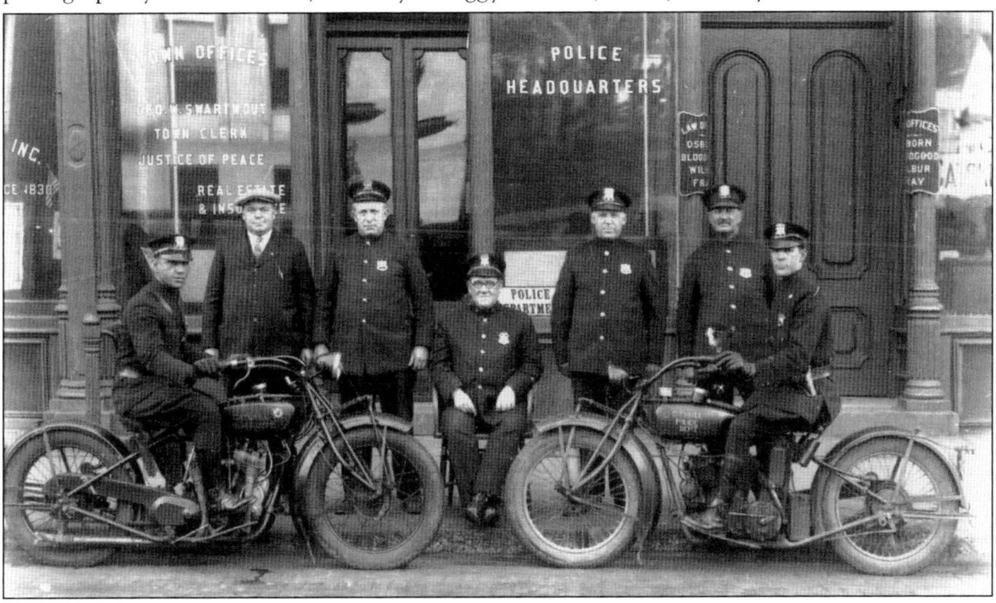

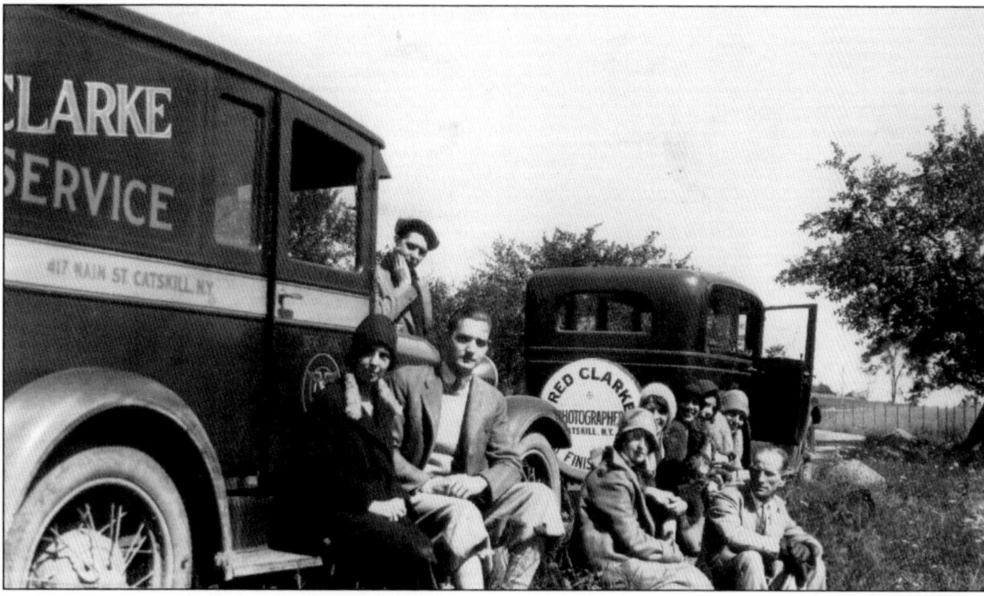


There have been a number of professional photographers operating in the village from the 1850s to the present time. Fred Clarke (above) offered a range of services from weddings to funerals and is seen here looking very natty with family and friends. Fishing on the Hudson River was a profitable business for many years until pollution, which included the ingestion by fish of arsenic and mercury and other dangerous metals, killed the market. Behind the fishing boat (below) on the creek is one of the Knickerbocker icehouses in summer mode, which meant it supplied local and New York City markets. When the ice business slowed due to the development of mechanical refrigeration, many of the abandoned icehouses were converted to mushroom farms, another profitable local venture. (Courtesy of Robert Carl.)

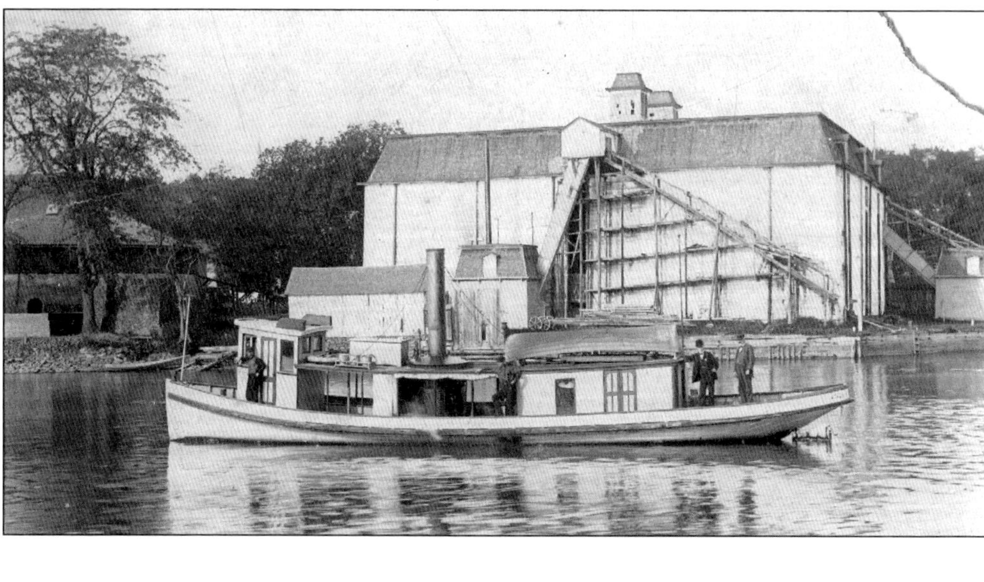

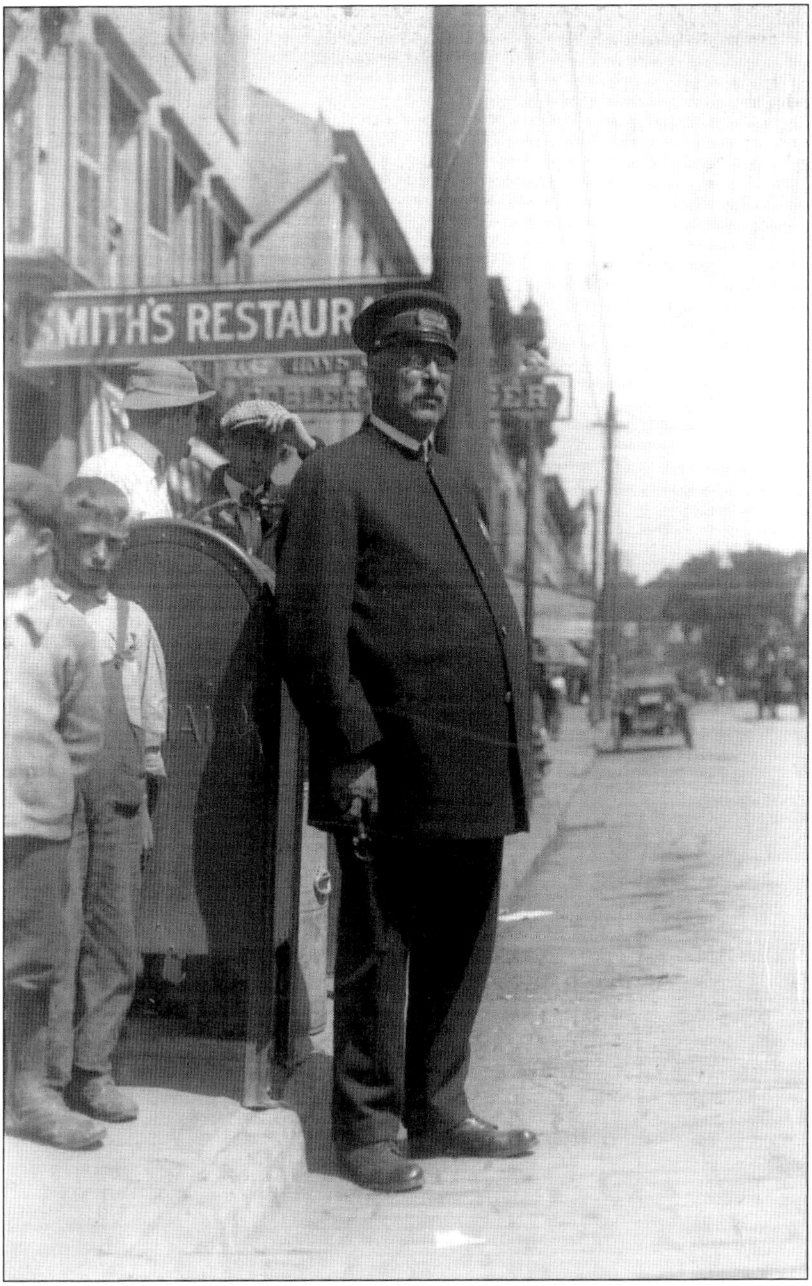


Ira Gray was one of six or seven uniformed policemen in the village in the early decades of the 20th century, and the memory of this local character lingers yet as a ready and willing helper when villagers were distressed over matters ranging from flat tires to stolen milk bottles and missing cats. He was especially good with children, several of whom are seen hovering at the left waiting for the light to change. As there is only one stoplight on Main Street at its intersection with Bridge Street where Gray might have been at work directing passenger traffic, it is clear where this photograph was taken but not by whom. The sign hanging over the sidewalk for Smith's Restaurant is a clue to the date because it burned to the ground in the fire that engulfed its neighbor the Nelida Theatre on January 1, 1918. (Courtesy of Robert Carl.)

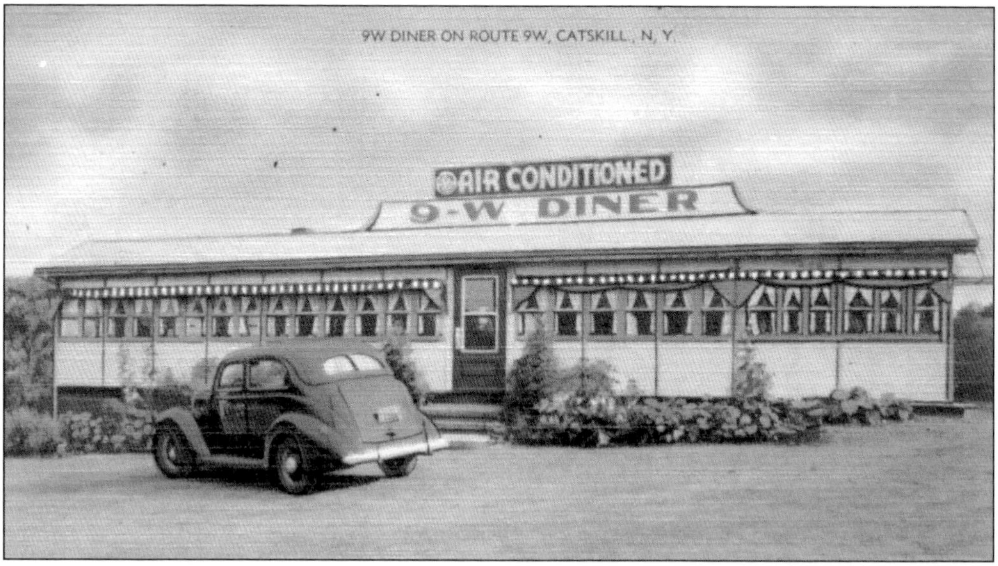


The ubiquitous diners across America were as recognizable as purveyors of quick, cheap meals as Burger King or McDonald's are today. By the early 1900s, diners had developed into portable sit-down restaurants designed to corner the family market. New York State played a big role in the development of diners in their manufacture and design, which tended to follow architectural trends of the times. The diner (above) at the edge of Catskill Village on Route 9W, seen here about 1938, featured marble counters and ceramic walls and floors, as well as air-conditioning. Below, busy at work, men are waiting for the train to bring a load of tourists who will want carriages to take them to resorts throughout the county. (Above, courtesy of Joan Jacobs; below, courtesy of Robert Carl.)

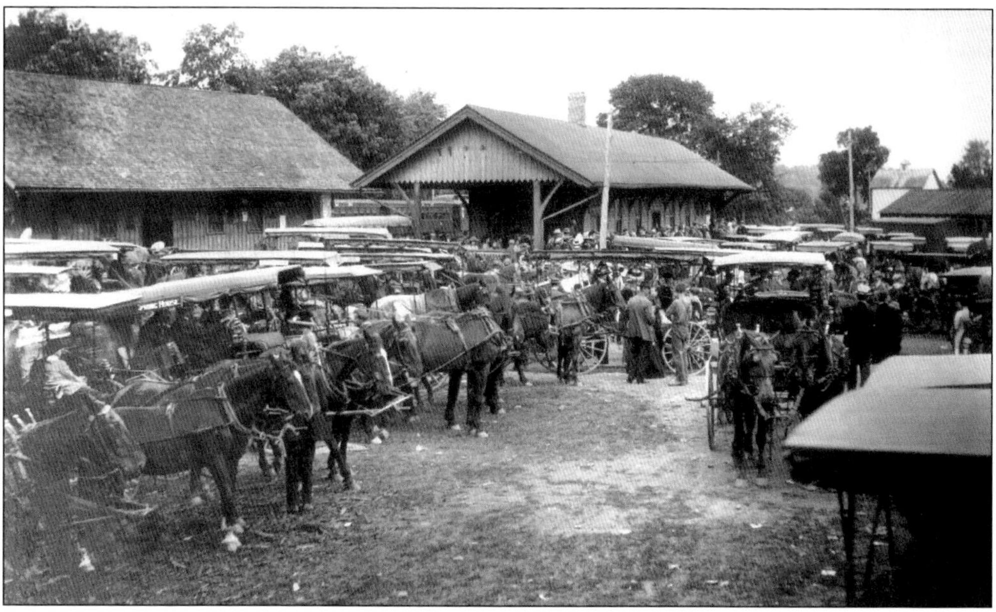

# *Nine*

# CELEBRATIONS

Catskill Village has always loved a parade, whether it was in celebration of the Fourth of July, Memorial Day, a firemen's convention, Thanksgiving, the holiday Festival of Lights, or any number of other occasions. One of the most celebrated occasions was the long-anticipated visit in 1824 of the 67-year-old Marquis de Lafayette, the last surviving general of the Revolutionary War, on his 13-month farewell tour of America. In the village, speeches were memorized, a feast was prepared, and excited crowds began gathering before dawn along Lafayette's Main Street route. But the general, having spent too much time at Clermont over breakfast with the Livingstons, was running late when his steamboat, the famous Fulton-Livingston *Clermont*, finally chugged into the Point. Lafayette got into his carriage, stayed there while being whisked hastily up Main Street with Erastus Beach at the reins, turned around at the top of the street, and just as hastily raced back to the Point and chugged off to Hudson without hearing any of the rehearsed speeches, receiving any of the flowers or gifts, or touching any of the liquor (although it was only midmorning) or prepared food. There is no record of how the villagers felt as a result of this slight, but undoubtedly they enjoyed the feast, and further celebratory events that day seem not to have been deterred.

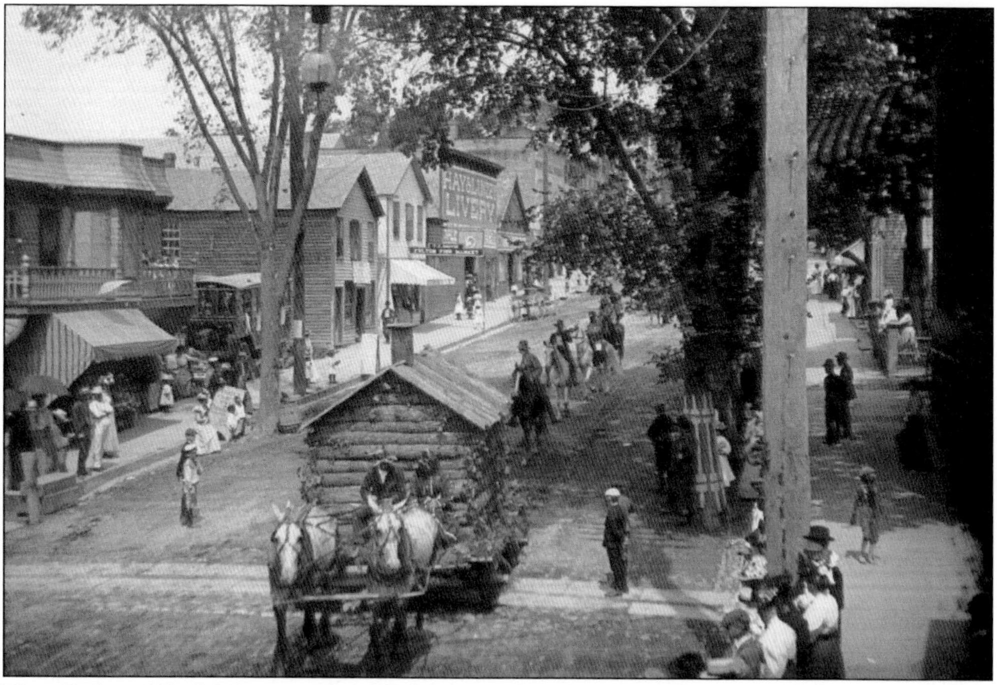


The Order of Red Men is a fraternal society founded in 1765 as the Sons of Liberty, an underground gang of patriots "with the purpose of establishing freedom and liberty in the early colonies." It is arguably most famous for having incited the Boston Tea Party. The Red Men patterned themselves after the "Great Iroquois Nation and its democratic government body." They are similar to the Masons. In Catskill Village, the society was active in the 19th and early 20th centuries. They appear above, in this glass-plate photograph of a parade taken on August 2, 1898, to have carried their patriotic spirit into a pioneer theme with a log cabin float. The Catskill Village Red Men (below) are lined up on the east side of Main Street for what must have been a club picture around 1898. (Courtesy of Robert Carl.)

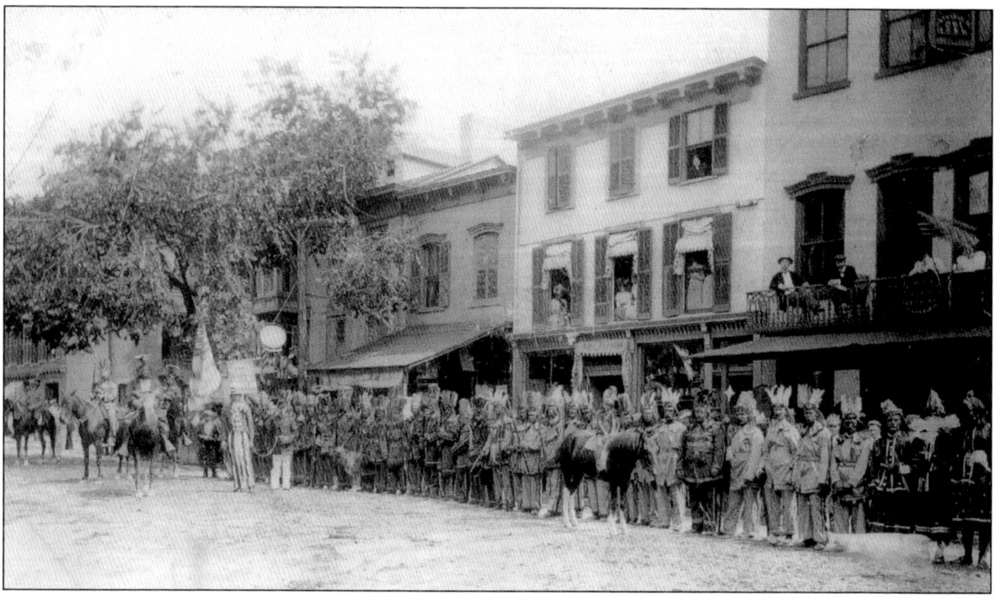

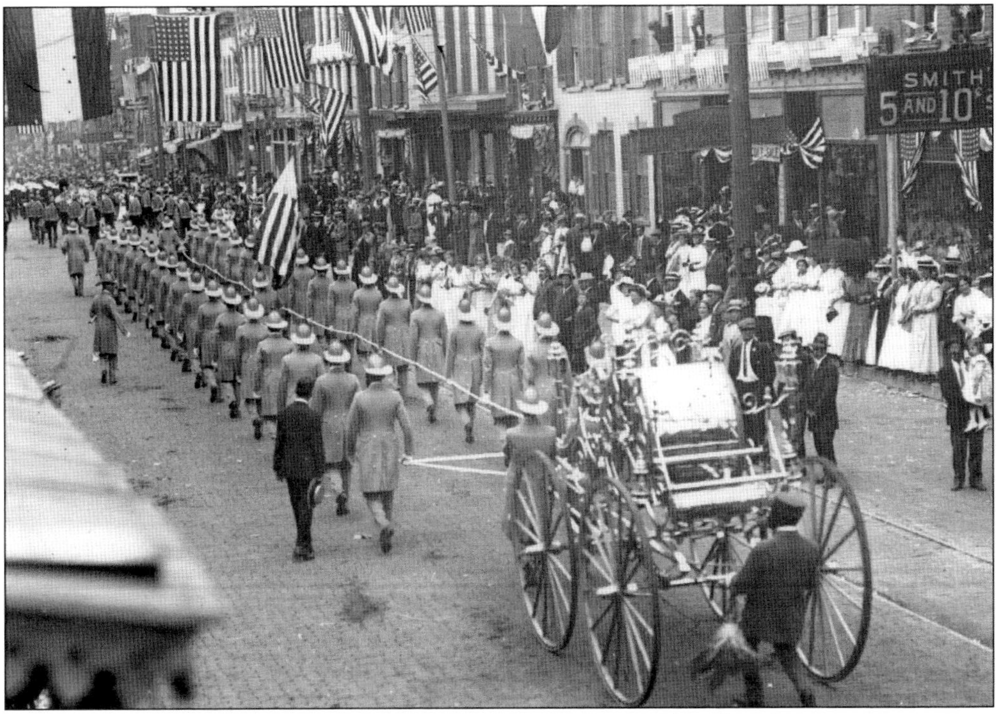


Marching down Main Street is Catskill's Hose Company No. 1 (above) with its antique pumping apparatus that is still pulled out of mothballs for events such as this Fourth of July parade around 1910. Note the traditional African American "duster dancing" along behind. This 19th-century pumper appeared recently again on Main Street in an August 2006 parade celebrating the 200th anniversary of the incorporation of the village. Below, the Marquis de Lafayette's carriage is in a Philadelphia museum, where this photograph was taken in the 1940s. (Above, courtesy of Robert Carl, below, author's collection.)

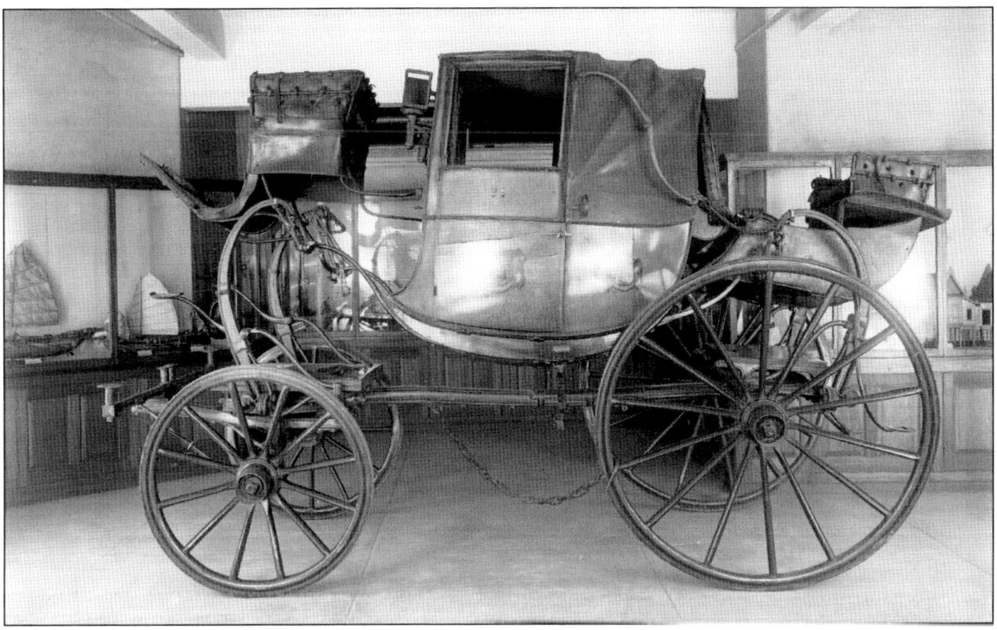

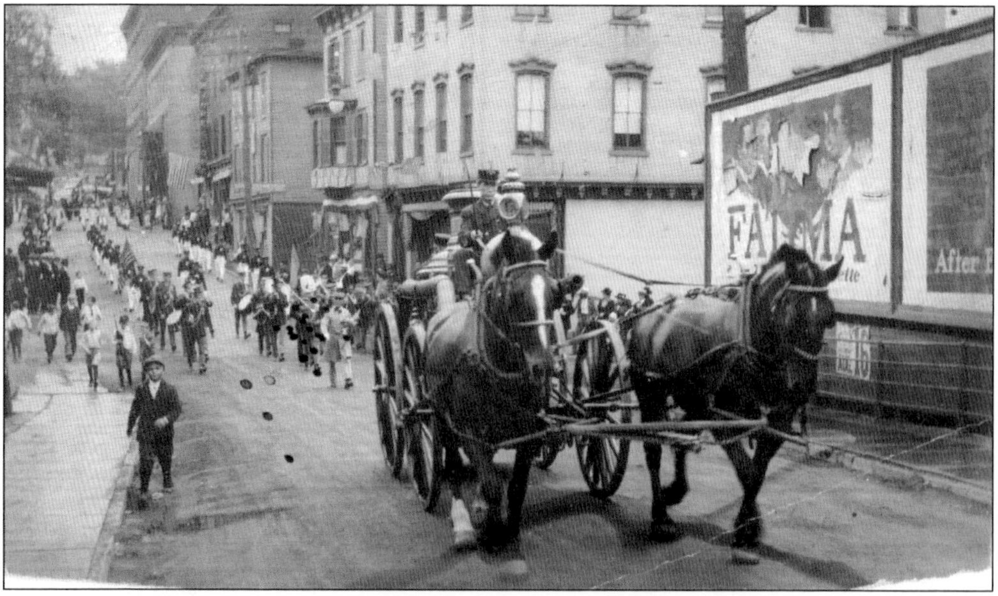


The parades in the village take a time-honored route that begins on the west side, crosses the Catskill Creek over the Uncle Sam Bridge, winds north on Water Street to the top of Main Street, goes down Main Street to Bridge Street, and then goes back down Bridge Street and across the bridge to the west side. There have been many variations, including the parades that used to end up the hill at the Thompson Street Cemetery honoring the dead from wars as far back as the American Revolution. A number of youngsters (above) are marching along beside the big guys as they approach the bridge on their way back across the creek around 1920. Double parking (below) interferes with an otherwise perfect formation as the volunteer Francis N. Wilson Hose Company No. 5 marches down Main Street around 1930. (Above, courtesy of the Arthur Hamm collection; below, courtesy of Robert Carl.)

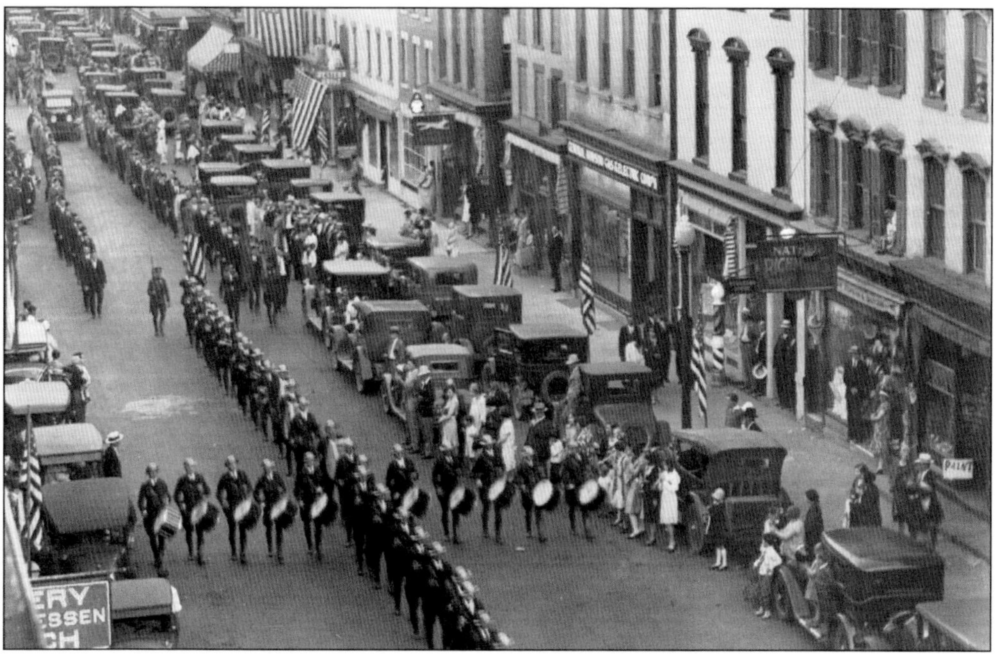

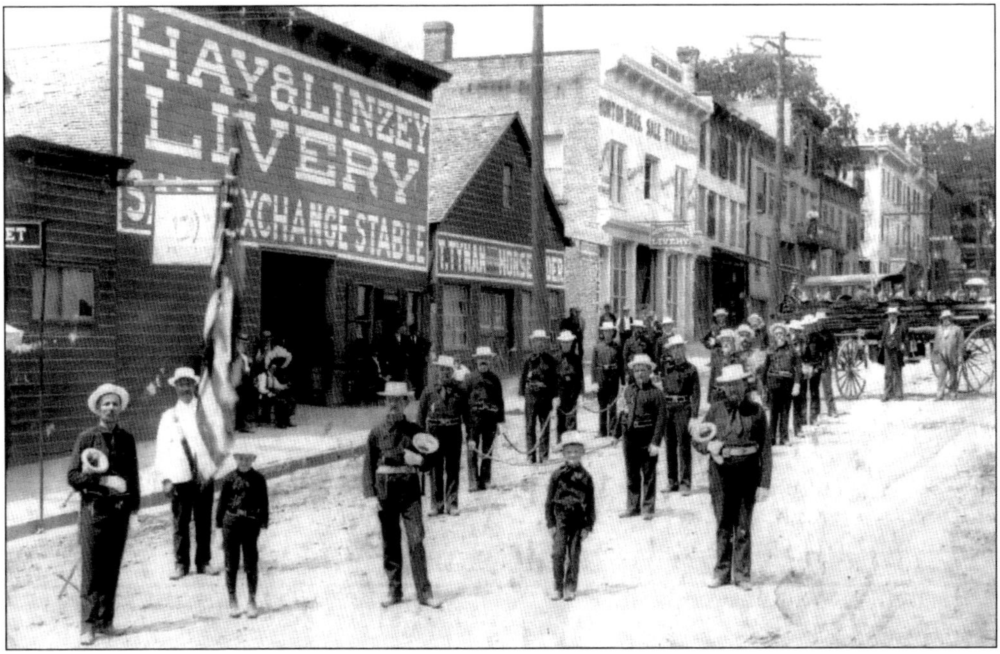


This *c.* 1900 photograph (above) shows the ever-ready Francis N. Wilson Hose Company marching band preparing to parade down Main Street dressed to the nines in its snappy black outfits and white hats; even the kids are ready to go. Below, the Pruyn Drum Corps poses on parade day in front of the courthouse about 1940. (Courtesy of Robert Carl.)

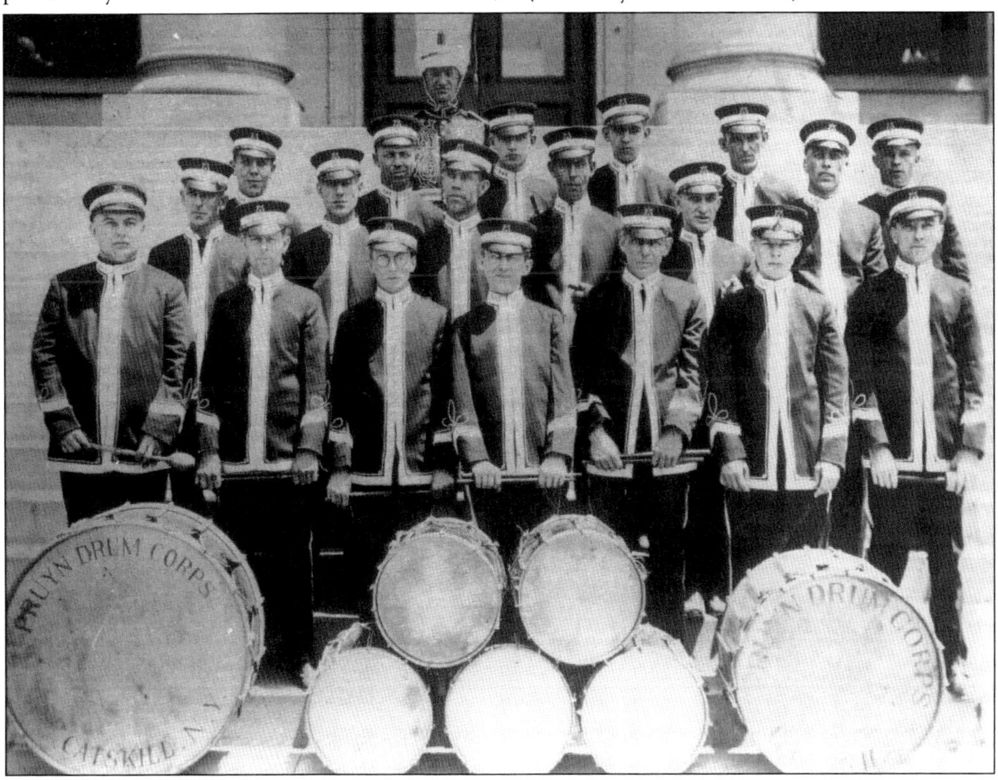

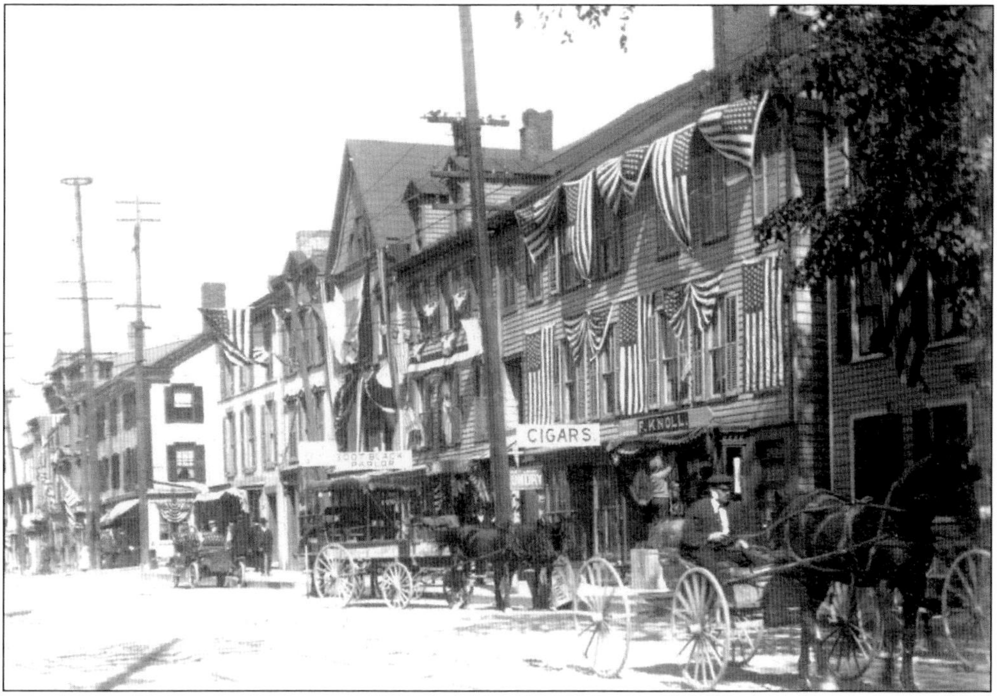


Catskill's Main Street (above) is decked out extravagantly with flags and bunting for the Hudson-Fulton celebrations in 1908. Manager Mike Krstovich (below, about 1945), seen in the white shirt in the center, shakes the cocktail shaker at his taproom and restaurant, Sarro's, located on Route 9W where Dunkin' Donuts is today. (Above, courtesy of Robert Carl; below, courtesy of Mark Krstovich.)

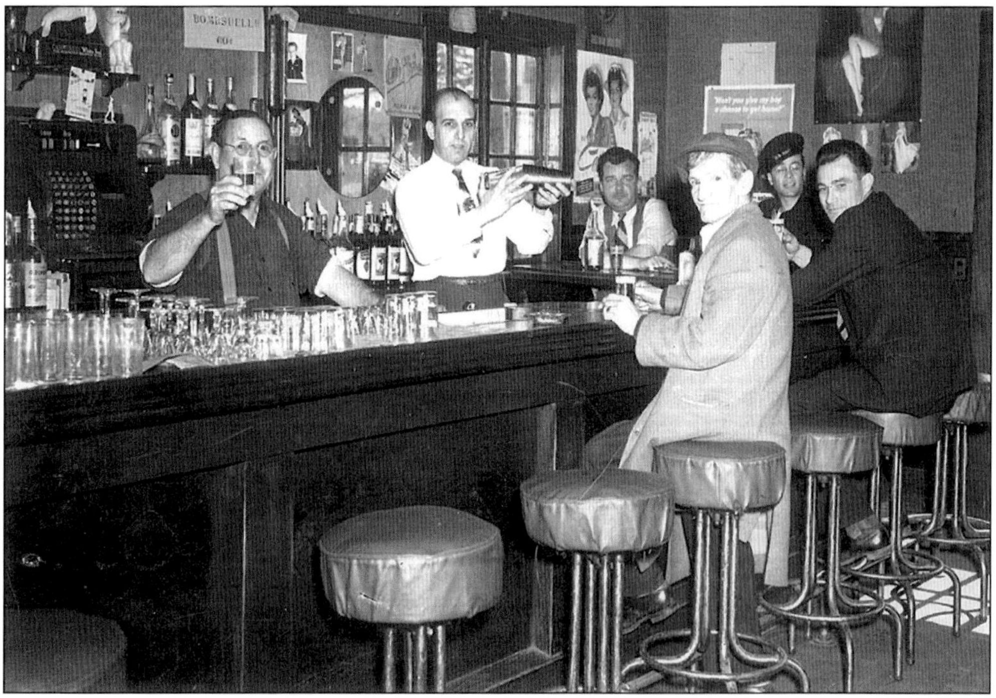

# BIBLIOGRAPHY


Beers, J. B. *History of Greene County, New York*. New York: J. B. Beers and Company, 1884.

Chadwick, George Halcott, and Jessie Van Vechten Vedder, eds. *The "Old Times" Corner, First Series, 1929–1930*. Catskill, NY: Greene County Historical Society, 1932.

Dunbar, Chas. S. *Buses, Trolleys & Trams*. Feltham, Middlesex, UK: Hamlyn Publishing Group, 1967.

Evers, Alf. *The Catskills: From Wilderness to Woodstock*. Woodstock, NY: Overlook Press, 1982.

Fiero, Winifred Wardle. *Attic Odyssey: Letters Tell a Tale or Two*. Catskill, NY: Self-published, 1985.

Gallt, F. A. *Dear Old Greene County: Embracing Facts and Figures, Portraits and Sketches, of Leading Men Who Will Live in Her History, Those at the Front Today and Others Who Made Good in the Past*. Catskill, NY: 1915.

Helmer, William F. *Rip Van Winkle Railroads*. Berkeley, CA: Howell-North Books, 1970.

Hutton, George V. *The Great Hudson River Brick Industry: Commemorating Three and a Half Centuries of Brickmaking*. Fleischmanns, NY: Purple Mountain Press, 2003.

Lossing, Benson J. *The Hudson, From the Wilderness to the Sea, Illustrated by Three Hundred and Six Engravings on Wood, from Drawings by the Author, and a Frontispiece on Steel*. New York: Virtue and Yorston, 1866.

Philp, Richard, ed. *Village: A Bicentennial Celebration of the Village of Catskill (1806–2006)*. Catskill, NY: Heart of Catskill Association, 2006.

Pinckney, James. *Reminiscences of Catskill, Harmony Lodge Papers & Catskill Cemetery Papers*. Catskill, NY: Catskill Recorder and Democrat, 1868.

Ringwald, Donald C. *Hudson River Day Line: The Story of a Great American Steamboat Company*. New York: Fordham University Press, 1990.

*Souvenir Book of Catskill: Being a Compilation of Interesting Facts Showing What Catskill Is—A Well Conducted Village, Beautiful and Healthful for Residence, with Unequaled Location for Business, Having All of the Advantages and None of the Discomforts of a City*. Catskill, NY: Committee for Old Home Week Celebration, 1908.

Vedder, J. Van Vechten. *Official History Greene County New York with a 1926–1927 Statistical Update Arranged by Community and a New Name Index by Audrey M. Klinkenberg*. Catskill, NY: Greene County Board of Supervisors, 1927. Reprint, Hope Farm Press, 1985.

Venema, Janny. *Beverwijck: A Dutch Village on the American Frontier, 1652–1664*. Albany: State University of New York Press, 2003.